'Kevin Shillington is to be commended for
bringing Patrick van Rensburg's story to a wide audience.
This book should be read by anyone interested in education,
as Patrick's Education with Production model is relevant
to the whole education ladder, from early childhood
through to university.'
— *Gaositwe K. T. Chiepe, educationist and politician,*
Minister of Education, Botswana, 1995–1999

'This is a story that has to be told and Van Rensburg
has found a worthy biographer ... The dominant image is of a
man who had a great appetite for life – work, projects, parties,
women, debate, travel – but who is simultaneously a
semi-heroic, semi-tragic figure.'
— *Linda Chisholm, Professor in the Centre for Education Rights and*
Transformation, University of Johannesburg

'Patrick van Rensburg is remembered by most people
for his pioneering work in Education with Production ...
His most enduring legacy, in my view, is as a journalist and
pioneer of the independent pluralistic press in
Botswana and Southern Africa.'
— *Methaetsile Leepile, Swaneng Hill School alumnus and*
former editor of the Mmegi *newspaper*

For Hazel,

In memory of Derek.

Kevin
1/9/2020

PATRICK VAN RENSBURG

Rebel, Visionary and Radical
Educationist
A Biography

Kevin Shillington

WITS UNIVERSITY PRESS

Published in South Africa by:
Wits University Press
1 Jan Smuts Avenue
Johannesburg 2001

www.witspress.co.za

First published 2020

http://dx.doi.org.10.18772/12020076048

978-1-77614-604-8 (Paperback)
978-1-77614-608-6 (Hardback)
978-1-77614-605-5 (Web PDF)
978-1-77614-606-2 (EPUB)
978-1-77614-607-9 (Mobi)

Published with the support of the Foundation for Education with Production

Foundation for

FEP

Education with Production

Project manager: Lisa Compton
Copyeditor: Pat Tucker
Proofreader: Lisa Compton
Indexer: Margie Ramsay
Cover design: Hybrid Creative
Typeset in 11.5 point Crimson

For all those who benefited in some way from the life of Patrick van Rensburg

Contents

Acknowledgements

I met Patrick van Rensburg on only one occasion and that was at his home in Serowe, Botswana, in 2016, just one year before his death. I had heard of him and his work from as long ago as 1969 and had heard him speak at a conference at the University of Botswana in the early 1980s. But that meeting in March 2016 was the only occasion that I actually got to speak with him; and by then Alzheimer's had taken hold of his mind. He understood that I was doing something connected with his life and work and he was pleased.

In addition to that meeting, over a long weekend, I have had the privilege of being welcomed into the fold of his family: his wife, Liz van Rensburg; their sons, Tom Masego and Mothusi Joe; and the partner of his later life, Rosemary Forbes, and their daughter, Joanna. I am grateful for the time they have given freely in personal interviews, the photographs they have shared with me and their ever-helpful responses to email requests for further clarification. In addition, Liz and Rosemary have each sent me copies of Patrick's unfinished, unpublished memoir, which he had entitled 'The Making of a Rebel'. My thanks to Liz in particular for painstakingly editing her copy, with extracts from her diary, to add clarity, for my benefit. It is her version that is referenced in the notes as 'Memoir'.

I am grateful to the Foundation for Education with Production (FEP) – founded by Patrick in 1980 to further his educational principles – which financed my research trips to Botswana in 2016 to 2018 and whose trustees – Frank Youngman, Mothusi van Rensburg, Bobana Badisang, Ditshwanelo Makwati and Hamish Bowie – have individually and collectively supported this project from the beginning. Without that financial underpinning and their unhesitating support it is doubtful that this biography could have been undertaken.

Thanks, in particular, to Mothusi for introducing me to Serowe; and to Bobana and her assistant Keaobaka Didi Tau for their ever-helpful work on bibliography, press clippings and so much more.

The biography was first proposed by Anne Mager of the University of Cape Town. In June 2014 she and Frank Youngman put it to Mothusi, with whom Patrick, in declining health, was then living. Mothusi readily agreed to the proposal and Anne Mager approached Peter Kallaway of the University of Cape Town to help find a biographer. I am grateful to them both – Peter for first broaching the subject of my undertaking the biography, Anne for providing the funding for a research trip to Cape Town, and both for hosting me during that visit in 2017.

My thanks are due to Kajsa Övergaard of the Right Livelihood Award (RLA), especially for inviting me to the 2018 RLA award ceremony, held in the Vasa Museum, Stockholm. Thanks, too, to Karin Abbor-Svensson and Anita Callert of the Dag Hammarskjöld Foundation (DHF) for allowing me free access to the DHF Archives in Uppsala.

I am grateful for the help offered by the staff of the National Archives of Botswana in Gaborone and of the British Newspaper Library in London, the Bodleian Library in Oxford for the archives of the Anti-Apartheid Movement and the staff of the Khama Memorial Museum in Serowe. I am grateful, too, to Tom Holzinger for sharing with me his own extensive Van Rensburg archive and photographs, as well as his personal memories and interpretations; to Evelyn Oakeshott, who generously entrusted me with his brother Robert's letters home to his mother over the period 1968 to 1970; and to Gerry Pozzani for creating and maintaining the Swaneng Hill School website.

I have relied heavily on personal interviews, in person, on Skype, by phone and email, with people who knew and worked with Patrick van Rensburg over the years. Many of these interviewees are not directly footnoted in the text, but all contributed in some way or another to helping me establish the broad picture and environment of Patrick's life and work. Apart from the Van Rensburg family already mentioned – Liz, Tom and Mothusi, Rosemary and Joanna – I am grateful to the following individuals for granting me their time and memories in interview, in the order in which the interviews took place between 2016 and 2019: Methaetsile Leepile, George Moalosi, Modise Maphanyane, Ditshwanelo Makwati, Mike

Dingake, Otlhogile Bojosi, Bram Dilrosun, Titus Mbuya, Tsetsele Fantan, Motlhaleemang Ntebela, Ralph Nickerson, Joel Pelotona, Neil Parsons, Anne Mager, Richard Whiteing, Jeff Jarvis, Debbie Budlender, Peter Kallaway, Marcus Solomon, Paula Ensor, Tariq Mellet, Judy Seidman, Quett Ketumile Masire, Jeff Ramsay, Sandy Grant, Otsogile Pitso, James Olesitse, Deborah Nkolane, Moaci Montshiwa, Reggie Koee, Scobienol Lekhutile, Frank Youngman, Pelonomi Venson, Gaositwe Chiepe, Hamish Bowie, Philip Segola, Seth Sekwati, Florence Shagwa, Monageng Mogalakwe, Lord (Frank) Judd, Thomas Maseki, Charles Bewlay, Vernon and Tineke Gibberd, Derek and Hazel Hudson, Ian Martin, Tessa McArdle, Alison Kirton, Julia Majaha-Jartby, Pierre Landell-Mills, Ted Comick, Murray McCartney, Mike Hawkes, Tom Holzinger, Modisaotsile Hulela, Sebofo Motswane, Philip Bulawa, Frank Taylor, Rahim Khan, Queen Notha, Nthaga Keoraletse, *Kgosi* Mokhutshwane Sekgoma, Elijah Makgoeng, Bishi Mmusi, Olle Nordberg, Fay Chung, Jakob von Uexkull, and Wouter and Titia van der Wall Bake. Many others offered advice or referred me on to other sources. In addition, I wish to thank the two anonymous publishers' readers and, once again, Liz van Rensburg and Frank Youngman, all four of whom read an early draft of the completed manuscript and offered some invaluable advice. Responsibility for any errors of interpretation or fact, however, remains mine alone.

I am grateful to the following for granting me permission to use their photographs in the book: the Anti-Apartheid Movement Archive, the British Library Board, the Khama Memorial Museum, the Van Rensburg family, Rosemary Forbes, Mary Kibel, Benny Wielandt, Mike Hawkes, Sandy Grant, Karl-Hermann Handwerk, Peter Jensen and Andrew Gunn. Despite efforts made, it has not been possible to trace all the photographers whose images form part of the Van Rensburg family collection.

Thanks to the staff of the Motheo Apartments in Gaborone and the Serowe Hotel in Serowe, who always made my research visits to Botswana so pleasant and enjoyable. Finally, special thanks to my wife, Pippa, for her constant enthusiasm, advice and support.

Kevin Shillington
Dorset, United Kingdom
July 2019

Abbreviations and Acronyms

AAM	Anti-Apartheid Movement
ANC	African National Congress
BDA	Bamangwato Development Association
BDB	Bertrams Development Brigade
BDP	Bechuanaland/Botswana Democratic Party
BNF	Botswana National Front
CAO	Committee of African Organizations
Cosatu	Congress of South African Trade Unions
Danida	Danish International Development Agency
DC	district commissioner
DHF	Dag Hammarskjöld Foundation
EwP	Education with Production
FEP	Foundation for Education with Production
IVS	International Voluntary Service
JC	Junior Certificate
NP	National Party
PAC	Pan Africanist Congress
RLA	Right Livelihood Award
SADC	Southern African Development Community
SADCC	Southern African Development Coordination Conference
SBDT	Serowe Brigades Development Trust
Sida	Swedish International Development Cooperation Agency
SOMAFCO	Solomon Mahlangu Freedom College

UN	United Nations
Unisa	University of South Africa
UP	United Party
WNLA	Witwatersrand Native Labour Association
YET	Youth Education Trust
ZANU	Zimbabwe African National Union

List of Illustrations

Maps

Map 1: Eastern South Africa, mid-twentieth century. (Cartography by Janet Alexander)

xxi

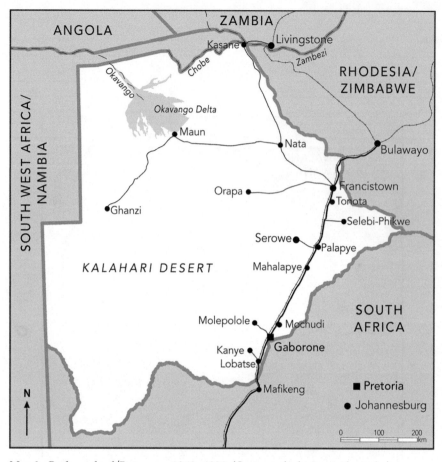

Map 2: Bechuanaland/Botswana, 1960–1990. (Cartography by Janet Alexander)

Introduction

In the late 1970s a Swedish collector and dealer in rare postage stamps who lived in the Isle of Man, an offshore tax haven in the midst of the Irish Sea, contemplated the problems of the world. Not so much the grand problems of the Cold War or the meaning of the universe; more the everyday problems of human development and mankind's relationship with the environment. Jakob von Uexkull was a man interested in solutions.

He put it to the Nobel Foundation that they award two new annual prizes for those who had found practical solutions to these world problems. When the Nobel Prize committee turned him down, he decided to undertake the task himself. He sold his business to set up a prize fund of US$50 000 and named it the Right Livelihood Award,[1] with a mission to 'honour and support courageous people and organisations offering visionary and exemplary solutions to the root causes of global problems'.[2] The award soon gained international prestige and the media dubbed it 'the Alternative Nobel Prize'. Patrick van Rensburg (1931–2017), the subject of this biography, was one of three laureates honoured with the award in 1981, the second year in which it was presented. His was awarded 'for developing replicable educational models for the third world majority'.[3]

In view of his origins Van Rensburg might seem a most unlikely candidate for such a prestigious honour. Born into a broken family of modest means, he was a white South African who grew up in the 1930s and 1940s within the cushion of white privilege and prejudice that dominated much of Africa in those years. His surname indicates that he was an Afrikaner, a member of that specifically South African 'white tribe' whose chosen form of 'nationalism' tied its future on the African continent to a racially defined system of separation and dominance known as apartheid (separateness). But was Patrick van Rensburg really an Afrikaner and did it matter, other than what he did from his position of racial privilege?

The story of his childhood and early adult life is heavily dependent upon his own writing, both published and unpublished. During the three decades of his exile, from 1960 to 1990, he lost touch with most of his family, and although he re-established contact in the 1990s it has not been possible in the research and writing of this book to track down any survivors who might add independent evidence to his own account of those early years.

There are two main sources for the life of Patrick van Rensburg, up to his break with apartheid in 1957. The first is his published book, *Guilty Land*, written at the age of twenty-nine in 1961, his first year in exile. The second is his incomplete and unpublished autobiographical memoir, which he began writing in the 1990s after he had re-established contact with his family in South Africa.

Guilty Land[4] is primarily about the history and reality of apartheid as he perceived it, and why and how it should be opposed both within South Africa and on the international stage; but he introduces the subject through a short autobiographical account of his own upbringing and early adult life in an attempt to explain what led him to become an ardent opponent of the system. *Guilty Land* is a powerful polemic, directly related to the struggle for liberation in South Africa, and the account of his personal life that he presents there must be read with that in mind.

His unpublished memoir, on the other hand, although written when he was in his late sixties and early seventies, was the product of many years of work, undertaken at a time when his memory had been refreshed by reconciliation with his family and visits to the places of his childhood and first employment. There are two main versions of the memoir: one, entitled 'The Making of a Rebel'; the other, a slightly edited version of the same manuscript, which I refer to in endnotes simply as 'Memoir'. Rosemary Forbes, his partner in his later life, forwarded me a copy of the former, and his wife, Liz (née Griffin) van Rensburg, sent me a copy of the latter, which she had lightly edited for the benefit of this biography.

Her editing removes little from the original, but tidies up some of the chapters, corrects some of the chronology and adds a few comments and vignettes from her own personal diary. The level of detail and self-deprecation in both manuscripts carries conviction and, in the absence of alternative sources, the two versions between them have provided the chronological framework for this account of his early life. Once he turned his back on apartheid, both publicly and dramatically, however, numerous additional and alternative sources, oral and written, have become available.

The fractured origins and early life of Patrick van Rensburg would have a lifelong impact on the personality of the man and the direction and manner in which he chose to live his life. This book explores the intellectual struggle against his upbringing that finally led him to choose the side of justice and humanity.

From the moment he broke with apartheid the Afrikaner establishment regarded him as a traitor – a 'political snake-person'. This impelled him to nurture the image of himself as rebel, not only as a leading light in the non-racial South African Liberal Party and the boycott campaign in London that gave birth to the Anti-Apartheid Movement, but also from his position of exile in Bechuanaland (later Botswana), then one of the poorest countries in the world. Having chosen to reject his position of white privilege in South Africa, he lived the rest of his life determined to prevent the emergence of a privileged black élite in the societies of post-colonial Africa, including, in due course, South Africa itself.

This ambitious aim brought him to the field of education, that crucible of future generations. The process of changing attitudes, however, was an ever-present struggle, not only in society at large but with the very meaning and purpose of education. Anyone who has ever attempted to develop an alternative, more egalitarian education system will appreciate the level of deeply entrenched conservatism that permeates the whole international education establishment, with its primary focus on measures of academic attainment and its concomitant companion, failure.

Patrick van Rensburg, however, was a man of enormous energy and almost naïve enthusiasm, driven by an impatience to achieve, which seemed to reveal a constant awareness that he only had one life and the sands of time were running out. As a colleague and friend recalled of his first meeting with Van Rensburg, in Botswana in 1967: 'Pat was in a hurry to finish the foundation trenches for a new science lab. He swung his pick furiously at the red soil and soft rock below him. "Rome wasn't built in a day," he panted, "but then I wasn't the foreman on that job." '[5]

Hard work and humour are rare and inspiring companions and Van Rensburg used both to great effect: 'Pat was physically big and radiated charisma. He was driven by both long-term vision and here-and-now compassion. Lord how he worked! Students, brigade trainees, and volunteers ... easily accepted his leadership.'[6]

His achievements in the field of education were all the more remarkable for the fact that he was entirely self-taught: not a strong position from which to take on a powerful establishment. But then part of Van Rensburg's charm was not to realise the strength of that establishment until he was deeply committed to the battle. From building schools and closely related co-operative ventures and vocational training institutions, his ideas and deeply held principles were based on his own personal, practical experience and hard physical graft, as he constantly reminded anybody who would listen.

Most of his writings – books, articles and seminar papers – started with the story of the self-built school that he founded in Serowe, Botswana, in 1963, and the 'brigades', those training and production institutions devised for post-primary school youth. The brigades 'put Botswana on the educational map of the world'.[7] From that base he developed his concept of alternative education, which he called 'Education with Production' (EwP).

Van Rensburg became a recognised authority on his alternative approach to education, with its focus on quality and functional schooling for the majority, but he did not do it alone. He received financial support from many international agencies, among them the Dag Hammarskjöld Foundation, the Swedish International Development Cooperation Agency (Sida), the Danish International Development Agency (Danida) and the Canadian International Development Agency (Cida).

Help came, too, from numerous idealistic volunteers from Europe, South Africa and North America, and from the international recognition afforded by the Right Livelihood Award.

4

The ideas encapsulated in EwP were not unique to Van Rensburg, but he was a leading proponent of its principles and practical application from the mid-1960s through to the new millennium.

This book is the story of that remarkable man, from his humble origins in Durban, South Africa, to international fame and acclaim and reluctant decline into infirmity in old age. His name may have faded from public consciousness but, as can be seen from this story of his life and work, his legacy and ideas still have much to offer to those intent on solving the problems of the educated unemployed and the widespread inequality so characteristic of the twenty-first-century world.

1 | Origins and Identity in South Africa

On a hot and humid South African summer's day in January 1949, one month after his seventeenth birthday, Patrick van Rensburg realised for the first time that he was officially an Afrikaner.

Born in the commercial port of Durban on 3 December 1931, he had been brought up by his maternal grandmother as an English speaker in the historically Anglophile province of Natal (today's KwaZulu-Natal). The only surname he had known, and under which he had been schooled, was his grandmother's married name, Lagesse, and hitherto he had not questioned his parentage. But now, in the process of applying for his first job, he had acquired a copy of his birth certificate.

There, alongside the date and place of his birth, was the surname of his father, Henry Francis van Rensburg. Patrick was, by birth, a Van Rensburg. He had known that his maternal grandmother was an anglicised Afrikaner. Now, with this revelation, there could be no doubt: he was himself an Afrikaner.

Formerly known as 'Boers' (Dutch for 'farmers'), the Afrikaners were descendants of former employees of the Dutch East India Company and others who had settled in the Cape from the mid-seventeenth century. During the following century and a half, while some of these colonists established wheat, fruit and wine farms near the Cape, others expanded their pastoral and hunting settlements far to the north and east, largely at the expense of indigenous South Africans who were attempting to pursue a similar pastoral/hunting existence.

Afrikaans emerged out of the oral *taal* (language) of the semi-literate early settlers and their slaves and bonded servants. The appellation 'Afrikaner' came later: a badge of cultural distinction in the late nineteenth century. In particular, it distinguished them from the British, who had occupied the Cape in 1806. From the mid-1830s many of the Eastern Cape Boers trekked north to found independent republics on the Highveld. Against the background of their joint oppression of the black African majority, rivalry between 'Boer and Briton' led to two wars in the late nineteenth century and an uneasy peace and union in 1910.

Thus, within the context of the racial identities and hierarchies of South Africa, Patrick's discovery that January day was hugely significant, made all the more so by the victory just eight months previously of the Afrikaner National Party (NP) in the South African general election of May 1948. The NP had won power in the whites-only election on a pro-gramme of extreme racial segregation, known in Afrikaans as apartheid.

Hitherto, Patrick's sense of identity – if he thought about it at all – would have been complex. His maternal grandmother, Suzanne Isobella, née Lourens, was an Afrikaner from Harrismith in the Orange Free State. She was eighteen in 1899, when the Anglo-Boer War broke out between British imperial forces and the Afrikaner republics of the Transvaal and the Orange Free State. Following the British defeat of the conventional forces of the republics in 1900, the Afrikaners had turned to guerrilla tactics. Among their commanders were three future prime ministers of the post-war Union of South Africa (formed in 1910) – Louis Botha, Jan Smuts and J. B. M. Hertzog.

In order to deprive the commandos of familial support, the British had burnt their farms and imprisoned their women and children in concentration camps in which conditions were harsh and death rates high.[1] Suzanne Lourens, at the age of nineteen or twenty, was one of those interned in a concentration camp with the rest of her family. The roots of Afrikaner nationalism are to be found in a nineteenth-century struggle for freedom from British domination and the attempted anglicisation of white settler culture in the Cape Colony. But the burnt farms and concentration camps of the latter half of the war turned many post-war Afrikaners from flirting with a cultural movement towards a fierce anti-British nationalism. Not so Patrick's grandmother.

Suzanne, one of fifteen children in a typically large Afrikaner family, had been brought up and educated in the formal language of the republics – High

Dutch, a language she regarded as superior to Afrikaans.[2] She disapproved of the use of Afrikaans as a tool in the promotion of Afrikaner nationalism. Indeed, despite her experiences in the concentration camp, Suzanne disapproved of Afrikaner nationalism per se. She favoured the post-war Anglo-Afrikaner reconciliation that was promoted by the likes of Louis Botha and Jan Smuts.

At the end of the war, in 1902, Suzanne Lourens, now twenty-one, was released into Pietermaritzburg, the administrative capital of Natal, which had been a British colony since the 1840s and was thus officially a town where English was spoken, at least by the government and most of the white population.

The vast majority of the people living in the colony, which contained the former kingdom of the Zulu, were, of course, African, and spoke isiZulu or related African languages. But Africans lived in segregated townships and in restricted rural areas and, in the colonial situation of the early twentieth century, urban white residents seldom had any dealings with them apart from employing one or two as menial domestic workers.

On the whole, Natal's white population accepted this situation as the natural order of things and complacently thought of the province as an English-speaking white person's country. In doing so, they conveniently overlooked the significant minority of Indians, who had been imported as indentured labourers in the 1860s to work the sugar plantations of the coastal region north of Durban. By the early twentieth century many of their descendants had moved into retailing, market gardening and petty trading in the Durban suburbs, where they were looked down upon by urban whites as alien immigrants who did not belong.

Soon after her release Suzanne met and married France Lagesse, a recent Franco-Mauritian immigrant from the British Indian Ocean colony of Mauritius. The Franco-Mauritians were descendants of the original French settlers of Mauritius, who, despite the seizure of the colony by the British in 1810, proudly retained their French language and Roman Catholic faith. They developed a particular social prejudice against Mauritian Indians, who, like the Indians in Natal, had been brought out in the nineteenth century to work the sugar plantations. By the time France Lagesse left for Natal, Indians constituted two-thirds of the Mauritian population.

According to family accounts, the Lagesse family had once owned a sugar plantation in Mauritius but it had burnt down. It was this misfortune that had prompted the migration of the family to Natal, to which they brought their particular anti-Indian prejudices. France Lagesse got the relatively humble job of train conductor, and he and his new wife, Suzanne, settled in the small town of Avoca, then just north of Durban, now swallowed up in the suburbs of Durban North.

Suzanne forsook the Dutch Reformed Church into which she had been raised and became a devotee of her husband's Roman Catholic faith. She had a way with languages and quickly developed fluency in both French and English. She gave birth to five children, although only three – one son, Louis, known as 'Jumbo', and two daughters – appear to have survived into adulthood, and she brought them up as French- and English-speaking Roman Catholics.

The eldest of the three, Suzanne, nicknamed 'Pake', married Louis de Froberville, a Mauritian technician at a sugar mill. The younger daughter was Marie Cecile Louise, known simply as Cecile. She married an Afrikaner named Henry Francis van Rensburg, who was a prison warder in the town of Eshowe, north of Durban. At about the time her son, Patrick, was born, they divorced.

Figure 1.1: Cecile (née Lagesse) van Rensburg, the mother of Patrick van Rensburg. (Van Rensburg family collection; photographer unknown)

As a single mother, Cecile needed the income of full employment and she left her child with her mother, who, by then, lived in Pietermaritzburg and was separated from her Mauritian husband. Cecile got a job as a post office telephonist for the Natal county exchange, initially in Eshowe, but later in Howick, not far from Pietermaritzburg.

Patrick was thus brought up by his grandmother, Suzanne Lagesse. He called her 'Mama' and, as a child, was not aware that she was not his mother. Suzanne was about fifty at the time of Patrick's birth, 'a large, matronly woman with a high forehead and a strong face, her long grey hair tightly tied into a ball at the back'.[3] She had a game leg and always walked with the aid of a heavy stick.

Intriguingly, Patrick had two explanations for this. In his first published book, *Guilty Land*, which includes a brief account of his family and upbringing, he wrote that his 'grandmother was crippled by rheumatism and unable to bend her left leg'.[4] In the memoir, written forty years later, on the other hand, he opens the first chapter with a detailed story of one of his earliest memories: a motor car accident in which his 'grandmother alone was hurt, and could never bend her right leg again, having always afterwards to rely on a stout walking stick'.[5]

Whatever the truth about her disability, his grandmother was very much the mainstay of a large extended family, whom she partly sustained by dressmaking and taking in lodgers, mostly young Mauritian relatives. They helped to pay the rent for what was a fairly large house. Jumbo lived with them and contributed to the family income when he had work. Auntie Pake also came to stay for a while when her husband, Uncle Louis, was out of work.

Aside from those in the household, the relative Patrick saw most frequently was the one he knew simply as 'Cecile'. Once she was living in nearby Howick she would visit them quite often, or Jumbo would drive them to visit her. Patrick was fascinated by the Howick waterfall, but he also noted that Cecile gave him a lot of attention: 'She hugged and kissed me a lot, always brought me presents, and took many photographs of me. She was very pretty.'[6] Unaware of the maternal connection, and clearly much loved by the woman he knew as 'Mama', he probably simply took it for granted that he was very special.

Patrick has left us with two apparently conflicting references to his father. In *Guilty Land*, published in 1962, he wrote that his grandmother 'was helped financially by my father, whom I rarely saw'.[7] Later, however, in the memoir, written before Alzheimer's began to take hold of his mind, Patrick wrote that he had never met or even seen Cecile's first husband.[8] When he wrote the early chapters of his memoir he had a clear recollection of many details of his childhood, and a careful reading of those details reveals a probable explanation for the apparent contradiction.

During his teenage years Patrick would gradually learn more about his parentage and by the time he turned thirteen he realised that Cecile was his mother, though he still called her 'Cecile' and his grandmother 'Mama'. Knowledge of his father, on the other hand, was considerably more complex. His statement in the memoir that he had never met his father, whom he refers to as Henry Francis van Rensburg, appears to be true.

On the other hand, he refers frequently to a certain Patrick Maxwell, whom he often met and who paid him a lot of attention. Maxwell was part owner of the Maxwell Campbell motor car business in Durban. He had been a close friend of Cecile when she lived in Eshowe, before Patrick was born. Members of the Lagesse family maintained that Van Rensburg had beaten Cecile, implying that that is why they divorced.

Whether he beat her just because he was that kind of man, and she turned to Maxwell for comfort, or whether it was because of her friendship with Patrick Maxwell, is now impossible to tell. But it must be significant that she called her son Patrick. What is clear is that the Lagesse family would have nothing to do with Van Rensburg, whereas Maxwell was readily accepted as 'Uncle Pat', a close family friend who contributed financially to the household on behalf of Patrick.[9]

Even as an adult Patrick seems to have retained a level of uncertainty about his paternity. Although he provides the reader of his memoir with all the details, hints and implications, as he learned them, he seems reluctant to spell out in so many words that Patrick Maxwell was probably his biological father, which would have meant that he was illegitimate. As we shall see in Chapter 3, as a young adult he was initially happy to take on his new identity as an Afrikaner and, some years later, when writing *Guilty Land* at the age of thirty, he did not want to spoil his new, carefully nurtured image of an Afrikaner who had rebelled against Afrikanerdom's racist ideology of apartheid. In his memoir, on the other hand, he is happy to portray the doubts, and the gathering certainty, about his parentage.

* * *

Patrick grew up accepting as natural the racial prejudices of white South Africans. It was part of the colonial mindset in which South Africa was so deeply entrenched. White people were, in their own view, superior to Africans, Indians and people of mixed race, known in South Africa as 'coloureds'. Indeed, racial prejudice and social hierarchy were so deeply ingrained in the country's social relations that Anglo South Africans even looked down upon their fellow-white Afrikaners.

As a schoolboy Patrick picked this up, joining his schoolfellows in jeering and mocking the boys who attended the Afrikaans school as they walked to and from home on the other side of the road. Added to this, the Lagesse family had inherited the particular Franco-Mauritian prejudice against Indians. Patrick recalled an example of this in an incident from his early childhood. Following the motor accident in which his grandmother injured her leg, the car, which had suffered a tyre blow-out, ended up on its roof in a ditch beside the road.

The driver of the first vehicle to stop happened to be an Indian. His offer of help was rejected. To have accepted his offer would have put *him* on some level of equivalence and put *them* in a state of obligation towards him. This was totally unacceptable, on grounds of racist principle. Fortunately, the adult Patrick observed ironically, it was not long before 'racially accept-able help came by'![10]

On a later occasion, when they were living in Durban, another incident of anti-Indian prejudice occurred that clearly disturbed Patrick, and the memory stayed with him for life. The family had baked a cake for a raffle to raise money for some local cause. Tickets were sold for sixpence and the winning ticket was bought by the Indian man who sold them vegetables at the door. He was very poor and thin and could have done with a cake to take home to his family. But the committee of white ladies organising the raffle insisted that the Indian could not possibly be declared the win-ner. They probably told themselves he would not know what to do with a cake. They drew out an alternative ticket and a white woman 'won' the raffle. Patrick was deeply ashamed of his family's collusion in this deceit and wrote in his memoir: 'I weep at the memory of this happening, as I write this sixty years later.'[11]

Although lacking a traditional two-parent nuclear family and being brought up in a household full of adults, with no siblings, Patrick had an abundance of extended family support and attention. Up to the age of five or six he slept in the same bed as his grandmother, who was very protective of his safety. She would not allow him the freedom to explore the nearby Umzindusi River with a cousin, and when she was busy dressmaking she would tie his leg to her sewing table to prevent him from wandering off and playing in the road outside.

The family, however, frequently went on outings at the weekend. Despite Suzanne's estrangement from her husband, Jumbo would drive them to visit their Mauritian relatives. They would go for tea on Sunday afternoons and from an early age Patrick developed a taste for the garlic and chillies of Mauritian food. French was often spoken in the household, between Mama Suzanne and her children, though not with Patrick.

Fully accepting that the Union of South Africa was a British Dominion, Suzanne Lagesse was determined that her grandson would grow up as a fully English-speaking Natalian. Nevertheless, they still had regular contact with the Afrikaners of his grandmother's Lourens family, especially her youngest brother, Uncle Charlie, who lived nearby in Pietermaritzburg. Despite being Afrikaners, he and others of the Lourens clan who lived in Natal had become much anglicised, and Patrick rarely heard Afrikaans spoken.

2 | An Anglophone South African, 1936–1948

In 1936 Jumbo, who worked for the railways, was transferred to Durban and the Lagesse family moved with him, as his salary had become a vital ingredient of the household income. They settled in Moore Road (now Che Guevara Road), a residential lane in the Berea district, not far from the city centre. Once again the house they rented was large enough to accommodate lodgers.

Patrick, now aged four, began to attend the Davaar Kindergarten. He was particularly taken by any practical work that he was set. He loved making things, a fascination that was to remain with him throughout his adult life. At the age of six he moved to St Henry's Marist Brothers' College, a private school, catering for all levels, from junior primary to senior secondary. His school uniform and other school expenses were paid for by Uncle Pat. Indeed, every birthday Patrick would be taken by car to Uncle Pat's mother's flat in Durban, where he was treated to a birthday tea and presents from Uncle Pat and his sister, whom Patrick knew as 'Auntie Maidie'.

Patrick seems to have been above average at all the usual school subjects at St Henry's, but the one that particularly attracted him was Science. His first visit to the Science laboratory was a revelation as he watched one of the Marist Brothers heating and blowing glass into various shapes. He was 'becoming more and more interested in how things were made'.[1] The subject the school regarded as most important, however, was the study of the Catechism, a question-and-answer booklet that laid out the core beliefs of the Roman Catholic faith. These had to be learned by rote and chanted back to the Brother, regardless of any real understanding.

In this way Patrick was prepared for his First Communion, and later for his Confirmation, performed in the cathedral by the bishop.

His grandmother was a strong devotee of her adopted Catholicism and the family attended Mass every Sunday in the cathedral, which was not far away. Once he had taken his First Communion Patrick would regularly attend confession on Saturday evenings. Then, having confessed his sins and silently recited the allocated prayers for his penance, he would leave the cathedral exhilarated and uplifted, no matter how trivial the misdemeanours he had just confessed.

In due course, as he approached puberty and sexual maturity, a major feature of these visits to the confessional was to confess what the priests referred to as 'self-abuse'. His grandmother's solution, in anticipation of this problem, was to strive to keep him away from girls. This did not help matters at all and merely added to his instinctive shyness with girls, a problem he would have to confront in his early adulthood.

As war in Europe approached in the late 1930s, the family gathered round the radio to listen to the news on the BBC Overseas (World) Service and on returning from school in the afternoon Patrick would be sent out to buy the evening newspaper from the local shop. News of impending war split the South African political scene. J. B. M. Hertzog's Afrikaner Nationalists and Smuts's South African Party had combined in 1933 to form the United Party (UP). On the approach of war, however, Smuts's pro-British stance alienated Hertzog, who broke away from the UP and in due course joined Dr D. F. Malan's 'Purified' National Party. This left Smuts as prime minister of the remaining United Party government.

On the outbreak of war in September 1939, thousands of white South Africans, mainly from among the English-speaking population, volunteered for active service in the South African Union Defence Force (SAUDF). Among them was Patrick Maxwell, 'Uncle Pat'. Jumbo volunteered too but was initially turned down as his work with the railways was considered an essential service.

Initially, Smuts, keenly aware of Afrikaner sensibilities, confined South African forces to the strategic defence of Southern Africa. Once the Italians had attacked British forces in occupied Egypt and in Somaliland, however, Smuts got parliamentary approval for the deployment of South African troops anywhere within Africa. In January 1941 two divisions of the SAUDF travelled north to serve in North Africa and the Horn. Uncle Pat, now an army captain, went with them, as did Jumbo, whose application had finally been accepted. He was to serve as a despatch rider.

And so, in January 1941, with the loss of two sources of financial support, Patrick's secure and loving family life began to fall apart. Uncle Pat was no longer available to pay his school fees and the loss of Jumbo's contribution to the household income meant that his grandmother could no longer afford to keep the house in Moore Road. She rented a room for herself from a local Jewish shopkeeper named Waldman and sent Patrick to a state boarding school at Ixopo, far off in the hills of the Natal Midlands north of Pietermaritzburg.

It was nine-year-old Patrick's first time away from the security of his family and he suffered from homesickness. He was housed in a make-shift dormitory with a number of other boys on the veranda of a large old colonial-style house belonging to one of the masters, known to the boys as 'Mr Chips', an archetypal teacher's nickname from the book and film *Goodbye Mr Chips*.[2]

It was while staying at Mr Chips's that Patrick first became accustomed to the staple African diet of maize meal, two to three times a day, either cooked as a stiff mash or diluted with milk and a little sugar to form a soft porridge. It was accompanied by a small amount of vegetable relish and, only rarely, a little meat.

Groups of children shared plots in the garden where they were able to grow vegetables to supplement their diet. Mr Chips appears to have run a small farm and sawmill not far from the school and the boys were obliged to work there on Saturday mornings, usually loading logs at the sawmill. If chickens were being slaughtered for market the boys would return home to a lunch of boiled chicken offal, feet and heads, served with bread – surely a veritable feast compared with the humble fare usually served at the school. Many years later Patrick was to draw on this model of school farm, com-bined with 'voluntary' labour on Saturday mornings, to supplement the students' diet, when he set up his own school in Bechuanaland/Botswana.

The sense of war was never far away, as Durban's daily paper, the *Natal Mercury*, was regularly delivered to Ixopo. Patrick would pore over it for news of the South African troops, trying to picture Uncle Pat and Jumbo in faraway North Africa. Halfway through his second year at Ixopo, at the end of June 1942, he learned of the fall of Tobruk in Libya, one of the worst British defeats of the war. Some 34 000 men, including the South African division, surrendered to Rommel's Afrika Korps.

Uncle Pat was to spend the rest of the war in a German prisoner-of-war camp. The *Mercury* carried a banner headline 'Avenge Tobruk', and this was duly achieved by General Montgomery and the Eighth Army at the Battle of El Alamein in October 1942.

In December 1942 Patrick, just turned eleven, left the Ixopo boarding school for the last time and returned to Durban in high spirits. Jumbo had been released from military duty and they had rented a big house at the uphill end of Moore Road. Once more they took in Mauritian relatives as boarders, while Patrick shared a room with Jumbo.

One of the first things Patrick was told he had to do on his return from Ixopo was to go to a hotel in Durban to meet Cecile and her new husband, a Scotsman named Norman Bain, who worked for the Anglo-Iranian Oil Company (the future British Petroleum, BP). They were currently on leave from Iran, had already been to visit Norman's family in Scotland and were due to return to Iran shortly.

It was at this time that Patrick became aware that Cecile was his biological mother. The knowledge did not create a new emotional bond. Indeed, the sadness he felt as they departed from the Durban docks was not at their going and leaving him behind, as Cecile might have imagined; rather, Patrick was mourning for the true parental bond of which he had been deprived. It was a sense of personal loss and rejection that was to haunt him for many years to come and led to a sense of inadequacy and lack of personal self-confidence.

He learned to deal with it through a fiery determination always to prove himself capable of achievement and worthy of admiration and love. Throughout much of his adult life he would strive for the emotional rewards of fame. On this occasion he was simply pleased to be able to go home to the emotional warmth of his grandmother, who would always be his true 'Mama'.

In January 1943 he started at Bulwer Park Primary School, where he was fortunate to have a Miss Frank as his form teacher for the next two years. She was impressed with the strength of his general knowledge and his understanding of events around him. He had learned much from reading newspapers, listening to the news on the wireless and being exposed to regular adult conversation. She encouraged this knowledge and helped him expand his understanding of how society was organised and how government worked, with political parties, elections, Parliament and a Cabinet of ministers.

Between them, Miss Frank and his grandmother encouraged his reading habit, sending him to the public library to choose his own books. At this stage he was reading classic boyhood books like *Just William* and *Biggles*, but they instilled in him a love of reading and, in due course, he moved on to English literature and poetry. He would sit on the floor while his grandmother sewed, her mouth filled with pins so that she could seldom talk while working, and he would read to her from *Outspan* magazine,[3] or romantic stories from *Women's Weekly* and the latest reports, especially war reports, from the *Daily News*, Durban's evening paper.

In 1943, at the age of twelve, Patrick decided he would publish his own newspaper as a one-off edition to raise money for the war effort. He would call it *The Goodwill Magazine*. He found a printer in town who would print it free of charge, while a technician at the *Daily News* agreed to make metal photographic plates, also free of charge. He showed Patrick around the paper's printing works, introducing him to the whole printing process, one step at a time, from typesetting the lead lettering to assembling the print onto the huge rollers.[4] He was interviewed for the *Daily News* about his fundraising and was proud to see the report of the interview printed in the paper the next day. A week later his own paper appeared, and all 1 500 copies were sold.[5]

As many of the young Mauritians who boarded with the family in Moore Road left to set up their own homes, his grandmother began taking in on short-term leases Afrikaner couples, some with children of Patrick's age. It was a bit of a revelation for Patrick, who began to hear Afrikaans spoken in the home for the first time. He had never actually conversed with Afrikaners before. Afrikaans was a subject he had to learn at school and Afrikaners were known in the stereotype of his school peers as strange snub-nosed people with short-cropped hair. He was surprised to find that they were really no different from himself.

One couple, the Mullers, were staunch Nationalists and one evening Patrick, who was about twelve at the time, sat with them after dinner

Figure 2.1: Patrick, about twelve years old, with his maternal grandmother, Suzanne Isobella Lagesse, and a young cousin. (Van Rensburg family collection; photographer unknown)

and listened as they extolled the virtues of Afrikaner nationalism and condemned Smuts's betrayal of the Afrikaner by his support for the British in the Second World War.

Patrick had never heard criticism of Smuts before and he listened carefully to their reasoning. They explained that the British had always wanted to control the whole of South Africa, in order to profit from the country's gold and diamonds. And after the Anglo-Boer War, which the British had caused, they sought to divide the Afrikaners by winning over people like Botha and Smuts to supporting the British Empire.

The British controlled the economy, exploiting Afrikaner workers. What South Africa needed, argued the Mullers, was a government for the Afrikaners that would take care of the poor whites from rural areas, who were moving into the cities in search of jobs that were being given to the blacks. The Mullers' voices were raised with passion as they spoke of the way the British had treated Afrikaner women and children in the concentration camps, describing the British behaviour as 'bestial'.

At this point Patrick's grandmother, who had come in at the tail end of the loud monologue, could stand it no longer. She told them she had been in a concentration camp and had personally experienced the conditions there, which the Mullers, who had not even been born until long after the war had ended, had not.

She claimed that the Nationalists 'distorted the truth about the camps, making up stories and telling lies', and doing it just for 'their own political gain'. In doing so they were reviving the old animosity between English-speaking South Africans and Afrikaners 'that 40 years of reconciliation had helped to heal'. It was one of the only times Patrick had heard his grand-mother speak of the concentration camps and he had never seen her so angry. Her outburst ended the discussion.[6]

The household at this time had hired a young Indian woman as a cook, perhaps because she could make the kind of spicy food the family enjoyed. One evening, after his grandmother had retired to bed, there was some disturbance outside, near the small servants' quarters at the back. Muller led the way outside to see what the disturbance was about. There they found a slightly built young bespectacled Indian man who had come to visit the cook.

Without enquiry and without hesitation Muller, who was a burly man, punched the Indian to the ground, smashing his glasses in the process.

Patrick was deeply shocked. It was his first experience of the violence of racism in its crudest form, and he recalled that he 'sensed a stirring of sympathy ... for its hapless victim'.[7]

* * *

The year following his thirteenth birthday (3 December 1944) was one of happiness and grief for Patrick and his family. It had started well, with the usual birthday celebration at the Maxwell household, something Auntie Maidie and her mother maintained throughout the time that Uncle Pat was away.

Shortly afterwards Patrick heard that he had passed his primary school examinations well enough to be admitted to Glenwood High School, a whites-only English-medium state school, founded in Durban in 1910. In the new year Auntie Maidie took him to buy his school uniform: green blazer with badge and tie, grey flannels and a straw boater, or basher, with green ribbon. Recollection of the pride he felt in his new uniform and the élitism it represented may have contributed to his decision years later not to allow a school uniform at his own school in Bechuanaland.

Patrick did not develop many new friendships at Glenwood High. He already had a core of close friends from among the sons of family friends and neighbours in the Moore Road district of Durban, with whom he would play backyard cricket and stage mock battles in their gardens. The favourite playground was the backyard of one of his closest friends, Colin Francis, whose parents, Eric and Vivienne, were very tolerant of the boys' rowdy games. The Francis parents were to become important figures in Patrick's life during his Glenwood years. As he was to discover, Vivienne, Uncle Pat and Cecile had been close friends in Eshowe before Patrick was born. And Eric Francis was Patrick's English teacher at Glenwood High.

Eric's English lessons brought the set books alive to such an extent that six decades later Patrick could vividly recall the characters of *The Virginian* by Owen Wister, a novel about cowboys in the American Wild West, but could not recall any of the boys in Eric's class. Eric not only built on Patrick's love of reading but helped develop his enthusiasm for English literature, recommending classic works that were beyond the curriculum.

Backyard cricket had given Patrick a great love for the real game. He never made it into the school team, but found an alternative route into the game – as an umpire. In due course, as a young adult, this was to take him to high levels of the game.

* * *

In April 1945 Cecile and Norman came home on leave from Iran with their new infant daughter, Jean, Patrick's half-sister. But the joyful family reunion was almost immediately buried in the disaster that followed.

'Mama', the loving grandmother who had been Patrick's sheet anchor in life, became gravely ill with liver cancer and was admitted to hospital. She went downhill quickly, becoming thinner and frailer every time he visited. She suffered greatly and gradually it dawned on him that she was dying. Finally, one evening Cecile and Jumbo came home from a visit to relate that she had died while they sat with her. She was sixty-four. She was buried in the churchyard of Emmanuel Cathedral, and every Sunday in the weeks that followed Patrick visited the grave and observed the gradual sinking of the mound of earth as the soil settled around the coffin.

Patrick felt 'cut adrift' by the loss of his precious 'Mama'. Cecile was small comfort – he never felt a bond with her. And she would soon be off to Scotland with Norman and Jean for the rest of their leave, then back to Iran. The family gathered in Moore Road to decide what to do. It was agreed that they would give up the house after Cecile and family left for Scotland; Jumbo would take a room in Clark Road and Patrick would move in with Eric and Vivienne Francis, who lived just around the corner in Cato Road.

The loss of his home was yet another painful blow that Patrick found hard to bear, but Eric and Vivienne made him feel a real part of their family and that was his salvation. Years later he was to write that 'no one could have done more than Vivienne to help me regain composure and self-confidence'.[8]

It was around this time, in May 1945, that the war in Europe ended. Uncle Pat came home from Germany a few weeks later. The first Patrick knew of it was when a smart car came to pick him up from school and take him to the Maxwell Campbell car salesroom in town. Many years later he could still recall the scene vividly: 'Uncle Pat came out of his office on seeing me, clasping my hand firmly, with the reassuring smile that played on his lips and lit up his face and eyes, which I remembered from before.'[9]

It had been four and a half years since they had met, and Uncle Pat would have seen a huge change in the boy. He drove them along Durban North beach and parked the car. They walked along the shore and talked into the early evening: 'He told me of his war experience. I unburdened my anguished soul to him.'[10]

He saw quite a lot of Uncle Pat after that and understood him to be his guardian, whatever that might mean – nobody ever talked about it in his family. Uncle Pat gave him books to read and tried to give him advice. He sometimes took him to lunch, but mostly they went for drives or walks. He still went to Uncle Pat's mother's house on his birthday, although, interestingly, he was never taken to Uncle Pat's own home.

Patrick does not mention in his memoir whether Patrick Maxwell had a wife and children, presumably because he did not know at the time, and he was careful only to relate the world as he had experienced it. In fact, Patrick Maxwell was married and in the post-war years he and his wife had three sons. It was not until 1990–1991, when Patrick was allowed back to South Africa after thirty years spent in exile, that the truth of his paternity was openly confirmed and he was welcomed into the Maxwell family by 'Uncle Pat' – whom he now recognised as his true biological father – and his three half-brothers.[11]

Patrick quickly settled into his new home life with the Francis family. One of their friends was a Mr Silburn, a leader writer for the *Natal Mercury*, which greatly impressed Patrick. Silburn encouraged the boy's enthusiasm about essay-writing competitions and, at the same time, discouraged his youthful penchant for using long words.

But perhaps the most important influence on Patrick in terms of his future work and career in Bechuanaland/Botswana was his introduction to the building trade. Eric's father, Percy Francis, was a woodworking craftsman who made spinning wheels and Eric had picked up many of his father's skills. But he did not confine himself to woodwork. He could turn his hand to anything.

He had renovated and made improvements to the home in Cato Road and at the time of Patrick's arrival was planning to build a garage at the end of the driveway. This required concrete foundations on which to lay the floor and Eric had already made the wooden shuttering. Patrick, always interested in how things were made, helped mix the concrete and pour it into the shuttering. Eric showed him how to measure out the rectangle of the plan – providing practical application for the theoretical geometry he was learning at school – and how to lay the bricks for the garage wall, being careful to maintain accurate measurements with the aid of a spirit level.

Then, under Eric's close supervision, Patrick was allowed to build an extension to the servants' quarters. He also helped Eric convert a two-storey house into two maisonettes. As Patrick remembered it: 'We spent many hours after school and at weekends to complete the job and I happily worked as his "apprentice", learning varied building skills including drain-laying and manhole construction, and marvelling at his handiwork.'[12]

* * *

Patrick turned fifteen at the end of 1946. He had passed his Junior Certificate examination well enough to go on to senior secondary school. Uncle Pat offered to pay for him to go to Michaelhouse or Hilton College, the top two English-medium private schools in Natal, both situated in the northern Natal Midlands.

But, remembering his unhappiness at Ixopo, so far from home, Patrick preferred to stay in Durban and went into the senior school at Glenwood High, where his teachers were mostly good at their job and their lessons often memorable.

He recalls the 'painstaking bookkeeping lessons' of Mr 'Zookie' Ellison, the highly disciplined Maths lessons of Mr Dwyer and the more relaxed classes of Mr Max Sandler, who taught Afrikaans. The latter's easy manner and good humour enabled Patrick to enjoy his Afrikaans lessons and appreciate some Afrikaans literature. Sport was an important feature of school life and in the summer season he was able to progress with umpiring at cricket, while in the winter season he enjoyed rugby, at which he did well, featuring in one of the school teams.

Ever since his primary school days Patrick had enjoyed writing stories and essays, many of which he sent to magazines for publication, though never with any success. During his first year at Glenwood Senior School, however, he won second prize in an under-16 essay competition run by the *Natal Mercury*.

His prize was book vouchers to the value of two guineas (£2.2 shillings).[13] He used them to buy two books, each of which made a deep impression on him. The first was Thomas Armstrong's *King Cotton*, a novel about cotton workers in industrial Lancashire who, during the American Civil War, refused to work with cotton imported from the slave-owning states, despite the hardship it caused them. It taught him the importance of principle over personal gain. The second was a non-fiction work about the great slave revolt in San Domingue, France's sugar plantation colony in the Caribbean.

The book, probably C. L. R. James's *The Black Jacobins* (first published in 1938), tells the story of Toussaint L'Ouverture, the San Domingo Revolution and the establishment of the Republic of Haiti (1791–1803). Books such as these took Patrick, at least in his imagination, way beyond his limited experience of life in Durban and colonial Natal.

Two incidents brought Patrick to the notice of the school authorities and possibly barred his passage to becoming a school prefect. The first was the 'liver revolt', in which he and a number of boys carried the liver they had been served at dinner to the headmaster's study to complain that it was tainted. Sure enough, when the meat was tested it was declared 'unfit for human consumption'. The food improved after that, but the incident did not win Patrick any friends in high places.

Then, during his final year, at the age of sixteen, as the nation of white electors geared up for the fateful general election of 1948, Patrick organised a campaign among the boarders 'to be allowed to hold elections for a student representative body that could discuss student concerns with the hostel administration'. Although the idea had a lot of student support, he noted later that 'our masters were not ready for such initiatives'.[14]

Patrick was boarding at the school by then and on the night of the general election (26/27 May) he and a friend named McGregor decided they should stay up to listen to the wireless in the common room as the results came in. At 5 am they finally retired to bed, happy in the knowledge that General Smuts's United Party was clearly on the path to victory.

By the end of the following day, however, once all the rural constituencies had been declared, it became apparent that, although the United Party had a clear majority of total votes cast, Dr D. F. Malan's Afrikaner

National Party had won a majority of four seats in Parliament. Such were the vagaries of the 'first-past-the-post' voting system, which was set out in the South Africa Act of 1909 and had been modelled on the British system.

As Patrick recalled, there was consternation in many parts of the country, especially in Anglophone Natal.[15] He had picked up from his grandmother, and from the behaviour of their Afrikaner boarder, Muller, that Afrikaner Nationalists were not good people and he simply accepted that all good people voted for Smuts.

During the final term of 1948, as a break from intensive study and to get the students thinking about adult life after school, the seniors were taken on educational trips to learn something about productive industry. Years later Patrick could still recall the huge soap-making vats of Lever Brothers, in which fats and oils bubbled away, and the moulding and packaging of the finished soap.

Figure 2.2: Patrick (*left*) in his final year at Glenwood High School, 1948. (Van Rensburg family collection; photographer unknown)

Some of the teachers took their students to see a couple of the films of Shakespeare plays that were on the English Literature syllabus, but the film that affected Patrick most was *A Song to Remember*, the story of the life of the Polish composer Frédéric Chopin, played by Cornel Wilde. From his earliest childhood Patrick had enjoyed going to the cinema (known in South Africa as the 'bioscope').

He had been excited by the animated films he had seen as a child, and, as he grew older, he eagerly absorbed the images and informative ideas of documentaries, as well as comedy and adventure films. But he was, at heart, an incurable romantic and now, approaching the age of seventeen, he was moved, not only by Chopin's stirring piano music, but also particularly by his love affair with the French woman writer George Sand, played in the film by Merle Oberon.

Patrick felt he had acquitted himself well in his final exams, especially in the English Language essay in which he chose to write about his preference for film over theatre. He had no problem extolling the visual scope of cinema, maintaining that it was far superior to that of live theatre 'with its flimsy, make-believe props'.[16]

At his farewell school assembly he was disappointed not to receive any of the awards given out to students who had been outstanding in sport or studies. It appeared that he had 'not made much of a mark at Glenwood High'. He left the assembly room 'feeling a little sad, unfulfilled and uncertain of the future'.[17] Perhaps, however, he had made more of a mark than he supposed, for when he told his headmaster that he was thinking of going into teaching, the head remarked, 'You'll be wasting your talents! ... You can do better with your life than going into teaching.' Patrick felt enormously flattered, although he was not at all sure what career path the head may have had in mind.[18]

He walked out of the great red-brick school building for the final time acutely aware that he was about to enter upon his adult life. From now on he alone would be responsible for decisions about his future path. In fact, he had already sat the civil service examination, and this was the career direction in which he was initially to head. But, according to his memoir, as he walked out of the school for the last time, the title of a book came into his mind. It was a novel set in pre-war industrial Britain and related the story of a working-class boy who became a socialist activist and, in due course, rose to become a successful politician.

The book, a best-seller by Howard Spring, was first published in 1940 and a film of the same name, starring Michael Redgrave, came out in 1947. Patrick had probably just seen the film, which would account for the title *Fame is the Spur* springing to mind.[19] If this was more than just an apocryphal recollection he would have strode out of that school building boosted by the notion that somehow, someday, he would become famous.

3 | The Making of an Afrikaner, 1949–1953

In January 1949 Patrick heard that he had passed the civil service exam and that he was to report to the magistrate's office in Durban. He went along with a copy of his matriculation certificate, but was told he also had to bring a copy of his birth certificate. He turned to his uncle Jumbo, who produced the document. Patrick was shocked to find that his surname on the birth certificate was 'van Rensburg'.

The magistrate insisted he must use his officially registered name, and Patrick and Jumbo each had to make a sworn declaration that Patrick van Rensburg and Patrick Lagesse (the name on his matriculation certificate) were one and the same person. He recollected being quite upset about the 'conspiracy of silence' that he felt the family had practised on him. Nor was he mollified by Uncle Pat's offer to adopt him formally and change his name by deed poll to Maxwell. He declined the offer. He had had quite enough of 'unexplained complications' and having just collected one new name had no inclination to adopt another.[1]

He received a posting to the Office of the Master of the Supreme Court in Pietermaritzburg, where, initially, he shared a room at Uncle Charlie's in Longmarket Street (today's Langalibalele Street). Most of his work entailed sorting out the legal ramifications of deceased persons' estates. He shared an open-plan office with a number of other clerks, half of whom were Afrikaners and half English-speakers, who rarely socialised outside their own group. Patrick Lagesse had been brought up with the anti-Afrikaner sentiment of a typical Anglophone Natalian. Now, as Patrick van Rensburg, he found himself in the unusual position of being an Anglophone Afrikaner, able to identify with either group.

He was quickly taken under the wing of Michael John Ensor, an Anglophone ex-serviceman who took Patrick home to lunch and won his friendship by playing cricket with him in the office corridors.[2] Interested in learning more about Afrikanerdom, that unknown side of his heritage, he also deliberately socialised with the Afrikaners in the office. Two of the people who were a big influence on him during his four years there were Afrikaners: Daan van Tonder,[3] a clerk like himself, though some years older, and Mr J. J. A. Nel, the chief clerk and assistant master.

Both were keen supporters of the new National Party government and Daan van Tonder used every opportunity to try to win Patrick over to the Nationalist cause. He was so convinced of the righteousness of the cause that he loved to discuss it and explain its virtues to this 'half-English' Afrikaner.

Van Tonder believed that in due course the two white groups would come together to ensure that they were not overrun by blacks. There were, after all, eight million black people in South Africa in 1945, compared with just two million whites. The all-white election of 1948 had been won largely on the propaganda of the *swart gevaar* (black peril) and the *oor-strooming* (swamping) of the cities by black people.

Van Tonder argued the National Party line that for white people to survive it was essential to keep the races apart. This, he explained, was what apartheid was all about. Patrick, who appears initially not to have been aware of the domination element in National Party policy, was swept up with the fascination of the new cultural identity he was forging for himself.

He was, for the moment, seduced by Van Tonder's insistence that 'blacks would only find their fulfilment in their own self-governing homelands'.[4] The unpalatable truth that those so-called homelands were confined to about 13 per cent of the country was glossed over, with people like Patrick left to assume that a more equitable distribution must feature somewhere in the grand plan.

Van Tonder took Patrick to his home in the Orange Free State, the heart of Afrikanerdom, for the celebration of his brother's wedding. The trip was a revelation. Twelve years later Patrick was to write:

I remember, as if it happened yesterday, the strange feeling I had at the reception as I noticed how very much these people looked like the

32

people I had mixed with in Natal. Afrikaners were *not* all pug-faced people with short haircuts! There were good-looking men and beautiful girls, just as there were among the people I associated with at home. It struck me like a blow in the face, and when I talked with them afterwards and danced in the evening with the girls, the transformation was complete. We spent the rest of the week-end with Daan's mother, and she reminded me of my grandmother. She had the same grey hair, the same kind of voice. I felt at home.[5]

He was introduced to an Afrikaner *braaivleis* (barbecue) and the fast spinning dance and musicians of the *Tiekiedraai*. By the end of the week-end he had begun to feel some link with his missing Afrikaner heritage. He acknowledged that he would probably never become a true native-born Afrikaner – his Anglophile upbringing was too deeply ingrained for that – but he began to feel empathy for Afrikaners and understood something of their desire to protect and preserve their culture.

His relationship with Mr Nel was quite different. Possessing the subtlety of his seniority, the chief clerk may have been more persuasive in his own quiet way. For some reason he decided to take Patrick under his wing. Perhaps he perceived something of the young man's intelligence and propensity for hard work. As Patrick fondly remembered him:

Mr J. J. A. Nel was a tall, brilliant, middle-aged man, with a slight stoop and a balding head. He immediately took a fatherly interest in me, was always available to me, even though I was a very junior official, and spent hours in teaching me the finer details of my work. He encouraged me to wrestle with all the legal problems that cropped up and to argue them to a conclusion … When I began studying for an extra-mural degree, he kept me going with encouragement and interest. He drew me very gently towards a deeper understanding of and a greater sympathy for Afrikanerdom …[6]

* * *

Soon after he had begun work at the Master's Office Patrick registered as an external student at the University of South Africa (Unisa) to study by correspondence for a Bachelor of Arts degree. In the first two years of the four-year course he could study a wide range of subjects. He chose Afrikaans/Nederlands, History, Psychology, Law, Politics, Economics and English Literature. In due course he settled on English and Economics as his two majors.

In all he had eleven modules to complete in the four years. In contrast to the Anglophones, who normally expected Afrikaners to speak English, he welcomed the opportunity to speak Afrikaans with Van Tonder, Nel and others in the office. And through his studies he learned to appreciate the beauty of Afrikaans poetry. As for Law, he could clearly see its importance and role in so many of life's major decisions. It also enabled him to understand better the intricacies of some of the cases with which he had to deal.

English Literature was an obvious major: it had been his favourite subject at secondary school. His lessons in Practical Criticism[7] taught him to read with sensitivity and awareness, enabling him to experience, vicariously, through the characters in the novels and plays that he read, people of other times and cultures, especially those of England. And the feedback he got from his correspondence tutor, Professor Edward Davis, helped improve his writing and make it more succinct, focused and clear. He developed into a very quick reader and his reading fed into an emerging desire to travel – 'overseas', as Anglophone South Africans put it when they wanted to 'go home' to England.

His shared room at Uncle Charlie's was not conducive to a life of work and study and he found a single room with a Boulanger cousin who lived nearby. The Boulangers were relatives on the Mauritian side of the family. Uncle Pat bought him a bicycle and undertook to provide him with an extra £5 a month to buy books. Thus settled in, he developed a regular work routine, allocating time for study before work in the morning and every evening during the week. He kept the weekends free for sport and other activities.[8]

He registered with the Umpires' Association in Pietermaritzburg and, using Uncle Pat's allowance, was able to buy himself a white coat, floppy hat and dark flannels so that he looked the part of an umpire. The experience he had gained at Glenwood High was soon recognised by the association and he found himself 'standing' for First Division matches at the famous Oval in Alexandra Park.

Then, as the summer turned to autumn, he joined the Wanderers' Rugby Club and began training for the winter season. During that first year he played regularly for the club's second team. At six feet (1.85 m) he was a tall young man for his generation and, through rugby training, he broadened out considerably and became fit and powerful. One weekend he cycled, on his standard bicycle, down to Durban and back with Clive Andrews, the hooker of the first team: five hours down, a quick swim in the ocean, overnight with relatives and eight hours back uphill on the Sunday.

By the second rugby season, at the age of eighteen, Patrick had become a promising member of the rugby club, a regular for the second team and occasional reserve for the first. He played tight-head prop in the front row of the scrum. But he was also nimble on his feet, and in the days before colleagues hoisted the 'catcher' in the line-outs he outjumped many of his opponents to catch the ball and pass it back to the waiting scrum half.

His efforts were well rewarded when, in the 1950 season, he was chosen for the Pietermaritzburg under-19 team to play Durban. The match was played at Durban's Kingsmead ground, the home of Natal rugby, where, as a schoolboy, he had watched a number of first-class matches. During the game Patrick broke through a loose scrum and sprinted to the line to score a try, an unusual feat for a front-row forward. After the match he was selected to play for the province's under-19 team against the Orange Free State in September. Natal won, with Patrick once again scoring a try.

In the summer seasons Patrick shone at cricket too and was gaining quite a reputation for his confident and accurate umpiring. To be a cricket umpire is a highly responsible position for in his[9] hands may lie the outcome of a match. Reputations can be made or lost on the decision of an umpire. He must know the exact path of the ball from the moment it leaves the bowler's hand and whether it strikes the batsman's bat, gloves, leg or wicket. He must know immediately how to respond to the fielders' eager appeal: 'Howzat!'

The one thing an umpire dreads is making a mistake. That happened to Patrick in a match against Durban at the Pietermaritzburg Oval in January 1952. As the appeal resounded for lbw (leg-before-wicket) Patrick's finger went up. In the stunned silence that followed two things happened. The Durban batsman accepted the decision and walked and Patrick realised he had made a mistake. His reputation as an umpire depended on what happened next. He ran after the batsman, apologised for his mistake and called him back to the wicket.

He expected to be criticised during the lunch break but he found quite the contrary. He was praised for instantly correcting the decision and that season the Umpires' Association nominated him to umpire the Currie Cup match between Orange Free State and Natal, to be played at the Oval. It was a three-day first-class game, and Patrick proudly noted that his name would be entered in *Wisden Cricketers' Almanack*, the international record of first-class cricket. Natal won the match.

During his four years at the Master's Office Patrick made a large number of friends, Afrikaners and Anglophones; but it was very much a male world. Apart from his colleagues at work (there were only ever three women in the office in the four years that he worked there), most of his friends were from the rugby club, a very male bastion. He felt shy and awkward in the company of females and did not know how to communicate with them. He was acutely aware that he had no girlfriend and hid away from the fact by burying himself in his books.

His growing interest in Afrikanerdom was boosted both by his new friends and by his reading of their literature. He found the re-reading of South African history from an Afrikaner perspective very revealing. It was, of course, a history of 'white' South Africa, which glossed over or ignored prior African occupation and the violence of the white man's subjugation of rural Africans. And it failed to mention altogether the seventeenth- and eighteenth-century acts of genocide against the indigenous San ('Bushman') hunter-gatherers.

Historical myths are the building blocks of cultural perception, and through his reading of the Afrikaner view of history Patrick began to understand something of their perception of their struggle against the odds, first against indigenous Africans and then against the British.

He learned of the significance of the Great Trek, in which half the Afrikaner population of the Eastern Cape (some 7 000 men, women and children, together with their bonded servants) migrated to the Highveld north of the Orange River between 1835 and 1841. They went on to found the republics of the Orange Free State and the Transvaal.[10] He learned, too, of the importance Afrikaners attached to their victory over the Zulu at the 'Battle of Blood (Ncome) River' on 16 December 1838, the day commemorated by Afrikaners thereafter as *Geloftedag* ('the Day of the Vow').[11]

Those original Afrikaner migrants were known as *Voortrekkers* ('those who went ahead') and Patrick, absorbed in Afrikanerdom during his first year of study, listened avidly on the radio to the broadcast of Prime Minister Malan's *'Quo Vadis'* speech, delivered on the occasion of the unveiling of the Voortrekker Monument in December 1949.

Standing in front of that huge stone bastion built on a hill overlooking Pretoria, Dr Malan urged twentieth-century urbanised Afrikaners to turn back to the spirit of the Voortrekkers; to the religion, morals and supposed racial purity of those pioneering days. The significance of the date chosen for the unveiling, 16 December, may have been lost on Patrick at the time, although he was later to realise that Malan was identifying Afrikaner nationalism with the annual commemoration of their largest single military victory over independent Africans. It was to be a while before Patrick appreciated that what Afrikaner nationalism was really all about was not so much separation of peoples as domination, for fear of being dominated.

Meanwhile, Patrick would have noticed the name Van Rensburg cropping up in his history studies. One of the original Voortrekker leaders, for instance, was a Van Rensburg. It must have awakened in him thoughts of his Afrikaner father, Henry Francis van Rensburg, and he wanted to know more about him.[12] He dared not ask close members of the family as they had made it quite clear over the years that mention of the name was taboo.

He approached one of his Mauritian Boulanger cousins and asked her where his father was. Her enigmatic reply puzzled him, for she told him that he knew where his father was, he was living in Durban and managing a motor business. Patrick insisted that that was his guardian Uncle Pat, and she replied, 'Well, I don't know about that!'[13] Patrick makes light of it in his memoir and claims that knowledge of his father was not something that preyed on his mind. But the fact that his memory of this exchange remained so clear some fifty years later suggests it was not as insignificant as he made out.

* * *

Patrick's studies often took him to the city library to borrow books and while there he would browse the papers and periodicals. It was a legal deposit library, so a copy of every South African publication, be it book, paper or periodical, was required to be deposited there. For the first time Patrick was exposed to viewpoints other than those of white people. It opened up a whole new world of perspectives he could no longer ignore.

He read the *Indian Opinion*, a Gujarati-English weekly paper edited by Manilal Gandhi, the second son of Mahatma Mohandas Gandhi. Patrick had known Indians as shopkeepers and vegetable hawkers in Durban and had conveniently thought nothing further about them or their point of view. Over a long weekend in January 1949 Africans in Durban rioted against Indians, burning and looting their shops, assaulting and killing many. Some of that venom spread to Pietermaritzburg, where numerous Indians were assaulted and, true to his prejudiced upbringing, Patrick felt no particular sympathy for them.

His attitude, like that of many white people in Natal, was that Indians should go back to India. They had no future in South Africa. Now, here in the public library, he was exposed to the articulate Indian viewpoint. Among the various things he read, one that particularly stuck in his mind was a powerfully written article about the harsh realities of apartheid. The writer was Christopher Gell, an Englishman who had come to South Africa with his South African–born wife after a number of years in the Indian civil service.

Gell had been struck down by polio as a young man in 1945. By the time he came to South Africa two years later, he was confined to an 'iron lung' for all but six hours a day for the rest of his life. Undaunted, he was a passionate critic of racial injustice. He acknowledged in his article in *Indian Opinion* that he did not expect to live long but that he had requested in his will that his ashes be scattered over the sea so as not to rest on the land that had given birth to 'the abomination of apartheid'.

Patrick had never before heard or read such a strong and cogently argued condemnation of the very concept of apartheid. It would certainly have given him food for thought. Gell lived on until 1958, an undaunted journalistic critic of racial discrimination in all its forms.

While employed at the Master's Office Patrick often had to work on cases of Indian inheritance and he found himself regularly dealing with Mr P. R. Pather, the secretary of an Indian charitable society that helped people sort out the tangled affairs of their inherited estates.[14] Hitherto he had paid him the minimum of attention, but, after reading Gell's article, he found himself showing Mr Pather an exaggerated level of respect. Mr Pather must have noticed the difference, but whether he appreciated it or found it patronising Patrick had no way of knowing, because he did not as yet have any social contact with people of Indian origin.

Similarly, Patrick had only ever perceived Africans as servants, farm labourers and manual workers who performed menial tasks, yet here in the library were newspapers and periodicals written by Africans – authors and journalists of considerable literary sophistication. From their newspapers he learned something of their everyday struggles and aspirations, which were little different, in essence, from his own. But South African society was so constructed that he did not, in either his working or his social life, have an opportunity to meet any of these literate Africans and he had not yet reached the stage when he would seek them out. Nevertheless, his readings in the library appear to have sown the seed of a sense of unease about the government's racial policies.[15]

He began to be more observant of the world around him and became more aware of dire poverty contrasting with extremes of white wealth. He also became painfully conscious of the racist banter of his white friends. He had seen white people push blacks around, assaulting them without a second thought and treating them with contempt. It made him ill at ease and he grew concerned about the growing propensity for violence, as in, for instance, the government's response to the Defiance Campaign mounted by members of the African National Congress (ANC) and the South African Indian Congress through the second half of 1952.

As thousands of Africans and Indians defied the multitude of racist restrictions on where 'Non-White' people could live, where they could go, whom they could mix with and the amenities they could use, the authorities cracked down hard. Patrick was shocked by the level of police violence as they arrested thousands, whom the courts sent to prison for periods of up to three months. The Defiance Campaign only petered out towards the end of the year because most of its leaders were detained, and more draconian sentences were introduced.

At about this time, aged twenty or twenty-one, and in the process of developing a strong social conscience and feeling that he should do something about the social injustices he was beginning to perceive around him, Patrick contemplated becoming a Catholic priest. Years later he was to tell his daughter, 'I went for a long walk and decided to be an atheist.'[16] He had not yet thrown off all the sense of guilt that the Catholic Church so often harbours, but he was on the way to breaking that bond.

* * *

During 1952, with only two papers left to write for his degree, Patrick had more time to reflect upon these matters and he decided that when he completed the degree at the end of the year he would move on – if possible, abroad. Through his studies he had acquired a natural urge to travel and see something of the world beyond South Africa's borders. But where to?

He applied for the prestigious Rhodes Scholarship, which would entail a year's postgraduate study at Oxford University. He hoped that his sporting record would act in his favour, but it didn't. His other job applications showed that he was still searching for some justification for his country's apartheid policies.

He applied for a civil service job in Rhodesia on the eve of the British formation of the Central African Federation, in which the two northern territories, Northern Rhodesia and Nyasaland, were to be amalgamated with the settler colony of Southern Rhodesia. Patrick seems to have naïvely assumed that this was a genuine attempt to establish inter-racial harmony and he wanted to be in on the foundation of it. But his application came to nothing. He was later to learn the reality that the federation was little more than a power grab by the southern white settlers and he was well out of it.

Among his more imaginative job applications was one to a bank in Switzerland. He may have known nothing about banking itself, but banking was probably the only source of employment that he knew Switzerland was famous for. He was attracted to Switzerland as the model of a democratic country that could allow four different language groups to live separately and yet work successfully together as one nation. He appears to have still held out hope that the South African government's racial policies could somehow have a just and viable future.

His applications for these jobs abroad failed to provide any openings. He did not even get a reply from Switzerland. He fancied himself as an announcer at the South African Broadcasting Corporation, but they turned him down on the grounds that, although he had a liking for classical music and a good collection of 78 rpm records, he could not name all of Beethoven's symphonies.

Meanwhile, he went down to Durban to spend his twenty-first birthday with Cecile and Norman, and on the day itself (3 December 1952) he received the happy news that he had passed his final exams. Cecile and Norman took him to the Playhouse for dinner, but it was not the wild celebration of twenty-first birthday and BA degree that he might have hoped for; it was a quiet evening.

Cecile and Norman had returned to Durban for good after the Iranian government had nationalised the Anglo-Iranian Oil Company in March 1951. Following that birthday Patrick's former easy relationship with Cecile soured as she tried to insist that he stop referring to his late grandmother as 'Mama'. *She* was his real mother and he should be using that name for *her*. But this approach came too late; much too late. Patrick could not switch the allegiance of his deepest affections, no matter what the blood relationship. He preferred to avoid calling Cecile anything, and thereafter he rarely visited her in Durban.

* * *

Patrick decided that the solution to his future was to join the diplomatic service. Here the government would surely send him abroad, hopefully to Europe. He applied to the Department of External Affairs and was called for an interview in Pretoria in January 1953. During the interview, in the Union Buildings, the magnificent home of South Africa's seat of government, he was asked what he knew about the current state of South Africa's negotiations with the United Nations (UN) over the status of South West Africa,[17] which was at that time one of South Africa's most important theatres of international diplomacy.

Patrick, a regular listener to radio news reports on the BBC Overseas (World) Service, was well informed on the subject. He knew that after World War I South Africa had been granted a League of Nations mandate to administer the former German colony of South West Africa. With the demise of the League of Nations on the outbreak of World War II and the post-war founding of the United Nations, the mandatory powers were requested to transfer their mandates to the UN.

The other powers – Britain, France and Belgium – complied, but South Africa refused, for the UN mandate contained the obligation to prepare the territory for internal self-government leading to independence. On the contrary, the Smuts government indicated its intention to incorporate the territory into the Union of South Africa, as its fifth province.

The UN might have been persuaded to agree but for the intervention of Tshekedi Khama, regent of the Bamangwato, the largest of the Batswana tribes in the British protectorate of Bechuanaland (later Botswana). Tshekedi had as his guest at the Bamangwato capital, Serowe, the Herero paramount chief Frederick Maherero, whose people had fled genocide in German South West Africa in 1904–1905.

Tshekedi, 'one of the most forceful and adroit black politicians in southern Africa',[18] saw that if South West Africa fell to the South Africans it could have a domino effect, with the High Commission Territories of Bechuanaland, Basutoland (Lesotho) and Swaziland falling to South Africa soon after.

The British favoured the latter transfer as a convenient way to offload responsibility for three minor, impoverished territories and the South African government saw these countries as falling within its natural borders – extra territory for the implementation of its apartheid schemes.

Tshekedi invited the Reverend Michael Scott to meet Chief Maherero. Scott was an Anglican priest and human rights campaigner who had made a one-man stand against the 'near to slavery' conditions in labour compounds on white-owned farms in the Transvaal, where '"the rule of the sjambok" … seemed to have displaced the rule of law'.[19] Scott took up the Herero cause and went to South West Africa, where he managed to elude government strictures and gather the material and signatures needed for a petition protesting against the region's transfer to South Africa.

He took the petition in person to the UN headquarters in New York,[20] and in the years that followed, into the early 1950s, Scott proved himself a very effective thorn in the flesh of South African international diplomacy. As a result of his work the UN refused to approve the transfer of South West Africa to South Africa, leading Dr Malan to take the view that his government was '[not] accountable to the UN'.[21]

Apartheid South Africa was never to escape the condemnation of the United Nations, and at the time of Patrick's interview in Pretoria there was a stalemate between the two. It is not known exactly what Patrick told his interviewers, but they were surprised by and impressed with the extent of his knowledge and he was offered the post of cadet diplomat to the Political Section of the Department of External Affairs.

4 | Diplomat and Rebel, 1953–1957

Patrick began work at the External Affairs offices in the Union Buildings on 1 March 1953. The Political Section was headed by Second Secretary Bernardus Gerhardus Fourie, known in the department as 'Brand', and comprised a third secretary and himself. Patrick's initial role was to gather newspaper cuttings and paste them onto sheets of paper for the information of the department. Brand would either pass them straight back for filing or would initial them and pass them up to the first secretary.

The cuttings were taken from a wide range of papers and journals, domestic and foreign, and when they came back for filing Patrick was able to judge their importance, and thus the success of his selection, by how far up the line of authority they had gone. The initials he particularly looked out for were those of Mr D. D. Forsyth, the chief civil servant in the department, who was also the personal secretary to the prime minister. Patrick quickly got the hang of the job and soon tired of its mechanical nature.

Jawaharlal Nehru's government of India, which supported Michael Scott's campaign on behalf of South West Africa, was at the time the leading critic of South Africa at the UN.[1] Patrick regarded India's criticism of apartheid as hypocritical, bearing in mind the partition of India in 1947 into Muslim-majority East and West Pakistan and Hindu-majority India. He proposed to Brand that he compile a dossier setting out a critique of India's position at the UN. Brand agreed.

Patrick studied a wide range of publications, including Indian newspapers, from which he drew evidence of the caste system and racism against dark-skinned people in India. He also used the recently published scathing attack on Nehru, *The Lotus Eater from Kashmir*.[2] Although it was a hate-filled polemic lacking any sense of balance, D. F. Karaka's book added grist to Patrick's mill, especially his charge of hypocrisy over the disputed territory of Kashmir, to which Nehru denied self-determination. Patrick seemed to enjoy compiling the dossier, which went down well with his superiors – so much so that they published it and sent bound copies to South Africa's representatives at the UN.

The success of the India dossier led to others, including one on South Africa's case for the transfer to it of the High Commission Territories. This possibility had been written into the final clause of the Act of Union of 1909, which laid down the Constitution of South Africa.

The issue had been brought to a head within months of the National Party victory of 1948 with the marriage in London of the heir to Bechuanaland's Bamangwato chieftaincy, Seretse Khama, to a white English woman, Ruth Williams. In South Africa the marriage, which has spawned numerous books and films over the years, was regarded as a slap in the face to the South African government, which was about to make such inter-race relationships a criminal offence.

Malan demanded the dissolution of the marriage and the barring of Seretse from the chieftainship. And if the marriage could not be annulled, Seretse and his English bride should be permanently banished from Bechuanaland. After two of years of tension, negotiation and secret deals, Britain gave way to South African pressure and exiled Seretse and Ruth to Britain.[3] What Patrick did not realise at the time was that British intelligence had a mole at the highest level of the Department of External Affairs in the person of D. D. Forsyth. It was his secret advice to the British government that tipped the scales so strongly against the recognition of Seretse.[4]

Incorporation of the High Commission Territories remained on South Africa's agenda throughout the 1950s. Indeed, as we shall see below, South Africa still hoped to achieve it as late as 1963.

* * *

A few weeks after commencing work in Pretoria, Patrick was able to attend Unisa's graduation ceremony, where he was awarded his BA degree. If he had thought that was the end of his intensive studies, however, he was soon to learn otherwise. There was a wide range of subjects in which he had to pass examinations before he qualified as a full diplomat. These included Diplomacy and Protocol, Diplomatic History, International Law, French, and Codes and Ciphers.

Unlike many of his fellow cadets, he was already reasonably fluent in French. During his search for personal identity in Pietermaritzburg he had studied French in order to converse better with the Mauritian side of his family. Because Afrikaans had been covered in his degree course, he was not required to study it further. The language of the Union Buildings was predominantly Afrikaans and all reports, memos and dossiers were, in the first instance, written in that language. As a result, Patrick upped his fluency in the language and got a paying part-time job on the side translating Afrikaans documents into English for his alma mater, Unisa.

Once again sport provided him with his main social life. He joined Pretoria's Harlequins Rugby Club as well as the North-Eastern Transvaal Cricket Umpires' Association. The New Zealand cricket team toured South Africa in 1953 and Patrick umpired its match against North-Eastern Transvaal. Some months later, when he had joined the other diplomats and most of the civil service in Cape Town for the parliamentary session, he was able to use his contact with the New Zealand captain to arrange a friendly match with the tourists when they came down to Cape Town to catch their ship home.

The South African scratch side that he put together was drawn from cricketing enthusiasts from Parliament and External Affairs. Patrick, as a player rather than an umpire, was the last man in and managed to score a few runs. Needless to say, the New Zealand batsmen sailed past the South African score without the loss of too many wickets.[5] Patrick's batting experience on that occasion encouraged him to become a regular player in Pretoria and he became a bit of an all-rounder, excelling at bowling and fielding as well as with the bat.

Before Pretoria's government departments decamped to Cape Town for the parliamentary session of 1954 Patrick had an experience that he had longed for. He lost his virginity. She was a colleague in some other department in the Union Buildings. Both intensely shy, they had met in the dining room. They lived in the same road and would walk home together.

One night around Christmas she came into his flat and they both had their first experience of sexual intercourse. As he recalled many years later, it 'was not for either of us an act of love but a mutual satisfaction of deeply-felt emotional and physical need'. He had begun to loosen the bonds of the Catholic Church and does not appear to have been overcome with religious guilt. In fact, he felt he 'had come at last to manhood'. They did not repeat the experience. Indeed, she avoided him thereafter, and it was not long before his 'loneliness and longing' for love returned.[6]

He had an altogether different, but nevertheless significant, experience on the journey south to Cape Town in January 1954. Members of the various departments of government travelled by special train and, as they paused at the station in Johannesburg, Patrick and a colleague observed the huge crowds of Africans piling on and off their crowded trains at the other end of the station. His colleague, John Mills, with whom he shared a sleeper compartment, wondered aloud when 'Der Tag' would come.[7]

Patrick had not heard the expression before and asked him to explain. In response, Mills predicted 'a bloody day of reckoning and painted ... the spectre of a Black uprising'.[8] The matter-of-fact acceptance of this inevitability seems to have shocked Patrick and from then on he began to notice two things: the large number of urban Africans who were clearly downtrodden and not at all happy with their situation, and the apparent white acceptance of the inevitability of Der Tag, even among supporters of the National Party.

It dawned on him that what they were doing with their apartheid policies was attempting to put off the inevitable for as long as possible, and that among those who talked about it there was a general acceptance that Der Tag lay a comfortable way off in the distant future.

Patrick had begun to wonder seriously about the wisdom of the government's racial policy but, as he was a government employee with a comfortable, secure and high-status career ahead of him, it was difficult to do more than feel a sense of unease. As Helen Joseph, an English immigrant of a generation older than Patrick and much more advanced down the road to defiance, was to remark of her own lack of action in 1952: 'I lived on with my sense of guilt, which I did not yet see clearly as white guilt. That came later.'[9]

The pathway from unease to guilt to outright opposition was a difficult one to tread. It took great courage and confidence in one's own righteousness to break ranks and openly question one's own government's policies, especially when one was a dutiful employee of that government and a beneficiary of those policies. Patrick had not yet reached that destination. And so, in suppressing any sense of 'white guilt', he lived on in the false security of the artificial white world of a trainee diplomat.

It was an exciting time in his career, and he made the most of his five months in Cape Town. His work involved preparing position papers for parliamentarians and he enjoyed the educative research this involved. He fraternised with diplomats and, through events like the cricket match against the New Zealanders, he moved in high circles. He travelled the Cape Peninsula with friends who had cars and went swimming and crayfishing off the rocks near the Cape of Good Hope.

On one occasion he met a wealthy former student of Glenwood High who was studying medicine at the University of Cape Town and, although he enjoyed being driven in the young man's flashy white car, it brought back a disturbing memory. The boy had bullied him at school, taunting him with being a 'bastard'.

Patrick had been upset at the time, knowing the word was intended as an insult but not understanding its meaning. His law studies since then had taught him exactly what it meant, and being in the young man's company now raised once again the question of his paternity, something he had managed to put to the back of his mind. He realised now that he could never escape from the questions about his true identity.

Was he illegitimate, with all that that entailed? If it was true that Patrick Maxwell was indeed his genetic father at a time when his mother Cecile was married to Henry Francis van Rensburg, then, in the hypocritical Christian world of the 1950s, it was a major stigma from which his family had presumably been trying to protect him. Now, in his independent adult life, the confusion of his origins, cultural as well as genetic, was distancing him from his family connections in Natal.

Uncle Pat still wrote to him and showed an interest in his career, but he appears to have had little contact with Cecile or his uncle Jumbo. He began to question his identity and sense of belonging – English, French or Afrikaans – and now even the very concept of being a South African. These thoughts would eventually lead him to the conclusion that he could make up his own identity; indeed, that he could be a citizen of the world. But that discovery lay some years in the future.

In November 1954 Dr Malan retired and the hard-line Nationalist J. G. 'Hans' Strijdom took over the premiership. Soon afterwards the Political Section of External Affairs was split in two and Patrick was pleased to find that his new head of section, Albie Burger, was a much more amenable man to work with. Brand Fourie had never offered encouragement or praise and Patrick had felt that he was, at times, working in a vacuum. Albie Burger, however, positively encouraged his initiatives, and before long he was producing weekly international briefing papers for members of the Cabinet.

There was plenty to brief about. The Cold War was at its height, and Britain and France were making significant moves towards granting their African colonies self-government, something that was of particular concern to South Africa's Department of External Affairs. Patrick did not go to Cape Town for the parliamentary session of 1955. Towards the end of that year he passed his examinations and became a fully-fledged diplomat, at the level of third secretary. He had gained the confidence of his superiors and a secure career of some status lay ahead of him.

* * *

Although he was somewhat isolated from reality in white, predominantly Afrikaans Pretoria, Patrick was well aware of the 'political stirrings amongst the Blacks and their supporters and sympathisers among other races'. He knew of the formation of the Congress Alliance: the coming together of the African National Congress, the South African Indian Congress, the recently formed Coloured People's Congress, the South African Congress of Trade Unions and the Congress of Democrats.

The latter was a radical white organisation, many of whose members had previously belonged to the Communist Party, banned since 1950. Patrick knew that these organisations had held a 'Congress of the People' at Kliptown, near Johannesburg. There, on 25–26 June 1955, they had drawn up a 'Freedom Charter', a manifesto for a free South Africa.

He knew also of the ruthless police suppression of these activities. He raised his concerns about *Der Tag* and the future of South Africa with a senior colleague, who told him not to worry; it wouldn't happen in his lifetime. He told Patrick, 'You have a good career ahead of you and you'll become hardened and cynical about the nastier aspects of your job, in time. Make the most of it while you can!'[10]

Colleagues of his own age seemed unconcerned about political developments in the country, focusing instead on vying for the best postings abroad, such as London or Paris. Patrick preferred to trust to fate and was prepared to accept the first posting he was offered. In February 1956 he was offered the position of vice-consul in Leopoldville, the capital of the Belgian Congo (now the Democratic Republic of Congo). At the age of only twenty-four he would be the youngest vice-consul in the South African diplomatic service.

His colleagues sympathised: a posting to 'Darkest Africa' was what they most feared. But Albie Burger reassured Patrick that it was an important position in which he would be expected to do political reporting, a freedom unlikely to be extended to third secretaries in larger missions. Moreover, there was an urgent need to fill the post with a good man, for the consul-general had just died and the vice-consul, whom Patrick was to replace, had had a nervous breakdown and abandoned his post. Patrick had apparently been chosen for his good command of French and because Albie Burger had expressed full confidence in him.

Thus encouraged, Patrick began preparations for his new role. Any theoretical moral concerns he might have had about defending apartheid abroad were for the moment smothered by the excitement of this 'new and wholly unfamiliar experience'.[11] He bought new clothes and had business cards printed as 'Monsieur le Vice-Consul de l'Afrique du Sud'. It was late February when Patrick boarded the plane for Leopoldville with his diplomatic passport in his pocket.

The flight was uneventful, but, as he stepped off the plane at 'Leo' airport, he was struck at once by the heat and humidity. Durban at its hottest had nothing on this. Just a few degrees south of the equator at the hottest time of the year, the humidity hit him 'like walking into an open-air bath'.[12] He was met at the airport by John Oxley, the vice-consul for the Congo's second-largest city, Elizabethville (now Lubumbashi).

As the consul-general had not yet arrived, Oxley was the only diplomat in the country and had been holding the fort in Leopoldville until Patrick's arrival. Patrick was initially put up at Leopoldville's main hotel, the Regina, and that evening he and Oxley met up at the pavement bar for a few ice-cold local beers, aptly named 'Polar'. The next day Oxley showed him round, introducing him to the office staff, other foreign diplomats and members of the Belgian administration. He also arranged his membership of the Royal Leopoldville Golf Club, the social centre for privileged whites in the capital.

That afternoon they took the ferry across the river to the French Congo's capital of Brazzaville, to which Leopoldville's South African consulate was also accredited. Patrick was pleased to be able to take over his predecessor's expensively furnished flat overlooking the river, 'as well as his golf clubs'! Before long he was taking golf lessons at the club after work. He bought a new Peugeot motor car with an interest-free loan that was paid off through a car allowance. With an expensive flat and a brand-new car, Monsieur le Vice-Consul had moved up a class in the diplomatic world.

Having seen Patrick settled in, Oxley left him in sole charge – effectively acting consul-general – for a few days. When the new consul-general, Mr A. J. van Lille, finally arrived by train from the port of Matadi, Patrick quickly assessed him as a man not really fitted for the diplomatic world. He was a hard-line racist in his late fifties who had brought with him a huge supply of hard liquor and his own personal Mercedes-Benz.

Patrick gained the impression that Van Lille just wanted to see out his final two years of service quietly before retiring. He was not interested in Patrick's penchant for political reporting and Patrick felt free to pursue his own interests in sending reports back to Albie Burger.

He started by analysing the Belgian colonial system. The first thing he noticed was that although there were sharp social and economic divisions between black and white in the Congo, this was not enshrined in law. The Belgians' declared intention was to develop a federal relationship of equals between the Congo and Belgium. But this was pushed so far into the distant future as to be meaningless.

By 1956, after 48 years of direct Belgian rule, only 120 people in a total population of more than 10 million had been issued with a *carte d'immatriculation*, which allowed them equal rights with those accorded to whites.[13] Although the Belgians boasted of this as their 'civilising mission', it was becoming increasingly clear that any belief that they could keep a lid on African aspirations to rapid self-government was pure fantasy.

Patrick, however, was primarily interested in comparing the Belgian system to that of South Africa and, in order to please his political masters back home, he found the Belgian system wanting. He claimed that it contained no safeguards against the exploitation of black people by white. In contrast, he argued that 'in principle, Apartheid had more chance of success than the Belgian approach because it could protect blacks from white exploitation in their own areas and could lead to genuine development of the "homelands" in their interests'.[14]

It was a vain last effort on Patrick's part to argue that a genuine and equitable separation of the races in South Africa might work. But he was to admit later in his memoir that by the time he wrote that report, in the first half of 1956, he was already 'well aware that far from protecting Blacks in their own areas, Apartheid was a major instrument of their more intensified exploitation'.[15]

In the meantime, Patrick was able to enjoy an interesting social life, with his social network made up entirely of other nationalities. He appears to have had three principal friends: British Tony Northrup, Australian Roger McCloskey and American Dolores O'Halloran.[16]

Northrup, a sales representative for Lever Brothers, made regular short visits to Leopoldville, ostensibly selling OMO soap powder. He and Patrick hit it off from the start and, at his request, he stayed in Patrick's flat whenever he visited Leopoldville. He said it was so much nicer than staying in a hotel. Roger McCloskey, a building contractor with wide experience in West Africa and Ethiopia, was probably Patrick's closest friend and they spent a great deal of time in each other's company. McCloskey moved freely among the white social circles of downtown Leopoldville, various bars frequented by both black and white, and the African townships on the edge of town collectively known as Le Belge.

It was through Roger that Patrick started noticing for the first time the beauty of African and mixed-race women, with whom Roger clearly had intimate relationships. He envied Roger his facility with women, regardless of the colour of their skin. But he was, as yet, too reserved and inhibited by his South African background to cross that line. He rather pompously told himself he had a duty as a South African diplomat to observe his country's ban on such relationships. Nevertheless, Roger introduced Patrick to the concept of non-racial thinking, and this was an important step along the road to liberation.

Roger also introduced Patrick to the US consul-general, Jim Green, who held open-house receptions at his official residence on Sunday evenings. Patrick became a regular attendee and it was there that he met for the first time Dolores O'Halloran, a striking Irish American from Boston, who worked at the American consulate. Patrick was fascinated by Dolores and they became close friends.

Although he would like to have taken the relationship much further, she made it clear that she was a good Catholic and had an American boyfriend who worked elsewhere. But Dolores seemed to understand Patrick's dilemma of working for a government whose racial policies, he increasingly realised, he no longer believed in. She was a good listener and it helped Patrick to have a sympathetic ear to confide in, especially someone who encouraged him to start envisaging a life outside the strictures of apartheid.

South African newspapers were regularly flown in from Pretoria and Patrick developed an increasing interest in political events at home. He read in August 1956 how the recent extension of the oppressive pass laws to all 'Non-White' women had stimulated the Federation of South African Women to gather 20 000 women of all races to march to the Union Buildings in Pretoria, where they stood in silent protest against apartheid's racist laws. Patrick was impressed by the courage of the demonstrators.

Then, in December, he read of the arrest of 156 prominent anti-apartheid activists, mainly African, but also Indian, 'coloured' and white, on a charge of high treason. Most were supporters of the principles of the Freedom Charter, which had been drawn up the previous year, and were now effectively being told that to support an alternative view of South Africa's racial policies was tantamount to treason. The case was to drag on for years, resulting in the withdrawal of the charges against many of the accused and, finally, the acquittal of the remainder in 1961. Patrick would have found it difficult to believe in 1956 but, in the years ahead, a number of those 'Treason Trialists' would become his close friends and colleagues.

In the meantime, the news of the arrests prompted him to go to the consulate's library, where, through the early months of 1957, he made a systematic study of the Acts of Parliament that underpinned apartheid and compared them to the parliamentary debates of the time. There he found National Party ministers and parliamentarians 'clearly revealing with complete candour the oppressive purposes of Apartheid in the interests of White advancement'.[17]

He also read reviews, in English, of a couple of books by foreign critics of apartheid, 'both men of considerable repute'. *Problemet Sydafrika* ('Problems in South Africa')[18] was written by the Swedish political scientist Herbert Tingsten, the other by the socialist Dutch Reformed Church *predikant* (preacher) J. J. Buskes, known to Afrikaners as the 'Rooi Dominee [the Red Priest]'. They were both highly critical of apartheid as a 'measure of genuine partition', Buskes making his position very clear in his book's title: *South Africa's Apartheid Policy: Unacceptable!*[19] Although he was only able to read reviews of their books, Patrick was heartened by the cogent arguments of these overseas intellectuals. He was later to meet both men in Europe under very different circumstances.

In March 1957 two senior South African officials, Counsellor Bob Jones and Derrick de Villiers, the head of the Africa Section, stopped off in Leopoldville on their way home from attending Ghana's independence celebrations. Over dinner that evening they asked Van Lille whether black people were ever invited to consular functions. Van Lille replied, 'Certainly not!' He seemed to think it was a trap, intended to test whether he was upholding his government's racist policies. He was surprised to learn that the opposite was the case, as his two guests explained that 'a major aim of the Department's Africa Policy was the development of good relationships with the emerging African states'.

Van Lille was shocked, not at all sure that he could cope with such a policy. Patrick viewed it very differently. As he wrote in his memoir, on the principle of non-interference in each other's internal policies, 'we were seeking *carte blanche* for Apartheid from Black states, and I was one of the agents of the strategy'.[20]

He spoke with Dolores about his dilemma – his realisation that he could no longer morally support apartheid and his fear of leaving his job with no prospect of an alternative. She encouraged him to make a stand; but still he hesitated. It was a month or so later that Roger McCloskey invited him to spend the weekend at his flat on the grounds that he had purchased a case of Guinness and it needed to be drunk.

It was an amusing but emotionally seminal weekend for Patrick. The pair drank beer, read and listened to music on the record player. Roger had a small library of interesting reading matter. From an anthology of the works of Oscar Wilde, Patrick read and re-read 'The Ballad of Reading Gaol', with its vivid evocation of a man awaiting trial on a capital charge, with the threat of hanging at the end. It brought to Patrick's mind the Treason Trialists back home, also facing a capital charge, for merely peacefully challenging the government's racial policies.

To lighten the mood, Roger played Harry Belafonte's 'Brown Skin Girl', which Patrick insisted on playing over and over again. Roger then put on Beethoven's Ninth Symphony, the *Choral* symphony, judged by many to be his greatest work. It was a symphony that Patrick knew well and loved, especially now, for the 'Ode to Joy', with its heavenly Elysium in which *'Alle Menschen werden Brüder* [All Men shall become Brothers]'.

Among the books Patrick read that weekend was Chester Bowles's recently published *Africa's Challenge to America*.[21] Once he started reading it he could not put it down. He read the book right through over the weekend. Bowles, a liberal American diplomat, was writing at the height of the Cold War. His premise was that if America did not favour and support the rising class of young African nationalists, the emerging nations of Africa would fall victim to the spread of Soviet communism.

As if to prove Bowles's point, within months of the publication of the book in 1956, Soviet tanks had rolled into Budapest and crushed the brief flowering of the Hungarian anti-communist revolution. The book confirmed Patrick's distrust of communism, but it also showed him that a non-racially defined future for South Africa was not only a possibility but a moral and political necessity.

Bowles admitted that racism in some form or other was to be found all over the world, but only in South Africa was it 'sanctified by religion and philosophy, and institutionalised in the mores of the nation'. Chester Bowles provided Patrick with the rationale to make a moral stand:

Beer, Beethoven, Belafonte, Bowles and Wilde somehow blew my mind that week-end! I felt exhilarated, uplifted – suddenly liberated – in my mind, in my spirit and in my heart. I got some steel in my belly, too. On Sunday evening, I told [Roger] I intended to resign from my post and from government service altogether, and I only hoped that I would continue to have the strength to do it in the cold light of the next morning.

I had finally broken the crumbling barriers to my self-realisation that weekend. Reinforced by those words of Chester Bowles, I had finally acquired some emotional back-up for my intellectual and moral abhorrence of the racism enshrined in Apartheid. I could identify with men and women of other races, and felt, as well as knew, that we were hewn from a common tree.[22]

That Monday morning Patrick went straight to Van Lille's office to tell him of his decision to resign. To his surprise Van Lille's only concern was that the resignation might have had something to do with him personally. Apparently something like that had happened on a previous posting. Ironically, this strong supporter of apartheid was relieved to learn that Patrick was resigning because he could no longer support his government's racial policies. Patrick then went to his own office and wrote his formal letter of resignation, making his reason very clear: his moral 'abhorrence of Apartheid and nothing else'.[23] His last duty at the consulate was to organise and attend the official celebration of South Africa's Union Day on the evening of 31 May 1957.

5 | Anti-Apartheid Activist, 1957–1959

It was made clear to Patrick that once his resignation was accepted the government would take no further responsibility for him and he would have to pay for his own repatriation to Johannesburg. He booked his flight and dispatched his car overland, by river steamer and train. US Consul Jim Green and his family threw him a leaving party at the consul's official residence, and there his numerous friends gathered to show their support for the stand he had taken and to bid him a fond farewell.

Roger McCloskey, who had been so influential in his political and social maturing, stood out particularly in Patrick's memories of the Congo. Looking back on those fifteen months many years later he interpreted Roger's role as that of an elder brother, 'one who had helped a sibling become a man'.[1] He had a final dinner with Dolores O'Halloran at a quiet restaurant outside of town, and early in the morning of Friday 7 June Roger and a few friends saw him off at the airport. As he looked down from the plane on the city that had changed his life his thoughts were on what lay ahead. He knew he could no longer live under the confining restrictions of apartheid South Africa, but would he find the courage to confront segregation and discrimination?

* * *

Before leaving the Congo he had given a brief interview to a reporter for the Johannesburg *Star*, who happened to be in Leopoldville and had got wind of his resignation.[2] As a result, on his arrival at Jan Smuts Airport[3] in Johannesburg late that Friday evening, Patrick was accosted by a reporter from the *Rand Daily Mail* eager to build a more dramatic story than the bare outline of his resignation that had appeared in the *Star*.

Patrick gave him no more information than he had given the *Star*: as a matter of conscience, he could 'no longer defend the apartheid policy of the ... South African Government'. The *Mail* reporter, however, elaborated on Patrick's reply, claiming that criticism had been levelled against South Africa in the Belgian Congo.[4] It was Patrick's first experience of 'fake news' and journalistic opportunism.

He found reasonably cheap accommodation at the Douglas Hotel in Fox Street, but finding a job was not so easy. A few potential employers showed initial interest, but once they learned that he intended to maintain his opposition to apartheid they quickly showed him the door. Eventually, he struck lucky at the wholesale distributors L. Suzman and Company, where the managing director, Alfie Bernitz, was happy to take him on. Alfie had no worries about Patrick's political views. A relative of the company's owners, Helen (née Gavronsky) Suzman, was on the liberal wing of the United Party (UP) and since the 1953 election had been MP for Houghton in Johannesburg.

By this time Patrick had decided to write a book about his personal journey to Damascus and his thoughts on what should be done to forestall the dreaded *Der Tag*. He already had a title in mind. The book would be called *Guilty Land*, drawing on the prophetic warning of the American abolitionist John Brown, who, on the morning of his execution on 2 December 1859, had written: 'I, John Brown, am now quite certain that the crimes of this guilty land will never be purged away but with blood.'[5]

He began research in the Johannesburg reference library on South African history, politics and economics. He learned about the workings of the secretive *Afrikaner Broederbond* (Afrikaner Brotherhood), the 'think tank' behind the apartheid ideology, whose tentacles permeated all walks of life. Patrick was pleased to learn, however, that there remained a significant number of Afrikaners who clung to the late Jan Smuts's United Party tradition of 'White Leadership with Justice'.[6]

Patrick was new to oppositional politics and for a brief while he assumed he would find his political home in the UP, which was the Lagesse family's party of choice and the one for which we can assume he had voted in his first general election in 1953. It was the largest party of opposition in the all-white Parliament, having on that occasion won fifty-seven seats to the National Party's ninety-four and the Labour Party's five. In the course of 1957, however, it became clear to Patrick that the UP was in terminal decline and 'White Leadership', even 'with Justice', was no longer a plausible alternative to apartheid.

Before leaving the Congo he had written to that grand old man of the liberal South African conscience, the renowned novelist, journalist and political thinker Alan Paton, explaining the reason for his resignation and asking for his political advice. Paton was at the time chairman of the Liberal Party, which had been founded in the aftermath of the 1953 election.

At first the party had argued for a gradual transformation of South Africa, but in January 1957 delegates at its annual congress had voted to commit the party to universal adult franchise, regardless of race, colour, sex or creed, as the only plausible route to a future peaceful South Africa. Once this became clear to the general public the party began to gain a considerable number of African members, especially in the rural areas, where suspicion of the ANC's cosy relationship with former communists was rife.[7]

This was the position in June 1957 when Patrick arrived from the Congo. He had not given Paton a forwarding address; but when Paton was next in Johannesburg he sought him out. Patrick was easily persuaded of the Liberal Party's non-racialism, but he hesitated to commit himself to joining the party. He had a lot to think about.

For a start, until this moment, he had not yet thought beyond the concept of the qualified franchise.[8] Secondly, the Liberal Party's strategy in 1957 was still to pursue the constitutional route, which meant fighting elections for the whites-only Parliament; but how did this square with the party's non-racial membership? Furthermore, they had conspicuously failed to win any parliamentary by-election since 1953. And finally, what hope had they of persuading white voters to abandon the National Party, which had been steadily gaining support at every election? One thing that Patrick took away from his meeting with Paton, however, was the great man's advice not to squander the publicity of his resignation but rather to use the press attention for some political gain before his sacrifice was forgotten as a one-protest wonder.[9]

While still undecided about his future political home, Patrick renewed his friendship with a group of dissident Afrikaners with whom he had debated at Pretoria University. Most had left university by now, but they had formed a 'Pretoria Political Study Group'. It was through this group that Patrick met two inspiring Liberal Party activists, Maritz van den Berg and J. J. 'Osie' Oosthuizen.

His introduction to Wolf Hamm later that year moved him closer to joining the party. Wolf was a German Jew who, together with his mother, had escaped the Holocaust. He was a strong, outspoken member of the Transvaal branch of the Liberal Party, and he appreciated that in order to gain support the party must become involved in local issues, such as the Alexandra bus boycott of 1957 and the government's destruction of the multiracial township of Sophiatown on the western outskirts of Johannesburg.[10] Wolf invited Patrick to his home, where he met his frail mother and 'wondered at the fortitude of people who had been so close to a monstrous extermination and could stand up for justice for others'. He asked himself, 'If Wolf could be a Liberal, could I not also be so brave?'[11]

Finally, towards the end of 1957 Wolf introduced him to Patrick Duncan, the Liberal Party's national organiser. He found Duncan to be 'charming, outgoing, enthusiastic, brave, uncompromising in opposing both Apartheid and communism, and a good, strong speaker'.[12] He was also very persuasive and, at their first meeting at a restaurant in Johannesburg, he convinced Patrick not only to join the party immediately but also to attend an upcoming multiracial conference in Cape Town and to speak at the party's National Congress in Durban in December. No record of that speech appears to have survived but, as Patrick noted in his memoir, 'there was no going back now' and with 'the enthusiasm of a convert' he became 'very active in the Liberal Party' in the months that followed.[13]

Some of his inspiration in the early months of 1958 came from Jock Isacowitz, former Communist Party secretary-general and now one of the more radical, idealistic and energetic activists in the Transvaal Liberal Party. The totality of Patrick's commitment to the non-racial cause, however, must have come from the new friendships he was making beyond the colour bar. They started when Wolf Hamm introduced him to Robert Resha, the outspoken Transvaal regional secretary of the ANC, who had attracted wide public notice with a speech in which he predicted that 'Africans would have to "cross rivers of blood" to win their freedom'.[14]

Robert Resha introduced Patrick to Joe Matlou, another ANC activist, and to Stanley Lollan, a member of the South African Coloured People's

Organisation (SACPO). Both Robert and Stan were defendants in the ongoing Treason Trial, although, like all the Treason Trialists, they were out on bail and so had evenings and weekends in which to socialise. These three residents of Sophiatown (popularly known as 'Sophtown' or 'Kofifi') formed a close friendship and trusting bond with Patrick, who spent much time in their company and was inspired by the 'strength and authenticity of their commitment to non-racialism'.[15]

They introduced him to Ahmed (Kathy) Kathrada, who had been a member of the Communist Party before it was banned in 1950, a member of the Transvaal Indian Congress, and a fellow Treason Trialist. Patrick's almost new Peugeot arrived safely from the Congo, enabling him to move easily around Johannesburg with his new-found friends. On one occasion he drove Robert, Joe and Stanley down to Durban for a long weekend. They reached Pietermaritzburg late at night,

> … and having driven all the way from Johannesburg, I felt quite weary. In fact we were all tired, and someone suggested we sleep in the car. I was wondering who of all the friends I had there, might be prepared to put up this multi-racial gang. Mike Ensor's name sprang to mind. Arrived at his gate, I went inside while the others waited in the car. Mike, who still worked at the Master's Office, agreed to my request and made us comfortable with blankets on the sofas and on the floor, also giving us something to eat and drink. We left before dawn, and I heard Mike telling his small daughter, Paula, who'd awoken early and seen us, that she must always keep secret what she had seen.[16]

Paula Ensor, who grew up politically radical, walked across the border into exile in 1976. One of the first things she did was visit Patrick in Serowe, Botswana.[17]

Patrick had assumed he knew his way around Durban, but on this occasion he chose not to introduce his companions to any of his family or childhood friends. Rather, he allowed them to introduce him to a whole new side of Durban life. This included their Indian friends David and Monty Naicker. Both were prominent anti-apartheid activists who, besides being leading members of the Natal Indian Congress, were strong supporters of the ANC and its non-racial aims. 'Monty',[18] like Robert and

Stan, was a Treason Trialist and David would in due course spend fourteen years imprisoned on Robben Island. It was, for Patrick, a memorable weekend.

During this period, in the first half of 1958, Robert, Joe and Stanley took him to Alexandra, a freehold African township on the northern outskirts of Johannesburg. There he met, among others, 'the earnest young Tennyson Makiwane who had a fondness for classical music and read a great deal'.[19] His friendship with Makiwane, another Treason Trialist, and the trust that built up between them, was to lead to their working together in London the following year.

Some of Patrick's Sophiatown friends were hard drinkers and he would often illegally buy so-called European liquor on their behalf – something they were barred from doing according to a racist law that dated back to long before apartheid. His memories of those days and of life in Sophiatown are worth quoting quite extensively. He was later to confide to his English wife, Liz, whom he married in 1962, that this year (1958–1959) was one of the happiest and most formative of his life.[20]

> When Robert, Joe, Stanley and I were together, sometimes with Kathy, we talked, and often laughed, about everything under the sun, including of course politics. These were intelligent, knowledgeable, sensible men, with feelings and sensibilities no different from mine, with the same aspirations and dreams, with human fears that they overcame with shared courage. They changed many of my attitudes and views. I began ... to feel that the [Liberal Party] should work more closely with the ANC, in joint activities and campaigns.
>
> I lived in two worlds, divided by a chasm that the Verwoerd regime[21] was widening and deepening with each passing day. There were few public places to which my new-found friends and I could go together ... [But] in Sophiatown, the racially-mixed 'black spot' in the midst of White suburbs that was such an affront to the Verwoerdian outlook ... I could move freely with trusted friends[22] ... It was overcrowded, the houses small ... There were *shebeens* [illicit taverns], always under threat of police raids, there were the *tsotsis*, criminals who plied their trade mainly elsewhere in Johannesburg, there were artists, writers, poets and musicians, and there were the

politicians like Robert Resha, the ANC's Transvaal Regional Secretary, who were closely in tune with their community and kept their fingers on its pulse.

Here I met people like Peter Nthite, the clerk who had a touching, caring affection for his dogs, and Jerry Mbuli who scraped a living as a hawker, both men who put their safety at risk for the ANC ... Here I first heard the penny whistle of Lemmy Special, the sweet magic flute of the street boys that took the townships by storm, and I danced to the *kwela* [a style of music very popular in the 1950s, in which the lead part is usually played on the penny whistle].[23]

The forced relocation and destruction of the houses and shacks of Sophiatown had begun in February 1955, the year that the township's Anglican priest, Trevor Huddleston, was forced to return to England.[24] A strong campaign of resistance prolonged the life of Sophiatown, which was not finally closed and bulldozed to the ground until 1960, when it was renamed 'Triomph' and rebuilt as a soulless township for working-class Afrikaners.

In the meantime, Sophiatown was still a vibrant multiracial community. Derek Hudson, a member of the Liberal Party and former anti-racist student activist at the University of Cape Town, recalls meeting Patrick at a Liberal Party function in Johannesburg in early 1959. Patrick, eager to introduce him to a glimpse of the possibilities of a non-racial South Africa, took him to a party in Sophiatown. Derek was somewhat nervous at the casual defiance of apartheid that he was witnessing and admitted to being 'a complete novice at multi-racial parties'.

On another occasion Patrick took Derek to a party at the home of Bram Fischer, the high-profile anti-apartheid lawyer who defended the leaders of the Defiance Campaign of 1952 and went on to lead the defence in the Rivonia Trial of 1963–1964. Derek recalls that most of the guests were black people and he marvelled at the way Fischer took enormous risks, and generally got away with it.[25] But this was the world in which Patrick moved, and clearly thrived in.

Patrick campaigned hard for the Liberal Party in the April 1958 general election. He considered that the main target should be United Party voters. To achieve this, he took to the press to expound his political views, writing in the new fortnightly news review, *Contact*, a couple of weeks before the election. *Contact*, founded in February 1958, was a vehicle for the liberal point of view and Patrick Duncan soon became its editor, although it was never formally attached to the Liberal Party.

In his article Patrick claimed that the UP lacked any philosophy that could cope with even a limited degree of racial integration, unlike the Liberal Party, which was 'the only alternative party because it has a philosophy'.[26] On election day the Liberal Party made serious inroads into UP support, but failed to win a single seat. Overall, the election produced another win for the National Party, which was returned with an even bigger parliamentary majority. Boosted by the favourable response to his *Contact* article, Patrick made a serious foray into editorial journalism.

The *Rand Daily Mail* had a new editor in Laurence Gandar, who 'swung the *Mail* from its bland and smug conservatism to a forum of debate and analysis which also crusaded fearlessly against the oppression and injustice of the Verwoerd regime'.[27] Writing under his middle names, Owen Vine, Gandar had for some time been urging the liberal wing of the United Party to break away from their conservative colleagues. He thus welcomed an article of Patrick's, written in the aftermath of the 1958 election.

The article appeared on Monday 5 May as the leading editorial piece of the day, entitled ' "Me-too" policy does not win elections'. Patrick's name featured prominently in the centre of the article. He called on the liberal wing of the UP to break with their conservative colleagues, whose 'White Leadership with Justice' was merely a variation on apartheid. He pointed out that the African National Congress still stood for racial cooperation but that 'a hand held out in friendship too long without response must become tired'. He called upon the liberals in the UP to throw in their lot with the real constitutional alternative to the Nationalists and join the Liberal Party.[28]

Patrick's article revived his name in the public consciousness, with references to him in the press always reminding the public that this was the Afrikaner diplomat who had resigned because of his moral opposition to apartheid. It helped gain him political credibility among those 'Non-White' opponents of apartheid who were still interested in a multiracial future, and towards the end of May he was invited to open the annual conference of the South African Indian Youth Congress in Johannesburg.[29]

He returned to his theme with a follow-up article in June that urged the liberals in the UP to stop wasting their efforts on internal arguments and join the Liberal Party.[30] South Africa needed a real multiracial alternative and this would be a quick way for the party to gain instant access to Parliament. Patrick was acutely aware through conversations with Robert Resha and others that the leadership of the ANC was coming under increasing pressure from an 'Africanist' group within their membership who rejected all cooperation with whites.

The Africanists pointed out, correctly, that all whites benefited from the system, from which they concluded that all whites were oppressors and only Africans acting alone could achieve real liberation from white oppression. Patrick could see that time was running out and, as he saw it, only two choices were available. By failing to reject racial prejudice, 'we [the white electorate] can create the most violent African nationalism we choose, or we can fashion a multi-racial society'.[31]

By this time Patrick was convinced of the need not merely to support the ANC but to coordinate the campaigns and conferences of both parties. He introduced Robert Resha and Joe Matlou to two members of the Pretoria Political Study Group, some of whose Afrikaner intellectuals were prepared to question the wisdom of the manner in which apartheid had evolved. Patrick had already met ANC President-General Chief Albert Luthuli and had had the honour of introducing him to Laurence Gandar. He now proposed to Robert and Joe that they ask Chief Luthuli if he would address the Political Study Group.

The group was in favour, although the details of the arrangements had to be left to somebody else as at that point Patrick fell ill with suspected encephalitis and was admitted to an isolation hospital. While in hospital he read in the newspapers that Chief Luthuli was due to speak to the Political Study Group on the evening of Friday 22 August. He managed to get himself released from hospital late that Friday afternoon. Though very tired, he drove straight to Pretoria and arrived in time to find 'total chaos in the hall'.[32]

According to press reports the next day, a group of about thirty white men had filed in, and when the chairman started to introduce the speaker, their leader leapt onto the stage, knocked Chief Luthuli to the floor and shouted that in the name of 'the Afrikaner people' he would not allow 'a Kaffir to address this meeting'.[33] As those on the platform attempted to restrain the man, his companions joined in, the chairman was struck in the face and a general fight ensued at the front of the hall. This was probably the point at which Patrick arrived.

Order was finally restored when police turned up in riot gear and half a dozen of the protestors were arrested. When Luthuli was finally able to address the meeting, he did so in his usual calm and courteous manner, despite the bruise on his forehead and the dust on his clothing. And his message of non-racialism and tolerance was very well received by an audience impressed by his dignity and courage.[34]

Luthuli laid a charge of assault against his assailant, H. B. Classens, but the prosecutor would not pursue the case and the six men involved were charged with the lesser offence of 'public violence'. At his trial in October Classens declared that 'if it had been in his power that evening, he would have annihilated the White liberals'.[35] Afrikaner Nationalists like him brushed Africans aside with contempt and reserved their real hatred for white liberals, especially Afrikaner liberals like Patrick van Rensburg.

* * *

The executive of the Transvaal Liberal Party had already been impressed by Patrick's energy and commitment to the cause, and the Luthuli meeting in Pretoria had demonstrated the value and breadth of his personal contacts both in the Afrikaner heartland and in the ranks of the ANC. He had shown in practical terms what he had already been preaching: the need to work *with* the ANC. That weekend he was approached by Jock Isacowitz, who asked if he would take the job of organising secretary of the Transvaal branch. It was to be a paid job, created with him in mind. Patrick's employer, Alfie Bernitz, appreciated that his heart was in politics rather than in business and had no hesitation in letting him go.

A week later, on Monday 2 September, Patrick began work at the Liberal Party office in Johannesburg. Coincidentally, it was also the day that Dr Hendrik Verwoerd, the man who, as minister of native affairs, had steered most of the key pieces of apartheid legislation through Parliament, took up office as the new prime minister of South Africa. The *Mail* recorded Patrick's appointment under the heading 'He'll fight Verwoerd'.[36]

For the next nine months Patrick's life was dominated by politics. He had no time for sport; indeed, he had little time for any social life, apart from that with a political dimension. His initial priority as Transvaal organiser was to fundraise and it was here that he learned the skills required to persuade potential donors to part with their money. It was a skill at which he was to become highly proficient, to the great benefit of his educational causes in Botswana in the decades to come.

He acknowledged that he received a great deal of help and guidance from Jock Isacowitz, a realist who, from his days in the Communist Party, knew what it took to build a *movement*; a concept that stretched way beyond a simple political party. It entailed keeping the cause constantly before the public eye, organising (and addressing) meetings, planning activities, recruiting members from across the racial spectrum and liaising with likeminded organisations – in this case, especially the ANC. Patrick not only wrote more for the liberal-minded press, he also produced a cyclostyled newsletter, *Liberal News*, and encouraged members to set up new branches of the party across the 'Rand', that stretch of urban and industrial conglomerates that radiates east and west from central Johannesburg.

He had come to realise that the political obsession with race – be it race domination or multiracial cooperation – was at the heart of South Africa's problem. 'The true safeguard of racial minorities,' he wrote in the *Mail*, 'will be the disappearance of race consciousness.' This message was intended for his friends in the black community as much as for those in the Liberal Party. As he put it, the only route to a peaceful alternative South Africa was 'to offer the [white] electorate the prospect of a non-racial democracy'.[37] This was a significant early use in South African print of the term 'non-racial'. For Patrick, it was an idealistic dream, but once he had imagined it, it was a dream to which he held true.

For months he had been warning his white readers of the dangers of an extreme version of African nationalism, which was arising from the 'Africanists' within the ANC who were challenging the party's moderate leadership. This reached a crisis at an ANC conference in Johannesburg in November 1958. Up to a hundred Africanists challenged the policy of cooperating with sympathetic whites, many of whom were communists. The conference ended with the Africanists walking out and leaving the ANC. Led by Robert Mangaliso Sobukwe, an African Languages lecturer at the University of the Witwatersrand, they were to go on to form the Pan Africanist Congress (PAC) the following April.[38]

On 13 October 1958 the Treason Trial had been temporarily abandoned on a technicality, although the state was soon to revive it with a new indictment. The defendants were, understandably, in a jubilant mood and many of them assembled for a party at the northern Johannesburg home of the lawyer Joe Slovo and his wife, the campaigning journalist Ruth First.

Slovo and First, fellow defendants in the Treason Trial, were secretly still members of the banned South African Communist Party. Later, in exile, Slovo was to go on to play a major role in the armed struggle for the liberation of South Africa. Ruth First, in exile from 1964, was assassinated by a letter bomb in Mozambique in 1982.

October 1958, however, was a time for celebration. Patrick always loved a party, and since he was on personal terms with many of the accused, which included his friends Robert Resha and Stan Lollan as well as Tennyson Makiwane, he joined them all at the Slovo party. Among the defendants also present was Alfred Hutchinson, an ANC activist and Johannesburg teacher whom Patrick had met through Robert Resha. He was there with his white girlfriend, Hazel Slade.[39] Shortly after the party Alfred and Hazel, their transracial relationship illegal in terms of apartheid law, seized the opportunity of the suspension of the trial to flee the country. After an adventurous journey across Africa they ended up in that beacon of African hope, Ghana, and it was here that Patrick met them again in 1960, when he was in need of a friend with whom to stay.[40]

During Slovo's party the police had turned up in force, officially on a liquor raid. The doors of the house were closed, giving the black guests time to dispose of any liquor they may have been consuming before the police gained access through an open window. While the police searched the house for bottles of liquor, some of which they found and removed, a police photographer took photos of this 'abomination' of a multiracial party.

The raid was splashed on the front page of the next morning's *Rand Daily Mail*, the reporter having heard the story from one of the guests. The source may well have been Patrick, for the story ended with the paragraph: 'After midnight the celebration was still going on – now with soft drinks and chips. And by then the green-overalled servant girl was doing the *kwela* with a bespectacled European.'[41]

Patrick was thankful that he had not been identified by name, for by this time he was increasingly coming to the attention of the South African Police's Security Branch, also known as the Special Branch (SB).[42] They raided his flat on at least one occasion and would stand outside meetings he had organised, taking note of the people going in.

On one such occasion Patrick approached them to insist that the people coming to the meeting were doing nothing illegal. The reply he got in Afrikaans was, 'You'd better watch your step, Van Rensburg, or we'll fuck you up!'[43] Patrick knew that they could easily arrange for him to be beaten up, or lock him up and put him under 'extreme interrogation'. While in his own liberal circles he was 'The diplomat who "saw the light"',[44] in Afrikaner Nationalist circles he was a major hate figure – an Afrikaner diplomat turned traitor.

6 | Boycott, 1959–1960

Meanwhile, north of the Limpopo the movement for liberation from colonialism had been gathering pace, and Kwame Nkrumah, prime minister of Ghana, hosted the first All-African People's Conference in the Ghanaian capital, Accra, from 8 to 13 December 1958.[1] Delegates representing African political parties attended from all over the continent and included many of the future rulers of independent Africa.

The ANC's delegation was led by the renowned South African literary figure Ezekiel (later Es'kia) Mphahlele, who was teaching in Lagos, having been banned from teaching in South Africa because of his opposition to Verwoerd's 'Bantu Education'. The delegation included the escaped Treason Trialist Alfred 'Tough' Hutchinson, who, after travelling for two months across the continent, walked into the hall to great excitement on the second day of the conference.[2]

His arrival helped inspire the delegates to pass a resolution calling for an international boycott of all South African goods. This international support provided the stimulus for the ANC in South Africa, and at its annual congress in Johannesburg later that month there were calls for a general boycott of firms belonging to Afrikaner Nationalists. In February 1959 the party published a list of firms and products to be boycotted.[3]

Patrick already saw the potential of boycott as a perfectly legal extra-parliamentary tool with which to bring pressure to bear on the white electorate. Many within the Liberal Party, however, were apprehensive about engaging in extra-parliamentary activity, especially alongside the ANC, with its 'communist sympathies'.

In an attempt to nudge the party into 'a "united front" with the African National Congress on matters of common concern', Patrick leaked to the press the news that the party was secretly planning to cooperate with the ANC in a national propaganda campaign against apartheid.[4] He clearly had boycott in mind and his leak to the press caused consternation among some of the well-heeled members of the Liberal Party.

Patrick was contemptuous of these 'comfortable, middle-class Anglophones, many of them smugly self-righteous, and excessively precious, ever protective about their cosy brand of liberalism',[5] but they could not be so easily written off and some of them saw an opportunity to curb what they perceived to be his dangerously radical influence.

At the Liberal Party's Johannesburg congress on 3 April, someone proposed that party employees should not be eligible for election to the executive committee. This was clearly a direct attack on Patrick, the only Transvaal employee of the party who was also a member of the executive. One proposal supporter claimed that it could lead to 'undemocratic decision-making'; another stated that 'elevation of Party employees to elected office is a feature of totalitarian movements'.[6]

The nature of the attack took Patrick by surprise; but what shocked him most was that, of all the executive committee members present, only Jock Isacowitz spoke up in his defence. Feeling betrayed, and forced to choose between his paid employment and policy-making on the executive, Patrick chose the latter and resigned his post as Transvaal organising secretary. He continued to work for the party; he was just no longer paid.[7]

At a mass rally in Durban on 15 April 1959, Chief Albert Luthuli announced that a boycott of 'products of Nationalist controlled institutions' would begin on 26 June.[8]

Two weeks later Patrick and Jack Unterhalter, chair of the Transvaal branch of the Liberal Party, met with the ANC to discuss how the party could support the boycott campaign. Patrick was delegated to draw up a resolution to put to the Liberal Party's national executive, urging it to 'support the African National Congress in its efforts to apply lawful economic pressure against adherents of the Nationalist [sic] Party ... until such time as the Nationalist Party abandons its policies of racial discrimination and *Wit Baaskap*'.[9] As Patrick was to discover in the months that followed, national chairman Peter Brown was in full sympathy with the idea of boycott as a tool to pressure the government.

With the movement for boycott gathering pace, Luthuli was issued with a banning order confining him to his home district in rural Natal and preventing him from attending any meeting of more than two people. Luthuli's stance on non-violence and commitment to non-racialism was well known. Indeed, within a year he was to be awarded the Nobel Prize for Peace, the first ever African Nobel laureate.

Patrick proposed that the Liberal Party hold a protest meeting against the banning order on the steps of Johannesburg City Hall, historically a favoured site for public meetings. The meeting, booked for 1 pm on Wednesday 17 June, was well advertised and attracted several thousand: 'a fair sprinkling of Europeans and a very large number of Africans'. The largest gathering the party had ever organised, it was addressed by Jack Unterhalter, Jack Lewsen, a former city councillor, and Patrick. Among the 200 police who monitored the meeting, Patrick noticed the head of the Special Branch from Pretoria. No contemporaneous record of the speeches seems to have survived, but Patrick wrote of it two years later:

> I said in my speech that there were a number of parallels between the Pretoria assault on Chief Luthuli and his present banning. In both cases an attempt was made to silence the President of the African National Congress; though he spoke with moderation and warned against sectional nationalism in a multi-racial country, neither his assailants that night at Pretoria, nor the Government in this act of banning and banishment, paid any heed to his language. He was black and he was to be silenced. He could say nothing unless it was to praise the white men. The hooligans who had kicked him in the face would be happy to know that the Government was continuing their own attempts to silence Mr Luthuli with an act of political hooliganism. Chief Luthuli came out of the assault without rancour, and with no hate for the white man; he reacted with the same moderation to the banning.[10]

Significantly, as Unterhalter reported to Peter Brown: 'I think we have learnt an important lesson from this meeting; we asked the A.N.C. to assist in the distribution of leaflets, which they did, and I am sure it is largely because of their co-operation that the meeting was such a great success.'[11]

It appears that Patrick's pressure for cooperation between the Liberal Party and the ANC had finally succeeded. With that and the party coming around to supporting boycott as a legitimate weapon, he could leave his post as party organiser with a sense of achievement.

In June 1959 Patrick was offered a job teaching Afrikaans at St Martin's School in Rosettenville, a southern suburb of Johannesburg. The school had previously been St Peter's College, a boarding high school for black people, known as the 'Black Eton' of South Africa.

Among its better-known alumni were the ANC's deputy president Oliver Tambo and the jazz musician Hugh Masekela. But St Peter's had been closed in 1956 in terms of the Bantu Education Act and was re-opened as St Martin's, a high school for whites. The headmaster, who had previously headed St Peter's, was Michael Stern, a British educationist and an active and radical member of the Transvaal branch of the Liberal Party.

He was happy to welcome Patrick onto the staff, but the position would not be available until the new school year in January 1960. That was six months away and Patrick decided that in the interim he would take a break from the hectic politicking of the past two years and travel to Europe.

He booked a passage on the RMS *Pretoria Castle* and slipped away quietly by train to Cape Town, informing only his closest friends of his intentions. He was thankful that he was not stopped by the immigration authorities as he boarded the ship on Friday 10 July.

The 'helpful, sympathetic *Rand Daily Mail* reporter', Joe Rogaly, who was on board, wired a report to the Johannesburg *Sunday Times* that appeared on the front page of the 12 July issue under the headline 'Liberal Party man slips quietly out of South Africa'. Rogaly reported that on being asked whether he would criticise the government while abroad, Van Rensburg, from the ease of his deck chair, replied, 'I do so at home, don't I? ... The crimes of South Africa will not become any less in my eyes because I have crossed its borders. Therefore I shall not be pulling any punches.'[12]

He was to prove as good as his word.

The fourteen-day journey to England (with a stop at Las Palmas) was probably the most relaxed and carefree holiday Patrick had experienced since his childhood in Durban. It would be his last for a while.

* * *

By the time the ship docked in Southampton Patrick and Joe had become firm friends. They travelled by train to London and Joe took Patrick to the home of his aunt in St John's Wood, a Victorian suburb in north-west London, close to Regent's Park.

Patrick rented an attic room in the aunt's house and quickly found himself a job in central London at a Lyons Corner House.[13] His work colleagues were a cosmopolitan lot from all over the Commonwealth and the crumbling British Empire, together with a smattering from Europe, and he fitted in well. But the manager had little regard for his staff as it was easy to find replacements and Patrick found he had to work long hours to earn any more than just enough for rent, food and transport.

The café was on the corner of the Strand and Duncannon Street, directly behind South Africa House, a grand neo-classical edifice that fronted onto Trafalgar Square. Designed by Sir Herbert Baker and Alexander Thomson Scott and built in the early 1930s, it was already a focus for anti-apartheid vigils and demonstrations.

Word soon got around that former diplomat Van Rensburg was reduced to 'flipping burgers' in a café, and one day in mid-August he was visited by Senator Leslie Rubin, an outspoken critic of apartheid and a founding member of the South African Liberal Party. Having started on the conservative wing of the party, Rubin had soon moved to the left in Liberal politics.[14]

In a debate in the Senate in 1958 he had described the Group Areas Act, which uprooted half a million people, mostly black, from their homes, as 'a mixture of stupidity and wickedness the like of which I have never seen before'.[15]

Rubin saw the former Liberal Party activist turned 'griddler' as a wasted asset and introduced him to John Collins, canon of St Paul's Cathedral. Collins had a long history of activism, having founded the charities 'Christian Action' in 1946, to promote reconciliation with post-war Germany, and 'War on Want' in 1951, to alleviate poverty worldwide.

He became the founding chairman of the Defence and Aid Fund (later the International Defence and Aid Fund – IDAF), formed to provide legal aid and family support for those caught up in the South African Treason Trial of 1956–1961.[16] Collins offered Patrick the job of fundraiser for Christian Action and IDAF at the rate of between £7 and £10 a week, a step up from the £6 he was currently being paid.[17]

Patrick had imagined that his 'holiday' in Europe would be a complete break from South African politics, but he could not resist the chance to do something much more worthwhile than griddling for Mr Lyons. The following week he began work in the basement office of Canon Collins's official residence at 2 Amen Court, a Georgian terraced house in the heart of the City, not far from St Paul's Cathedral and the London Stock Exchange.

Collins had a wide range of contacts and Patrick's role was to draft letters to them and expand the list of potential contributors. Through his direct and current experience of South Africa he was able to bring authenticity and urgency to his letters of appeal. It also earned him important experience in raising money for charitable organisations.

Towards the end of August Tennyson Makiwane called on the canon and learned that Patrick was working in the basement. Tennyson had slipped out of South Africa illegally earlier in the year and had arrived in London in early June. His mission on behalf of the ANC was to raise overseas support for the boycott campaign.

He had turned initially to the Committee of African Organizations (CAO), a grouping of Anglophone Africans working for the decolonisation of their continent. They worked out of a small borrowed office space in the basement of the surgery of the West Indian physician Dr David Pitt, at 200 Gower Street in west-central London.

The CAO was currently campaigning for the breakup of Britain's Central African Federation and for the release of more than 1 000 political prisoners in Nyasaland, detained under a state of emergency. Nevertheless, at Makiwane's request, the committee set up a boycott sub-committee, chaired by its chairman, the Tanzanian Dennis Phombeah. Their publicity secretary, Femi Okunnu, a final-year Nigerian law student, began sending out letters, including to contacts in the Labour Party and the trade union movement.

They were helped by several South African volunteers, including Abdul Minty and Rosalynde (Ros) Ainslie, and had soon gathered enough support to hold a public meeting addressed by Tennyson in Holborn Hall and a twenty-four-hour vigil outside South Africa House. These two events were timed to coincide with the ANC's official launch of the boycott in South Africa on 26 June. Thereafter they handed out leaflets at shopping centres listing South African products to avoid and put up posters urging people 'Don't Buy Slavery. Don't Buy South African'.

The high point in the campaign was a mass rally in Trafalgar Square on Sunday 19 July addressed by Tennyson on behalf of the ANC and, among others, Julius Nyerere, soon to lead Tanganyika to independence, and James Callaghan, Labour's shadow colonial secretary. Tennyson addressed other meetings at various centres around London through August, but it was clear that the campaign was running out of steam. It was at this point that he visited Amen Court and met up with Patrick.

Aware of Patrick's record as Transvaal organiser for the Liberal Party, Tennyson appealed to him to help revive the boycott campaign. Patrick sympathised, but was hesitant to commit himself. He already had a worthwhile full-time paying job, so any work that he did for the boycott would have to be in his own time, in the evenings and at weekends. And, as a member of the Liberal Party's national executive, he would have to get clearance from the party in South Africa. Initially, too, he was sceptical about the wisdom of such a campaign.[18]

He appears to have felt that a general indefinite anti-apartheid boycott in Britain would be too broad to have much impact, particularly bearing in mind the extent of British vested interests in South Africa. He also feared that if the boycott failed it could undermine the moderate leadership of the ANC and others who were committed to non-violence. That could lead to the emergence of a more extreme, possibly violent, brand of African nationalism. He had written of such dangers often enough in the South African press.

He discussed these issues with Michael Scott, the champion of non-violent campaigns in South Africa and South West Africa. Scott was honorary director of the Africa Bureau, set up in 1952 by David Astor, owner-editor of the Sunday *Observer*. The purpose of the bureau was to advise and support Africans in their various struggles against colonialism.

Scott, who had personal experience of the 'near slavery' conditions on South African farms, suggested that a short boycott aimed specifically at farming produce would be most effective. Within those limits, a total boycott should be possible.[19] Patrick came away from the meeting convinced and persuaded Tennyson that they should aim for a one-month boycott sometime in the new year after South Africa's summer harvest, when food exports to Britain would be at their peak. Thereafter, Patrick and Tennyson worked closely together.

On 1 September Patrick wrote to Peter Brown laying out these proposals and asking for Liberal Party approval of his involvement. A week later Conservative Prime Minister Harold Macmillan announced the dissolution of Parliament and called a general election for 8 October. Although Patrick and Tennyson knew little if anything about the inner workings of British politics, they did know that a Labour victory would definitely be best for their campaign. In the meantime, they decided to delay any public campaigning until after the election, for all media attention would now be focused on its outcome.

Authorisation from Peter Brown finally came through at the end of September. The party's national executive was not meeting until the end of October but, appreciating that Patrick must be champing at the bit, Brown, as chairman, gave his personal approval, adding, 'If anyone wants to give you a kick in the pants tell them they had better kick me instead'.[20]

At last Patrick was free to work openly on the campaign and he 'threw himself into action with gusto, firing off letters to prospective sponsors'.[21] He was fortunate at this early stage to have typing assistance from Jane Symonds, Canon Collins's secretary.[22]

The CAO had made a good start on eliciting support from people such as Lord Altrincham, better known as the journalist and politician John Grigg, Labour MP Fenner Brockway, a veteran campaigner against colonialism, the Africanist historian Basil Davidson and the South African anthropologist Professor Max Gluckman, in addition to that of the three prominent clergymen: Canon Collins, Michael Scott and Trevor Huddleston.

Through Christian Action and IDAF Patrick had access to a wide range of contacts in politics, business, the church and the arts. He slightly tailored each letter to suit the recipient but started them all by explaining that he was writing on behalf of the African National Congress of South

Africa and its representative in the United Kingdom, Tennyson Makiwane. He wanted to make it clear that the boycott was at the behest of the victims of apartheid. He also explained his own position as a member of the Liberal Party ('which supports the campaign') and as a former diplomat who had resigned because he 'no longer felt conscientiously able to support Government policies'.[23]

Disappointed at the sympathetic Labour Party's failure in the general election, which saw Macmillan's Conservatives back in power, Patrick and Tennyson decided it was time for some major publicity. Patrick drafted a press statement outlining the situation in South Africa and the reasons for the boycott campaign. The leading national liberal newspaper, the *Manchester Guardian*, published the statement in the form of an extended letter.

Having emphasised that the boycott was being asked for by the African people who would share its impact, Patrick pointed out that Britain was the biggest consumer of South African exports. Apart from gold, some £100 million worth of South African goods were imported into the UK every year, two-thirds of them agricultural. He concluded that 'it is fitting that farmers – the main Government supporters, and the worst offenders against human rights in South Africa – should be made to feel the pinch most'.[24]

The publication of the letter gave the campaign the shot in the arm it needed, and in the weeks that followed Patrick and Tennyson were in high demand as public speakers, addressing various organisations around the country, from towns on the south coast to the university cities of Oxford and Cambridge and as far north as Edinburgh in Scotland.

University students were a fertile field of support, and in Oxford alone as many as 44 student societies and clubs adopted resolutions condemning apartheid and pledging their support for the boycott.[25] At a meeting of the Oxford University Labour Club 1 000 students packed the hall and unanimously resolved to observe the boycott, although they were careful to exclude from the ban that source of cheap student alcohol – South African sherry![26]

Patrick was invited to Oxford to speak to the student body. One of those in the audience was Prince Bereng Constantine Seeiso, crown prince of Basutoland (Lesotho). He was concerned that a boycott would have a heavy impact on Basutoland, a majority of whose adults depended on employment in the mines and on the farms of South Africa. Patrick assured him that there would not be a boycott of imports of gold from South Africa (however much he might have liked to have been able to organise one), so the mines should not be directly affected.

As far as the agricultural economy was concerned, he stressed that the boycott would be scheduled to last for only one month – as a demonstration of the potential strength of international condemnation of South Africa's racial policies. He may have allayed the worst of Bereng's fears, for he seems to have established a certain rapport with him; a connection that would prove mutually beneficial in the years ahead.[27]

On 4 November Patrick called ten of the main activists on the CAO's boycott sub-committee to a meeting at the Gower Street office.[28] He suggested the campaign be put on a more formal footing, through a new committee, separate from the CAO, although Dennis Phombeah would be retained as chair.

Although Tennyson was not present at this meeting, the proposal had his full support and, at his suggestion, Patrick became director of the campaign, which was now to become known as the 'Boycott Movement'. Various roles were divided up between those present, most of them South Africans, notable among them Abdul Minty, Vella Pillay and Ros Ainslie. Patrick had already ordered letterheads and he urged those present to use all their contacts to find potential prominent sponsors. In the meantime, he was off to the Netherlands.

At the end of October he had received an invitation from a Dutch student organisation to undertake an expenses-paid ten-day speaking tour of Netherlands universities. The invitation had come at the suggestion of Karel Roskam, professor of International Law at the Free University of Amsterdam, whom Patrick had met at the Johannesburg lawyer Bram Fischer's house earlier in the year.

Patrick 'jumped at the chance' to present a critique of apartheid in what Afrikaner Nationalists regarded as their spiritual homeland, the country in which Dr Verwoerd had been born. The only Afrikaners the Dutch were used to hearing invariably spoke in favour of apartheid, and Patrick felt that 'reasoned criticism of it in Afrikaans would have a [strong] impact amongst the Dutch, and help consolidate their opposition to apartheid, so striking a hard blow at its Nationalist Afrikaner architects'.[29]

He arrived in the Dutch capital on 7 November and his first speaking engagement was alongside Dr J. J. 'Jan' Buskes, the Dutch socialist evangelical minister and strong critic of apartheid, and, 'for balance', a well-known Dutch supporter of Afrikaner nationalism. Patrick addressed the audience in Afrikaans and they seemed to understand him well enough, just as he found throughout his trip that he was able to understand Dutch. He recalled that it was a 'lively' discussion and that he and Buskes had received strong support from the audience.

Patrick himself received a standing ovation at the end of his address. Over the following week he visited just about every university in the Netherlands, usually accompanied by Karel Roskam, a man of his own age with whom he developed a firm friendship. His talks were all well received and his student hosts ensured he got good press coverage, with 'a ten-minute television interview and several press conferences'.[30] His hosts ensured he had a good time in Amsterdam, keeping him company over wine and music in the evenings, visiting restaurants and taking him to student parties in cellars never far from the canal.

Throughout his trip he was carefully tracked by the Dutch security police and the South African authorities soon picked up on what he was doing, with someone from the South African Embassy invariably in his audiences. *Die Burger*, the Nationalist paper in the Cape, devoted an editorial to attacking him and the Liberal Party.[31] It was clear he was storing up trouble for himself when he returned to South Africa.

Indeed, his former boss, the minister of foreign affairs, Eric Louw, later admitted that the government considered rendering him a stateless person.[32] The law at the time did not permit such a move, but the National Party had the parliamentary majority to push through such a law should it deem it necessary.[33] That it did not do so suggests that he was causing so much trouble abroad the party wanted him to come back home so he could be silenced more effectively through banning or imprisonment in South Africa.

Back in London, Patrick threw himself into his work – through the day at Amen Court and late into the night in Gower Street. Despite the long hours he was thoroughly enjoying life – having 'a great time', he wrote to Alan Paton.[34] He was mixing in high social circles, with newspaper editors, MPs, bishops, lords and professors.

The day after he returned from Amsterdam he could not resist writing to one of his boyhood film favourites, the actor Sir Alec Guinness, asking for his sponsorship. Sir Alec declined the invitation but expressed his moral support by enclosing a cheque for £10, the equivalent of Patrick's weekly wage.[35]

Patrick was enjoying being in the limelight. He was becoming a recognised 'name' and public speaking had given him added social confidence. The inhibition in the company of women that had constricted him throughout his youth was being stripped away. He was a tall, fit young man in his late twenties, with clean-shaven 'chubby looks'.[36] Someone who had known him in Johannesburg in 1958–1959 remembered him as 'handsome, charismatic, and a blinding light of inspiration'.

Parties with Patrick always 'went with a swing'.[37] In London he finally realised to his surprise and joy that women found him attractive. He recalled that at a party given by the MP David Ennals, who, together with his brother Martin, was a key Labour supporter of the boycott campaign, he met three attractive young women with whom he felt thoroughly at ease. He and they followed up their spontaneous friendship and he claimed that in due course he slept with each of them. What he recalled years later was the mutual enjoyment and the naturalness of this physical expression of affection. He felt a surge of freedom in these encounters, unencumbered as they were by any feeling of social awkwardness or religious guilt.[38]

During this second half of November he drew up a Boycott Manifesto, to be circulated to all potential sponsors, asking them to append their signatures to the document. It laid out the reasons for the boycott and its limited duration. The movement was not trying to bring down the South African government; rather, it was calling for an end to three specific issues:

(1) the Treason Trial and banning and banishment of leaders of the subjugated racial groups;
(2) the extension of the 'pass' system to African women, exposing mothers to arbitrary arrest; and
(3) the poverty wages of Africans, especially those in the agriculture sector.

As Patrick explained in the memorandum, these three 'most vicious aspects of apartheid' had the full or implicit support of most of the white electorate in South Africa.[39] The hope of the campaign was that these voters would be shown that international condemnation, backed up by economic boycott, could threaten the security of their comfortable existence.

The idea of issuing 'a short general statement of the Campaign to which sponsors could commit themselves' by adding their signature appears to have originated with Kevin Holland of Oxford University, who made the suggestion to Patrick in late October.[40] The strength of the idea was that it allowed the signatories to see for themselves the growing list of 'the great and the good' who had already committed themselves.

The campaign gathered momentum.[41] By 16 December 1959 there were just short of fifty sponsors and donations allowed the organisation to hire some part-time secretarial staff.[42] Questions by some newspapers about the authenticity of Patrick's and Tennyson's claims to be speaking on behalf of the 'subjugated people' of South Africa prompted Patrick to write to Chief Albert Luthuli asking him to indicate formally the ANC's support.[43]

On 17 December, just as the manifesto, with the names of its sponsors, was ready for publication, Patrick received a memorandum from Peter Brown fully supporting the UK boycott and formally signed by Albert Luthuli for the ANC, Gangathura 'Monty' Naicker for the Indian Congress and Peter Brown for the Liberal Party.[44] Luthuli's signature on this document was a major success for the Boycott Movement and its successor, the Anti-Apartheid Movement, especially following the award of the Nobel Peace Prize to Luthuli later in 1960.[45]

When he had taken on the job of director of the Boycott Movement, Patrick had indicated that he would have to quit at the end of the year as he was due back in Johannesburg for his new teaching job in January 1960. At the end of December 1959 he duly handed over the directorship to his co-director, Tennyson Makiwane.

The wisdom of Patrick's intention to return began to worry some of his friends, both in England and in South Africa. The government-supporting South African press held 'Patrick van Rensburg' solely responsible for the act of 'economic sabotage' against his own country. Sometime in December he received an undated handwritten note from someone in Johannesburg who signed himself simply as 'J', probably his closest ally in the Liberal Party, Jock Isacowitz.[46] The letter stressed the hostility towards him in South Africa and explained the very awkward position in which it

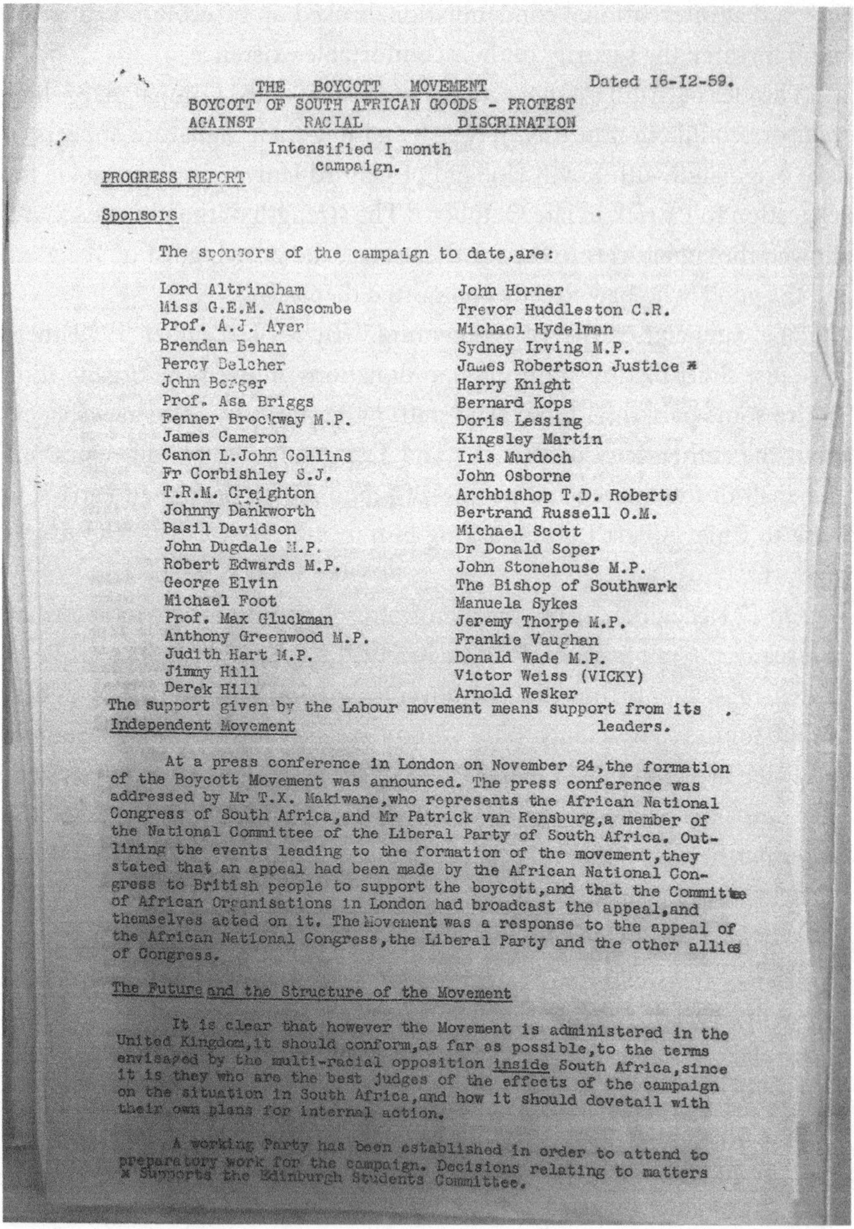

THE BOYCOTT MOVEMENT   Dated 16-12-59.
BOYCOTT OF SOUTH AFRICAN GOODS – PROTEST
AGAINST   RACIAL   DISCRINATION
                Intensified I month
                campaign.
PROGRESS REPORT

Sponsors

        The sponsors of the campaign to date,are:

Lord Altrincham   John Horner
Miss G.E.M. Anscombe   Trevor Huddleston C.R.
Prof. A.J. Ayer   Michael Hydelman
Brendan Behan   Sydney Irving M.P.
Percy Belcher   James Robertson Justice *
John Berger   Harry Knight
Prof. Asa Briggs   Bernard Kops
Fenner Brockway M.P.   Doris Lessing
James Cameron   Kingsley Martin
Canon L.John Collins   Iris Murdoch
Fr Corbishley S.J.   John Osborne
T.R.M. Creighton   Archbishop T.D. Roberts
Johnny Dankworth   Bertrand Russell O.M.
Basil Davidson   Michael Scott
John Dugdale M.P.   Dr Donald Soper
Robert Edwards M.P.   John Stonehouse M.P.
George Elvin   The Bishop of Southwark
Michael Foot   Manuela Sykes
Prof. Max Gluckman   Jeremy Thorpe M.P.
Anthony Greenwood M.P.   Frankie Vaughan
Judith Hart M.P.   Donald Wade M.P.
Jimmy Hill   Victor Weiss (VICKY)
Derek Hill   Arnold Wesker
The support given by the Labour movement means support from its   .
Independent Movement   leaders.

        At a press conference in London on November 24,the formation
of the Boycott Movement was announced. The press conference was
addressed by Mr T.X. Makiwane,who represents the African National
Congress of South Africa,and Mr Patrick van Rensburg,a member of
the National Committee of the Liberal Party of South Africa. Outlining the events leading to the formation of the movement,they
stated that an appeal had been made by the African National Congress to British people to support the boycott,and that the Committee
of African Organisations in London had broadcast the appeal,and
themselves acted on it. The Movement was a response to the appeal of
the African National Congress,the Liberal Party and the other allies
of Congress.

The Future and the Structure of the Movement

        It is clear that however the Movement is administered in the
United Kingdom,it should conform,as far as possible,to the terms
envisaged by the multi-racial opposition inside South Africa,since
it is they who are the best judges of the effects of the campaign
on the situation in South Africa,and how it should dovetail with
their own plans for internal action.

        A working Party has been established in order to attend to
preparatory work for the campaign. Decisions relating to matters
x Supports the Edinburgh Students Committee.

Figure 6.1: Sponsors of the boycott campaign, December 1959. (By kind permission of the
Anti-Apartheid Movement Archive)

left Michael Stern, his new prospective employer at St Martin's School. Although the headmaster was still prepared to take him on, Patrick took the hint. He wrote to Stern and declined the appointment as Afrikaans teacher.

This left him free to stay in the UK a little longer and Peter Brown asked him to represent the Liberal Party at the Second All-African People's Conference in Tunis from 25 to 30 January 1960.[47] This suited Patrick as he could treat it as the first part of his journey home. Then, on 4 January, he received a warning letter from Alan Paton: 'I have admired your actions but please tell me if you really mean to come back, because if you do, you certainly will never get out again.'[48]

By then Patrick was excited at the prospect of rejoining the struggle in Johannesburg and he brushed aside Paton's warning: 'I do really mean to return home and will immediately after the conference in Tunis.'[49]

At his last London press conference, on Tuesday 12 January 1960, he announced that the boycott was scheduled for the month of March and a conference of delegates and affiliated supporters would be held that Sunday, 17 January. The conference, chaired by Trevor Huddleston, was attended by 350 delegates from the Labour and UK Liberal parties, local councils, trade unions and other associations as well as many of the boycott's official sponsors.[50] By then Patrick had already left on the first leg of his journey home. He was restless, wanting to move on and see what fate awaited him. This desire for new challenges and fields of endeavour was a characteristic he was to carry into his later work in Botswana.

As he left London he reflected on the previous six months: 'I had found fulfilment in England in ways I never had at home, and my opposition to Apartheid had become a heavy cross to bear. But I never thought for a moment of laying it down, or of staying abroad, whatever deprivation and hardship it might cause me.'[51]

7 | Into Exile, 1960–1961

Patrick flew to Paris on Saturday 16 January 1960, the day before the London boycott conference. He found an unsanitary but cheap room on the Left Bank and spent the next week exploring the French capital, mostly on foot, visiting all the principal tourist sites and enjoying the pavement cafés, where he could drink coffee and read *Le Monde* like a regular Parisian.

After a week in Paris he caught a dawn flight to Tunis, where he registered at the Second All-African People's Conference as the official representative of the South African Liberal Party.

As Patrick recalled it, the first day of the conference was dominated by the Algerian delegation, whose *Front de Libération Nationale* (FLN) was fighting a large-scale guerrilla war against the French in Algeria and urged that violent struggle was the only route to independence on the continent.

That may have been true for them, but it did not suit the many delegates who hoped to achieve political independence by non-violent means – a hope fulfilled for most by the end of the year. Apart from that, the main theme of the conference, driven by Ghana, was the danger of neo-colonialism, whereby the colonial powers strove to maintain economic domination of their former colonies after political independence.[1]

But according to Patrick, the news that 'rocked the Conference' was the announcement by the Belgian government that it had decided to schedule the independence of the Belgian Congo for 30 June that year.[2] The news was received with euphoria in Tunis as a great victory in the struggle for liberation. And it prompted Patrick to place Leopoldville on the itinerary of his journey home to South Africa.

Figure 7.1: Patrick and Tennyson Makiwane at the All-African People's Conference, Tunis, January 1960. (Van Rensburg family collection; photographer unknown)

Patrick was still in Tunis when he read of British Prime Minister Harold Macmillan's historic speech to both houses of the South African Parliament in Cape Town on 3 February 1960. He had spoken of the African national-ism that was delivering such positive results in Ghana, then delivered his bombshell, which contained the phrase that was to define the era: '*The wind of change* is blowing through this continent and, whether we like it or not, this growth of national consciousness is a political fact. We must all accept it as a fact, and our national policies must take account of it.'[3]

It was a direct, if nuanced, criticism of South Africa's racial policies and it must have excited Patrick as much as it angered Afrikaner Nationalists.

* * *

The next stop on Patrick's trans-African flight was Accra. He had arranged to have his post forwarded there and, on arrival, managed to get hold of some South African newspapers. The Afrikaans press had been particularly hostile towards him.

In January the independent *Suid-Afrikaanse Stem* asked its readers what they thought should be done with Mr van Rensburg when he returned. Should he be imprisoned, banned or merely reasoned with 'to show him the folly of his ways'?[4] *Die Vaderland* urged Foreign Affairs Minister Eric Louw to remove Van Rensburg's citizenship, but then cautioned:

> Or is it just what the political snake-people desire, to pose as martyrs to their fellow-spirits here and overseas? Whatever the case may be, it is almost unthinkable that any civilised country would permit one of its citizens, like the arch-Liberalist Patrick van Rensburg, to associate himself actively with the boycott movement and then calmly and with impunity return to his fatherland which he tried so flagrantly to stab in the back.[5]

Contact wrote of 'plans for assaulting him or otherwise victimising him'. *Die Burger*, however, warned Nationalists against taking any such action, claiming: 'If one hair of Mr van Rensburg's head were touched ... a tremendous accession of strength would flow to the Boycott Movement, and to the Liberal movement generally.'[6]

The Liberal-supporting *Contact* did not help matters when it published news of his imminent return, with a large head-and-shoulders photograph of a clean-shaven Patrick van Rensburg plastered across the whole of its front page.[7] It may have been done with the best of intentions, but it helped ensure that the public, as well as border officials, would readily recognise him.

Patrick had already decided to grow a beard as a futile effort at personal disguise. The large, reddish-brown, bushy facial growth was in due course to become part of the defining image of the man and, apart from a brief fifteen months when he returned to London later that year, he retained it for the rest of his life. It suited his image of unconventional rebel and was, in any case, convenient on the many occasions in the future when regular access to hot water was not an option.

Letters from South Africa suggested he stay away for the time being, until things had calmed down a bit. He took some of this advice and remained in Ghana for six weeks, staying with Alfred and Hazel

Figure 7.2: Patrick van Rensburg gets unwanted publicity, February 1960. (Copyright ©
the British Library Board: P.P.7611.cau. 1960 February Vol. 3 No. 4 p001)

Hutchinson, whom he had last seen at Joe Slovo and Ruth First's party in Johannesburg sixteen months previously. Alfred had just completed a book about his adventurous trek across Africa posing as a migrant worker from Nyasaland.[8] By the time Patrick arrived in Ghana, Alfred and Hazel were married – something that would have been impossible in South Africa – and were teaching in Accra.

While in Accra Patrick visited a number of development projects and was particularly impressed by a training project for unemployed youth, most of whom had left primary school with no hope of entering secondary school. They were barely literate and had no specific skills. Without some form of training they would drift into urban unemployment and crime. The project organised them into what was known as a 'workers' brigade', where they learned specific industrial skills and, at the same time, put these skills into practice in productive work.[9]

Patrick flew to Leopoldville in the third week of March, three years after he had left the Congo. He was pleased to find that an old friend from the news agency *Agence Belga*, who was still working there, was able to put him up for a week or so. Out walking the next day, Patrick saw the South African consul-general, Theo Hewitson, walking towards him. As Patrick recalled, Hewitson 'stepped off the pavement to cross the road, spitting into the gutter as he did so'.[10]

* * *

It was in the *Agence Belga* office that Patrick heard of the massacre in Sharpeville on Monday 21 March 1960. The Pan Africanist Congress (PAC) leader, Robert Sobukwe, had called for an indefinite stay-at-home and mass defiance of the pass laws to commence on 21 March. He appears to have believed that the whole apartheid system, and perhaps even the government itself, would be brought crashing down if the people, en masse, simply refused to observe the unjust laws.

It was a rash decision with little planning; but thousands turned out in major cities across the country. The place that defined the events of that day, however, was Sharpeville, the African township that served the industrial city of Vereeniging, 40 kilometres south of Johannesburg. On that fateful Monday morning up to 5 000 people converged on Sharpeville police station, daring the police to arrest them for not carrying their passes. The police reacted by opening fire on the unarmed crowd. Within minutes they had killed 69 and wounded 180, many of them shot in the back as they fled.[11]

Just as Macmillan's 'wind of change' speech symbolised the independence movements of that year in Africa, so the Sharpeville massacre represented the South African state's response to movements for change. In the *Agence Belga* office in Leopoldville Patrick absorbed every detail of the news as it came through on the ticker-tape machine.

On 23 March Albert Luthuli called for a national day of mourning on Monday 28 March, a week after the massacre. Patrick, eager to get back home and play his part in the struggle, decided that would be a good day to fly back to Johannesburg. He believed 'the Afrikaner establishment would have more to worry about now than wreaking vengeance on [him]'.[12]

He sent a coded telegram to John Lang, a Liberal lawyer friend in Johannesburg, asking him to meet him at the airport, just in case 'anything untoward' happened when he landed. He was banking on the flight being too short for the passenger list to be signalled ahead. Nevertheless, he drank a couple of beers on the flight 'to steady [his] nerves'.[13]

On arrival at Jan Smuts Airport Patrick was held until all the other passengers had passed through immigration. When he was finally called, the immigration officer took away his passport and handed him a letter indicating that it had been confiscated. Alan Paton had been right: if he came back to the country he would not get out again, at least not legally. As he passed through the barrier he was thankful to see the reassuring bulk of John Lang. As he recalled, over the next two anxious days:

> The Liberals had arranged for different 'safe houses' for me to stay at each night. I was advised to limit my contacts for the moment to those I was staying with. A few close friends who knew of my whereabouts called on me. I saw the point of my seclusion on reading the papers the next day. *Die Vaderland* carried a story on its front page, headed *Patrick van Rensburg iewers in Goudstad*; I was 'somewhere in the Golden City [Johannesburg]'. Immigration officers must have told the paper's reporters of my arrival, and they were telling the Government's supporters.[14]

The state of emergency, declared on 30 March 1960, dashed Patrick's hopes of remaining in South Africa. Thousands were arrested, including eleven Liberals, and he learned that his name was on the wanted list.[15] He realised that his presence was putting others at risk.

He accepted the advice that he cross the border into Swaziland, at least for the time being, and his Liberal friends found someone willing to drive him the 320 kilometres late that night. It was an anxious journey, but nothing untoward happened. There was no border post at the Swaziland border and the driver was able to deposit Patrick safely at a Swazi hotel shortly before dawn on 31 March. Thus began a very hurried and unplanned exile that was to last for thirty years.[16]

* * *

Patrick registered with the British Protectorate Administration in the capital, Mbabane. This gave him documentation that allowed him temporary residence in Swaziland and the equivalent of British recognition of his refugee status. It would allow him in due course to travel north through Africa and, ultimately, to the United Kingdom. He could not have imagined at the time that he would spend the next five months in Swaziland.

After a few nights in the hotel it was arranged that Patrick should stay in a small cottage north of Mbabane belonging to Nell Green, 'a stalwart Liberal in Johannesburg', and her engineer husband. Patrick had been in Swaziland for a week when news came through that the ANC and the PAC had been banned. They were to remain 'illegal political organisations' in South Africa for the next thirty years.

The following day an attempt was made on the life of Prime Minister Verwoerd. He had been shot in the head, twice, by an Anglophone white farmer and Cambridge graduate named David Beresford Pratt. Although in due course Verwoerd made a full recovery, his life lay in the balance for several days. Afrikaner Nationalists were incensed and, although David Pratt had not been a member of the Liberal Party, indeed, had had no known political affiliation,[17] it was white liberals who were the subject of most of the Afrikaners' ire.

Patrick van Rensburg, the Afrikaner traitor, was singled out for particular condemnation. He received numerous direct verbal threats in

Swaziland, a country where political abductions were not uncommon, and he was lucky to escape a severe beating and several attempts at abduction and transportation back to South Africa.[18]

Meanwhile, Canon Collins's Defence and Aid Fund, for whom Patrick had raised money the previous year, provided him and other refugees who had 'limited resources' with a small monthly allowance. Patrick's needs were simple and he required little to survive.[19]

As the South African government clamped down ever harder on any internal political criticism it became clear that Patrick was in exile for the long haul. Peter Brown wrote warning him against trying to return home and pointing out that if he still wished to serve the Liberal cause he could best do that from abroad. But how to get out of Swaziland, surrounded as it was by South Africa on one side and Portuguese-ruled Mozambique on the other?

As the initial weeks of exile turned into months, time hung heavily. Inactivity did not suit Patrick. At one stage the boredom was relieved by a visit from Uncle Pat, who had driven up from Durban to see him. They had not met for a number of years, although they had maintained an irregular correspondence. Uncle Pat was the only remaining connection with the family of his youth and childhood. Old Jumbo had died and Cecile, with whom he now had no relationship, was living in Rhodesia, where her husband had a job.

Uncle Pat had been concerned in 1957 that Patrick had thrown away a good career in the diplomatic service, but he had never criticised the political road he had chosen; he was only ever worried about Patrick's personal safety. Even now he offered to plead for him with the government so that he could be allowed back home. Patrick was clearly touched by the older man's offer and concern, but he had moved on a long way from the life they had known together in Natal. He explained the depth of his commitment to the cause and Uncle Pat respected his position.

The two men spent 'a couple of very pleasant days together, looking around Swaziland', although their enjoyment in each other's company was overshadowed by the knowledge that they might never see each other again. Patrick would have loved to have asked about his paternity, but after all this distance from his life in Natal, the taboo was still too strong and he dared not broach the subject.

Uncle Pat did not raise it either, as if by unspoken agreement. But the visit restored their relationship and the sad farewell blew away any residual doubts Patrick may have had about their true relationship.[20] There were no regrets. Indeed, he felt liberated to reinvent himself in exile.

Following the visit from Uncle Pat, Patrick was pleased to hear, in July or early August 1960, that the Defence and Aid Fund was planning to fly some of the long-term refugees out of Swaziland and he would be on the list. Among the prominent refugees who were gathering in the country were the former Communist Party MP Sam Kahn and Oliver Tambo's wife, Adelaide, and their two young children. Tambo himself had been driven across the border into Bechuanaland in the aftermath of Sharpeville, under orders from the ANC executive to establish an external wing of the party.

Tambo had spent some weeks in Serowe, the largest town in Bechuanaland, capital of the Bamangwato Reserve and the hometown of the country's future president, Seretse Khama, who, some years previously, had returned with his English wife, Ruth, from their forced exile in Britain. Although he had been obliged to renounce his right to the chieftaincy as a condition of his return, Khama was a leading figure in the modernisation of 'Tribal Administration' in the protectorate and was, without doubt, the 'uncrowned king' in Serowe. With an official population of 30 000, Serowe was also the largest traditional African so-called village south of the equator.[21]

In April 1960 a light aircraft had been chartered to fly Tambo, Ronald Segal and Yusuf Dadoo to Tanganyika and thence to London.[22] By July Tambo had heard that his wife and children had arrived in Swaziland. It was thus probably at his urging that Canon Collins asked the *Observer*'s Africa correspondent, George Clay, then based in Cape Town, to go to Swaziland and see what could be arranged.

Clay would have known Patrick from the *Observer*'s support for the Boycott Movement and on his arrival in Swaziland Patrick introduced him to Oliver Tetley, who ran a smallholding outside Mbabane and with whom Patrick had developed a close friendship. Tetley and a small group of trusted friends identified a safe place to hide drums of aircraft fuel that Clay arranged to truck into Swaziland from South Africa.

Clay explained that once he had managed to identify a pilot he would get clearance from the British high commissioner in Pretoria for the group to fly to Bechuanaland. President Nkrumah of Ghana had already offered to provide a Ghana Airways plane to fly them out of Bechuanaland.

* * *

Clay found a willing pilot in Bulawayo, Southern Rhodesia: a German named Herbert Bartaune, who had flown for the Luftwaffe during World War II. He worked for Air Carriers Bulawayo and regularly flew into northern Bechuanaland. From 1961, as he became more involved in the refugee airlift, Bartaune teamed up with local businessman Cyril Hurwitz and operated two Cessna planes out of Lobatse as Bechuanaland Air Safaris.[23]

In 1960 he had only one plane available, but he was prepared to fly up to twenty refugees, four or five at a time, from Swaziland to Botswana. Seretse Khama had recommended that they use the small airstrip in Serowe rather than the only tarmac airstrip in the country, which was in Francistown, the main modern town north-east of Serowe.

The Francistown airstrip was under the control of the Witwatersrand Native Labour Association (WNLA), which recruited cheap African migrant workers from Angola and the Congo and flew them via Francistown to Johannesburg to work in the South African mines. WNLA employees had previously blocked the runway with drums of aircraft fuel to prevent the arrival of a Ghana Airways flight[24] and it was clear that the refugees would be safer if they were flown direct to Serowe.

Meanwhile, Serowe district commissioner David 'Robbie' Robinson had identified Ronald Watts as a suitable linkman for the operation. Watts was a British Quaker currently under contract to the Bamangwato Tribal Authority as 'Livestock Improvement Officer'.[25] He was a member of Christian Action, with connections to Canon Collins, the Defence and Aid Fund and the Africa Bureau, and he was willing to help.

The British authorities were keen that the refugees should pass through the protectorate with a minimum of delay. They had been concerned about the several weeks Oliver Tambo had spent in Serowe, leaving him vulnerable to potential abduction by South Africans. But it was important for diplomatic reasons that neither the colonial administration nor the tribal authority should be seen to be directly involved in any transfer of refugees.

Watts received funds from Canon Collins and was put in touch with the 'South African United Front', a refugee group in Dar es Salaam, which decided on the authenticity of refugees and identified who should be included on the flights.

Word came through to Serowe on 31 August that the flights from Swaziland would start in the next few days and on 1 September George Clay arrived with drums of aircraft fuel from Pretoria.[26] The first flight was due the following day.

* * *

During Patrick's final few days in Swaziland, a friend of Nell Green introduced him to Frank Lothar Krawolitski, 'a German who was organizing work-camps in Swaziland for South Africans and others to build primary schools'. It was an inspirational meeting for Patrick. Frank was a kindred spirit, with the same taste in classical music: '... a large man whom we found in his rondavel playing Beethoven's Ninth Symphony and singing "*Alle Menschen werden Bruder* (All Men are Brothers)" along with the chorus'.[27]

Frank's work in Swaziland and his work-camp contacts in South Africa showed Patrick, however briefly, the possibilities for rural development work in a small Southern African protectorate. It was an image he was to store firmly in his memory, to be resurrected when the time came for his own experiments in development work.

Patrick and his small group of friends in Swaziland had managed to keep their flight arrangements secret so that there would be no attempt by the South African authorities to interfere. Herbert Bartaune landed at the Swazi airstrip as agreed early in the morning of Friday 2 September. Patrick and Sam Kahn were to make the first flight, with two others, because they would be responsible in Serowe for organising the refuelling for the return flights. Once it had proved to be safe, Adelaide Tambo and her two children and the rest of the selected refugees would follow on subsequent flights.

The first flight arrived at the Serowe airstrip at about midday and was met by Ronald Watts, who had brought a drum of fuel in the back of his old Bedford van. They refuelled the aircraft and saw Bartaune take off back to Swaziland. Watts then drove his four guests into Serowe.

Figure 7.3: A typical view of Serowe as Patrick would have seen it in 1960. (By kind permission of Benny Wielandt)

Serowe was spread out over a dusty plain, backed by a ridge formed by a series of hills. It was towards the end of the winter dry season and the temperature was rising. The van in which they were travelling left a cloud of dust behind as it rode along the sandy track through the seemingly endless collection of homesteads, each made up of several round, mud-walled thatched houses.

The vision that stuck in Patrick's mind when he first glimpsed the town was the bright green of the succulent rubber-plant hedge that surrounded each neatly brushed yard – in sharp contrast to the grey, leafless scrub and thorn bush that dominated the rural landscape.

Eventually the group reached what looked like the centre of the settlement, where there were a number of rectangular brick houses with corrugated-iron roofs. On slightly higher ground they came to a number of large European-style bungalows, known mockingly by the locals as 'the white highlands'. As they drew up in front of one of these they were greeted by Ronald's wife, Theresa, a medical doctor who ran a clinic in the town.[28]

Patrick and Sam Kahn were staying with Ronald and Theresa, as was George Clay, who was already there. When Adelaide Tambo and her children arrived on a later flight they stayed with the London Missionary Society (LMS) couple the Reverend Alan and Ruth Seager, while the other refugees were housed elsewhere within Serowe.[29] Their accommodation was coordinated by Stephen Sello, a fellow South African refugee and resident who worked at the post office and ran a garage for the African Authority.

The South African refugees were generally welcomed by the Bechuanaland population, who had been shocked by the Sharpeville massacre and the mass arrests that followed, although there was some resentment among the cattle-owning élite in Serowe, who felt that Ronald Watts 'spent too much time assisting "refugees" and too little at work [as the Livestock Improvement Officer]'.[30]

After lunch Clay asked Patrick and Sam to load another drum of fuel into Ronald's van and take it back to the airstrip to meet the next batch of refugees. After a long wait at the airstrip the plane arrived and they assisted with the refuelling before driving the new batch of refugees to Mr Sello, who allocated their accommodation.

This was to become their routine for the next few days: taking fuel twice a day to the airstrip, where they waited in the slight shade of a thorn tree, often for hours at a time, watching the scurrying lizards and listening for the distinctive sound of the light aircraft.

With all nineteen refugees safely accounted for,[31] George Clay's role was to organise the next leg of their flight northwards. Kwame Nkrumah had agreed to provide a Ghana Airways plane to fly all of them to Accra, but that would require a much larger airstrip than the one at Serowe. Francistown was the obvious choice, but Khama was concerned about possible interference by the WNLA. Clay asked Bartaune to fly him to investigate the airstrips at Kasane, near the Chobe Game Reserve in the extreme north of the country, and at Maun in the north-west, the tourist centre for the Moremi Game Reserve and Okavango swamps.

Bartaune agreed to take Patrick and Sam along for the ride. At Kasane they were the first guests at the newly constructed Chobe Safari Lodge, where they had the pleasure of downing a few cold drinks as they watched the sun set over the Chobe River. At Maun the next day they stayed at Riley's Hotel before heading back on the third leg to Francistown.[32] It was clear that only Francistown had an airstrip suitable for the Ghana Airways plane, and one cannot help wondering whether the round trip was much more than an opportunity for a short break for Clay, Patrick and Sam, though not, of course, for Bartaune, who had flown thousands of kilometres in the past week.

For his final work on behalf of the refugees Bartaune flew George Clay down to Mafikeng, across the border in South Africa, where, to the south of the town, there was a collection of administration buildings enclosed within a high wire fence. This was the 'Imperial Reserve', the official head-quarters of the Bechuanaland Protectorate Administration.

Clay met the resident commissioner, Peter Fawcus, who had already given his full support to the project. Fawcus sent a firm message to the WNLA employees in Francistown warning them not to interfere with the Ghana Airways flight, and he arranged clearance for the plane to fly over the Central African Federation.

It is often claimed, or assumed, that during his brief stay in Serowe in 1960 Patrick discussed with Seretse Khama the founding of a secondary school in the Bamangwato capital. This does not appear to be true. Patrick had no such ideas in his mind at that stage. Seretse may have addressed the refugees as a group, but a few years later, when Patrick had settled in Serowe, Seretse was to complain that he had never come to visit him when, as a refugee, he had for a few weeks been a guest of the Bamangwato.

Watts organised a convoy of two cars and a lorry to take the refugees to the Francistown airport. They set off at about midnight, arriving on the outskirts of the 'one-horse town' shortly before dawn.[33] After several hours the plane arrived. It was a twin-engine Douglas Dakota DC4, the 1950s short-haul workhorse for national airlines around the globe.

As the convoy offloaded its racial mix of nineteen refugees plus George Clay, who was hitching a ride to Ghana, a group of burly white WNLA employees approached from the hangar. But the Francistown dis-trict commissioner, Phil Steenkamp, had brought a small detachment of Bechuanaland Protectorate Police to ensure there was no trouble and the refugees were able to board the plane without incident.[34] Years later Patrick was to record in his memoir that as the plane took off he looked down on dry and dusty Bechuanaland and doubted that he would ever see it again.[35]

The flight to Ghana took two days. The plane's first refuelling stop was Elizabethville, the capital of newly independent Republic of Congo's

Katanga province, which had recently declared its independence from Congo. Nkrumah had offered to send Ghanaian troops to help the UN end the illegal secession. Thus, the arrival of a Ghana Airways plane aroused suspicion and the refugee passengers spent an uncomfortable night under armed guard on the floor of an aircraft hangar. After another refuelling stop in Lagos, the plane was met in Accra by a number of ANC and PAC dignitaries.

Patrick and his fellow refugees spent the first few nights at a hotel on the edge of the city before being moved into a barracks-like holding centre near the airport. Prominent ANC members in the group had priority status and were quickly flown out to Europe, where they underwent training for Umkhonto we Sizwe (MK), the newly established military wing of the ANC. Patrick was left high and dry. His friends Alfred and Hazel Hutchinson had moved to London. He had no money and felt trapped within the dependent status of a refugee. He was determined to break free and, if possible, return to London.[36]

He got in touch with Leslie Rubin, who had introduced him to Canon Collins in London the previous year and who was currently professor of Law at the University of Ghana, Legon. Rubin invited him to stay with him, an invitation Patrick accepted gladly. He was even more pleased when Rubin telephoned Canon Collins on his behalf to ask whether the Defence and Aid Fund would pay for Patrick's flight to London. The canon was initially hesitant, but Rubin pressed Patrick's case and Collins finally agreed to send the money for the flight.[37]

According to Patrick's memoir, as he was about to depart from the Accra airport someone handed him a letter that had just arrived from London. He opened it on the plane. It was an anonymous handwritten note which simply said: 'Canon Collins thinks you're a police spy because Bishop Reeves told him so.'[38]

Ambrose Reeves was the former Anglican archbishop of Johannesburg whose outspoken criticism of the South African government after Sharpeville had led to his expulsion from the country in September. He had overlapped with Patrick in Swaziland by a few days and had clearly picked up gossip that must have been circulating among the exiles. Patrick was aware that there were jealousies and suspicions within the exile community, but he had never imagined that rumours had got this bad. He sat in a dispirited daze for most of the flight to London. After all he had sacrificed for the cause of liberation, his moral integrity was being doubted and challenged!

He was later to discover the basis for the suspicions that had gradually built into rumours in Swaziland. Why had he returned to South Africa when he did and then stayed for only two days? Where had he been in those two days? Why had he not been arrested along with so many others on the day the state of emergency was declared? Why had he chosen to go into exile as a refugee without a passport when he could have stayed out of the country and retained his passport, like so many other South African activists in London?

On arrival in London Patrick was pleased to find that the travel document he had been issued in Swaziland worked and he was allowed into the country as a citizen of the Commonwealth. It was early October 1960 and the first person he sought out was Joe Rogaly, whose aunt's attic room in St John's Wood was again available. He told Joe of the anonymous note.

As Patrick recalled, Joe knew him well enough to imagine the anguish the note would have caused, but he reassured Patrick that 'whoever believed its content had deeply suspect motives that would be exposed soon enough'.[39] Back in his attic room Patrick shaved off his beard, not wanting anyone to think that he was trying to disguise himself, and shortly afterwards he attended an Anti-Apartheid Movement (AAM) meeting.[40]

He kept a low profile, wondering who of those present might believe the 'crucifying lie' that was being spread about him.[41] Alan Paton was there and Patrick collared him afterwards, telling him about the anonymous note.

> 'John Collins is here,' [Alan] said. 'Let's find him and put an end to this thing.' We quickly found the Canon among a group of people, and Alan called him aside. 'What's this Patrick's telling me about, that you and others think he's a spy? I can assure you there's no truth in the allegation whatsoever!' I had never seen Canon Collins embarrassed before, but he was now, betraying it in his look and nervous laugh.[42]

Paton was off to New York the next day, but it was agreed that the canon and Patrick would have dinner together the following evening to sort out the misunderstanding. ' "We must kill this thing, John, before we kill a good man", Alan said, walking off with his arm around me.'[43]

Alan Paton's unreserved assurance of Patrick's trustworthiness helped smooth the waters for the explanations over dinner the following evening, which ended with Collins offering Patrick his old job back.

* * *

He started work again at Amen Court the next morning and quickly slipped back into some sort of London routine. But there was clearly something missing. When he had been in London the previous year it was for a limited six months, during which he had played a leading role in the Boycott Movement, which had now morphed into the Anti-Apartheid Movement.

He needed a focus to his life and his mind turned again to the writing of his book, *Guilty Land*, to which he had not given much thought in the past three years. Now was the time to write it, as a plea to South Africans and to the wider world. Support from the latter, he believed, was essential if the ideal of a liberal, non-racial South Africa was still to be achieved. Time was running out. The South African state had already resorted to open violence and the African response in kind could not be far behind.

He already had the structure of a three-part book in his mind. The first part would relate his personal story. Skimming over details of his childhood, it would tell of his learning to become an Afrikaner, as a way of introducing the reader to Afrikaans culture, with its complex mix of race-pride and fear. The explanation of his conversion from Afrikaner diplomat to radical critic and rebel would expose the contradictions and hypocrisy underlying the whole concept of apartheid.

The second part would present a potted history of South Africa by way of explaining how white domination and white-supremacist thinking had come about and the extent to which there was any difference between Afrikaner and British-settler political mentality.

The final section would look to the present, as it was in 1960, analysing the African opposition movements – ANC and PAC – their differences and their evolving strategies since their banning after the Sharpeville massacre. He would explain the role of the Liberal Party in helping break down fear and prejudice among white people, although he recognised that theirs could only ever be a very minor role in the coming struggle. The leadership lay in the hands of the African majority, while the international community had a role to play by providing moral and financial support and applying political and economic pressure on the South African government.

The time for gradual evolution was long past. Some form of revolution – violent or non-violent – was now inevitable. But he had seen some of the non-racialism that was emerging in the rest of liberated Africa and this gave him hope for the future of his own country.

With these ideas churning in his mind he met Pat Williams, who, like Joe Rogaly, was a former reporter for the *Rand Daily Mail*. She introduced him to Tom Maschler, the principal editor at Jonathan Cape, described as the blue-chip literary publisher of the day. Maschler was keen to take on the book and, encouraged by Pat and Joe, Patrick signed a contract with Jonathan Cape in February 1961. This brought him a £50 advance and pressure to start immediately, and he arranged with Canon Collins to reduce his hours at Amen Court to three days a week.

Although Patrick dedicated long hours to his work, he maintained an active social life, especially in the company of women, with several of whom he had sexual liaisons; but he sensed the hollowness of these physical relationships. Here he was in London, rebuilding and redefining his life as a long-term exile, and there was a vital ingredient missing. He felt the resurgence of the old yearning for a permanent, loving relationship – for someone with whom he could share the new life that was awaiting him, whatever that might be.

* * *

In December he had met up with Polly and Lindsey Loxton, whom he had known in Johannesburg. On visiting their flat he saw for the first time a young English friend of theirs named Elizabeth Griffin, known universally simply as 'Liz'. Liz worked with Polly as a secretary in the graphics section of the University of London publisher, Athlone Press.[44]

For Patrick, physical beauty was an important ingredient of a good relationship. He noticed that Liz wore a long dress topped with a duffle coat – a style that he felt was 'intentionally scruffy'; but, as he was to recall many years later, 'nothing could hide her striking beauty and her delicate, gracious movements'.[45] His interest was immediately aroused.

She seemed quiet and self-assured, but he found himself unable to establish immediately the sort of easy rapport that he had become accustomed to achieving with women. Over the following couple of months he met her on a number of occasions, at Polly's flat and at AAM rallies. From their casual bits of conversation he discovered that she was a humanist and was committed to a number of causes, including the Campaign for Nuclear Disarmament (CND), which had become a major force for campaign and protest since its founding in 1958.

Patrick, however, was totally focused on South Africa, and although she joined him at anti-apartheid demonstrations, which, by now, he was helping to organise, he did not join her on her other campaigns. He believed that apartheid was uniquely evil and that the case against it would be weakened if it were ever perceived to be 'just another "liberal" cause'.[46]

If he and Liz were to develop their relationship beyond the purely casual it would clearly have to be on his terms. Nevertheless, she remained much on his mind, and sometime in late January or early February she invited him to a party at the flat in Islington that she shared with her sister Mary and some friends. According to his account, it was here that their relationship began to develop.

He spent an increasing amount of time at Liz's flat as they gradually got to know each other. As he understood it, they both came from 'modest and precarious backgrounds, where money was always a struggle and life could be hard'. But there the similarity ended.

Liz and her sister 'had the advantage of a left-leaning, humanistic, politically aware and anti-colonial approach to life given to them by an enlightened, supportive and loyal family'. Home life for Patrick in Natal, by contrast, 'for all its extended family support, had given [him] racism, colonialism and Catholicism with all its guilt'. He had had to grapple with these influences 'by seeking out the helpful mentoring of good people and by [his] own receptive search for solutions, to educate and enlighten [himself]'.[47] As he was to recall: 'Meeting as we did, at this point in our lives, Liz and I had much to learn from each other.'[48]

Liz was deeply moved and distressed to learn that his mother had failed to acknowledge him during his early childhood and that his recognition of her indifference was followed by the sudden death of his beloved grand-mother, the only anchor of his life. Having had the support and advice of loving parents whenever she needed it, Liz 'understood intuitively and without discussion the depth of my emotional "neediness" and over time she resolved in her own quiet way to try to be for me the stable, loyal "rock" that her parents had been for her'.[49]

At about this time Patrick and Joe moved to rented rooms in a house on the north side of Primrose Hill, not far from St John's Wood. Patrick had a large room at the top of the house, on the floor of which he was able to spread out his research papers for *Guilty Land*, barely leaving room to put his feet.[50] On one occasion he left Liz sitting in a small clearing in the middle of the floor. By the time he returned she had read the early pages of his manuscript and he believed this was how she really came to know and understand him:

> She was utterly intrigued by my story, but what made a lasting impression on her at that moment was my complete attachment and devotion to South Africa and, despite its government's hatred of me, my determination to return somehow, whatever the cost. It meant that later, again intuitively and without discussion, she knew that come what may, she must never ask or expect me to break that commitment and leave Southern Africa for good, unless *I* had chosen to do so.[51]

He finished the *Guilty Land* manuscript in August 1961. South Africa continued to be very much in the news, so it was a good time to be publishing the book. In addition to the growing profile of the AAM and international condemnation of apartheid, South Africa had departed from the Commonwealth in March that year and declared itself a republic on 31 May.

Tom Maschler of Jonathan Cape, realising the book had the potential to appeal to a large general market, had negotiated a deal with Penguin Books, who agreed to publish simultaneously 40 000 paperback copies as a Penguin Special,[52] alongside Cape's 3 000 hardbacks. Printed locally in the UK, it was scheduled for publication on 11 January 1962.

In the meantime, Patrick needed some other employment to supplement his limited income working part-time for Canon Collins. Joe Rogaly introduced him to Andrew Boyd, a colleague of his at *The Economist*, who invited Patrick to work with him on an *Atlas of African Affairs*. As Patrick wrote of the finished book, published by Methuen in 1962: 'It was for its time, a pioneering work, offering in condensed and easily digested form, useful economic, social and sociological, cultural and geographical information in historical perspective.'[53]

* * *

Once he had finished *Guilty Land* and his floor had been cleared of his research papers Patrick and Liz began to live together in his room at the top of the house on Primrose Hill. He met Liz's parents several times, visiting their small farm, off the beaten track on the side of a mountain in Anglesey, north Wales, and was pleased to discover that Bernard and Joyce Griffin 'were very much in touch with the world, reading newspapers and listening to radio news programmes regularly. They were keen to hear about South Africa, [and were] sympathetic to [his] story.' And, importantly for Patrick, they supported the boycott.[54]

> The name of the farm was Tynymynydd which translated as 'the house on the mountain' – 75 acres of rough mountain and moorland with a few little green fields below the house. In winter-time, I found this an isolated and harsh environment. Liz took me to all her childhood haunts – climbing Snowdonia in wind and rain, and in summer-time, splashing in the cold waters of Red Warf Bay – a far cry from my own experience of sub-tropical Durban beaches. With the family, I carried water from the well, lit the tilly-lamps in the evenings, and helped with odd jobs around the farm ...
>
> Bernard and Joyce were a hospitable couple, who made me welcome. Joyce, a sociable and out-going person, was always cooking and baking and I recall long convivial meals in the evenings, beside the great old stove, drinking homemade wine. Bernard, a quiet and deeply thoughtful man, loved to philosophise about the state of the world. Sitting in the lamplight, smoking his old pipe, he would recall with great humour extraordinary stories of his childhood in Birmingham, working on farms in the 1940s, the war years and the early struggles

of life on the farm in 1945. Amongst Liz and Mary's friends, he was someone they very much looked up to for having turned his back on the upward social mobility of his generation.[55]

By the end of 1961 Patrick was sure in his mind that in Liz Griffin he had found the loving life's partner for whom he had been searching for much of his adult life. With her by his side, he was ready to move on to whatever the rest of his life had in store.[56]

8 | Return to Africa, 1961–1962

Having finished his writing tasks for the two publishers, Patrick began thinking seriously about his future. As far as his relationship with Liz was concerned, it was accepted between them that when they were settled and knew something of their future they would marry.[1] But how might he earn his living and where might they live?

Patrick was growing increasingly uncomfortable with the concept of being a permanent émigré.[2] He could not envisage any career path for himself in the United Kingdom. Besides, there were still suspicions among some of his fellow exiles about the speed and ease of his flight into exile and this may have burdened him with a degree of guilt.

He could not throw off the sense that he *ought* to go back home and join the struggle, even if it meant going underground with a high risk of capture and imprisonment, probable assault and possible torture. The only alternative he could think of would be to go to one of the protectorates (the 'High Commission Territories'), where he would at least be close to home and, as an exile, perhaps provide some support to those within South Africa who were struggling against apartheid.

The idea of a career in education had probably first been planted in Patrick's mind by the offer of a teaching job in Johannesburg in 1959. Since then he had seen the inspiring work of Frank Krawolitski, involving young South Africans in work camps to build a primary school in Swaziland. Krawolitski's playing and singing of Beethoven's Ninth in the remote bush while conducting a volunteer project for the local community was the sort of image that appealed to Patrick.

He could see himself in a similar role. While in Serowe he had learned that what was needed in the Bamangwato capital was a local secondary school, though there is no evidence that he discussed this issue with Seretse Khama at the time. The only secondary school in the northern half of Bechuanaland was Moeng College, a communal self-help project, the brainchild of Tshekedi Khama.[3]

The school, which had opened in 1949, was a boarding school in a remote site in the Tswapong Hills to the east of 'the line of rail' and more than 100 kilometres from Serowe. By 1962 there were five other secondary schools in the southern half of the country, although four of them only offered the first three years of secondary schooling. And there was no secondary school at all in Serowe.

A day secondary school for the primary-school leavers of Serowe would clearly be of great benefit to the local community and, in the absence of a government initiative, the building of it, like that of Moeng, would have to be a self-help project. Patrick liked the idea. Bechuanaland was a large enough country for him not to feel in constant threat of abduction, as he had in Swaziland and would have felt in Basutoland. He did not have much trust in the British colonial administration but, under the protection of Seretse Khama, he had felt safe in Serowe.

He tried these ideas out on a few trusted friends. Patrick Duncan, with whom he had discussed his options during the former's visit to London in June 1961,[4] was in favour of a return to South Africa 'when the time was right' and promised to keep in touch and see what he could organise. In the meantime, he recommended Patrick should go to Bechuanaland, which he had just visited, and keep his options open.

Joe Rogaly thought returning secretly to South Africa 'would be recklessly romantic, pointless, probably futile and just plain unworkable. "Try the school," he said tartly.'[5] Similarly, his editor, the 'wise and gentle' Dieter Pevsner, thought it would be 'crazy to try to go home a second time', especially after the publication of *Guilty Land*.[6]

Naturally, he discussed the issue with Liz, who made it clear that she was happy to go with him to Bechuanaland if he was going to set up a school. But she could not hide her alarm at the idea of his going underground in South Africa.[7] So it was decided: they would travel overland to Bechuanaland and take it from there, leaving straight after the publication of *Guilty Land*. That left about four months in which the two of them 'worked day and night to earn money for [their] trip'.[8] Liz left her job at Athlone Press and worked long hours as a saleswoman for Swan & Edgar, an old-fashioned department store at Piccadilly Circus, long since closed, while Patrick got a variety of fill-in jobs.

Uncle Pat came to London on business and managed to seek him out. They had a pleasant time together, with Uncle Pat sadly resigned to Patrick's exile status. As usual, neither mentioned their relationship. But Patrick had moved far beyond his youth in Natal and he had learned to put his family insecurity and genetic identity to the back of his mind.

On 3 December he turned thirty. He was about to enter the most exciting, challenging and rewarding period of his life. Since his early adulthood he had redefined his personal identity more than once and the past four years had been a turbulent and exciting time. On the surface he had grown enormously in self-confidence, although internally he was still plagued by diffidence and a constant need to prove himself. Now, on the cusp of an unknown future and entirely new adventure, he would redefine himself again.

In preparation for their transcontinental journey Patrick and Liz needed to make numerous visa arrangements. They would be travelling overland by the cheapest possible means and expected it would take about three months to reach Bechuanaland. Patrick's first priority was to sort out his citizenship. He still had no passport.

Unlike today, at that time any citizen of the Commonwealth could gain free entry to the UK and could even become a citizen after living in the country for a year. Patrick completed his year's residence in October 1961 and, although by then South Africa had left the Commonwealth, South African citizens were allowed up to the end of December 1961 to claim their citizenship.

Patrick applied in October and received his British passport in mid-November. He and Liz were now able to collect several of the visas they needed. As a 'journalist', Patrick even got approval to travel through southern Sudan, which was under military control because of fighting that was officially dismissed as 'rural banditry'. It was considered safe enough to travel by river to the southern capital of Juba, but they would have to pick up a military permit when they got to Khartoum.

Guilty Land was launched on 11 January 1962 and that evening Patrick was interviewed about the book on *Tonight*, the BBC's early evening current affairs programme.

The book was widely reviewed in most of the national newspapers and journals, mostly very favourably, but because publishers did not send out review copies in advance of publication, Patrick was not to see any of his reviews until he got to Cairo. Meanwhile, he and Liz had a final two weeks to prepare for their departure and say farewell to their numerous friends.

Their Nigerian dentist friend, Sonny Prince Akpabio, laid on 'a rollicking, all-night, all-African party'. Sonny was to rise to considerable heights in the Commonwealth and the World Health Organization, promoting oral hygiene in developing countries. His personal philosophy was simple:

Be honest with yourself and determine if you would like to serve your fellow human beings irrespective of nationality, social status or financial rewards. We are a multi-cultural, multi-national society. Let other factors determine your sense of belonging rather than your nationality.[9]

It was advice he may well have offered to Patrick at that moment in his life.

On the last Saturday in January Patrick and Liz caught the evening boat train to Paris. Liz, who had been used to travelling light, having hitchhiked across much of the UK and parts of the continent since her early teenage years, carried just a rucksack. Patrick, on the other hand, was still in colonial mode and packed all his possessions, including a white tropical suit and a bundle of paperback copies of *Guilty Land*, in a large tin trunk.

They spent a day exploring Paris by Metro and left by train for Athens on the Sunday evening. The long journey across Europe, with several changes of train, soon brought home to Patrick the impracticality of his trunk. Seated in packed compartments with the upended trunk jammed in a corridor, they got little sleep until the penultimate leg, across southern Yugoslavia, when they had a compartment to themselves and were able to stretch out across the seats and get some sleep. They woke in the morning to see the countryside 'draped in deep snow'. It was a novel sight for Patrick, who sat in the warmth of the train admiring the winter landscape.[10]

In Athens they found lodgings in a cheap youth hostel, which had been converted from a grand marble villa. Patrick was growing his beard again, as shaving was impractical on such a journey. The big red bushy beard that gradually greyed with age was to remain with him for the rest of his life – a symbol of his refusal to conform.

They were both enchanted by Athens, which came alive at 5 pm, after siesta. Liz recorded in her travel diary:

> .... tavernas below the pavements like dark warm caverns, no menu, but enormous bubbling copper saucepans all around you from which you choose; warm-smelling bakeries where the ovens are there in the shop and your bread steams hotly in the paper bag. Streets lined with orange trees laden with fruit; chestnut sellers; ... shoe-shine boys thriving in this city of unsurfaced streets ... Turkish coffee sip by sip with water; and resin wine.[11]

In the poorer quarter near the Acropolis they found an extraordinary market 'where smiths with roaring furnaces in dark tent-like caverns were turning scrap metal into farm implements'. Here, to their intense relief, they were able to exchange the tin trunk for a lightweight kitbag: 'We felt exhilarated and liberated at last, as we packed our bags, bought provisions, took leave of our Youth Hostel companions and made for Piraeus to take a boat to Alexandria.'[12]

The cold journey across the Mediterranean took three days and nights and they were thankful when they finally reached their youth hostel in a quiet suburb of Cairo. They found Cairo an exciting, bustling and friendly city: 'If you asked a man directions, he would lead you there.' They visited friends of Martin Ennals, brother of British MP David Ennals, who Patrick had met in London, and spent a relaxed evening with them, 'meeting both Coptic Christians and Muslim Arabs, and hearing about life in [President Gamal Abdel] Nasser's Egypt'.[13]

They ate falafel in cafés and drank strong Turkish coffee from tiny cups. When they went to the Sudanese Embassy to pick up their visas, officials doubted Patrick's credentials as a journalist, but the gift of a copy of *Guilty Land* for the ambassador got them their visas on the spot.[14]

After picking up their mail from the British Embassy, they caught the midnight train, third class, to Luxor. It was packed with people returning to their families for Ramadan and there was hardly room to put their feet on the floor, but the crowds gradually thinned out at the numerous stops along the way. They reached Luxor in the afternoon and quickly took a horse and trap to visit the Great Temple of Karnak before finding their way to the youth hostel for tea and oranges and an early night.

The train for Aswan left at 4 am. Third class was not packed this time, but the guard insisted they move up to second class for no extra charge. He took them to the first-class restaurant, where his friend the cook made them tea and cakes and regaled them with stories of his life as a cook in the Royal Navy.

The Aswan High Dam was still under construction, and Patrick and Liz were able to sail up the valley that would in future be covered by the waters of Lake Nasser. Third-class travel on a Nile dhow 'involved living, eating and sleeping on the deck, which turned out to be very pleasant indeed'.[15]

On the second day of their journey upstream they stopped at the Temple of Abu Simbel, which was still on its original riverside site. Plans were already under way to dismantle, move and reconstruct the temple on its present site above the high-water mark of the future lake.

On the journey south to Omdurman they spent many pleasant hours talking with the softly spoken, humorous and compassionate young Sudanese poet Salah Ibrahim, who was on his way home from an Arabic writers' conference in Cairo. Patrick gave him a copy of *Guilty Land*, which he promised to translate into Arabic. They reached the bright lights of Khartoum on 11 March and Salah Ibrahim took them to his family home in Omdurman, the old Sudanese city across the river from the modern capital. Liz captured the atmosphere in her diary:

> We are ushered into a cool shaded room with low chairs, and on the ceiling an enormous breezy fan, and we meet the family. Salah's father, a teacher, kindly, gentle and polite – and his mother, who speaks no English but smiles and welcomes us warmly and talks happily in Arabic to Salah's translation. Salah's gentle smiling sister, a journalist and about to leave for a trip to Wau, talks to us about her work. A serene atmosphere of cultured piety. From this home comes Salah the poet.[16]

After a family meal they slept in the courtyard of Salah's apartment 'under the stars in a silent Omdurman'. They took their leave of the family after two days, Salah having promised to contact his friend the military governor in Juba and ask him to look after them.

It was a nine-day journey up the Nile to Juba, their riverboat a string of barges chained together. Third-class passengers travelled on the front two barges, where chickens and goats were slaughtered and cooked over open braziers. As mosquitoes were a serious problem, Patrick and Liz were advised to upgrade to second class in one of the centre barges, where they had a cabin with nets and a fan. They were grateful for this luxury when, on the third day, the train of barges entered the Sudd, the almost impene-trable swamp where the Nile is joined by numerous tributaries.

During the five days it took to pass through the monotonous reed banks of the Sudd Patrick caught up on his reading. Among the post from Cairo was a collection of newspaper clippings sent by Joe Rogaly. Patrick now had time to read and re-read the numerous reviews of *Guilty Land* in the relative comfort of the riverboat.

Most of the reviewers felt that the first part of the book, about his per-sonal life and experience, was the best. The outspoken journalist and sati-rist Malcolm Muggeridge, writing in the *Daily Mail*, was cynical about the idea of the British public indulging in a serious boycott of South African goods:

> … nothing delights human beings more than to have a moral issue about which they can take up a wholly righteous attitude at no cost or danger to themselves. By eschewing South African sherry in favour of the far superior Spanish brand (though why Franco should be considered a less defiled source of this wine than Verwoerd is far from clear), people glow with a sense of martyrdom nobly and fearlessly undertaken.

But he was impressed by the fact that Patrick

> gave up his diplomatic job in the South African External Affairs Department, sacrificed a promising career and in the end found him-self an exile from the land he still loves. This makes his testimony, to

me at any rate, more impressive and instructive than that of a Canon
Collins or even Father Huddleston.[17]

The *Daily Telegraph* could not stomach Patrick's 'ultra-liberal views', which
pleased him enormously. He would have hated a positive review from the
right-wing paper that had failed to respond to any of the three letters he
had sent them as director of the Boycott Movement.[18]

He was particularly pleased to read that Canon Collins had written in
the *Christian Action Newsletter*: 'Patrick van Rensburg has written a book
which, in my opinion, no one who is concerned about the racial problem
can afford to neglect. The fact that it is partly autobiographical and is
dominated throughout by a personal quality gives it added importance.'[19]

* * *

Patrick and Liz were greeted at the Juba dockside by Salah's friend, the
military governor, who put them up in the comfortable 'government camp'.
After a couple of days in Juba spent wondering how they would proceed, a
taxi arrived from Kampala carrying some tourists who wanted to catch the
north-bound riverboat to Khartoum.

The taxi driver, who would otherwise be returning to Uganda with
an empty vehicle, agreed to take them to Tororo near the Uganda–Kenya
border for just £5. From Tororo they got a lift from some Kenyan Asians
who hosted them in Kisumu for three days before one of them gave them
a lift into Nairobi. During their stay in Kisumu, Patrick visited a mission school with a farm whose produce made the community virtually
self-sufficient.

The Nairobi Youth Hostel, in the suburb of Kabete, was a spartan
collection of round tin huts. Theirs had a charcoal stove on which they
brewed tea, and with food from the local market they grew quite fond of
their hut in the following days – but not so fond that they turned down the
offer of more luxurious accommodation. On a visit to the post office they
met the *Manchester Guardian*'s Africa correspondent, Clyde Sanger, and his
wife, Penny, an investigative journalist.

Penny offered to put them up in a comfortable summer house in the
couple's garden. It was the first week of April, they had been 'on the road'

for four weeks since leaving Cairo and they were grateful to stay with the Sangers for several days, during which Clyde showed them around Nairobi.

Kenya, in 1962, was going through the final negotiation process with the British government before independence the following year. In the light of the troubled 'Mau Mau'[20] past – the 'state of emergency' had only ended in November 1959 – Patrick was struck by the lack of animosity towards the former white colonists, hundreds of whom were heading south to the remaining bastions of white privilege, Rhodesia and South Africa.

But he was also struck by the scale of Nairobi's poverty-stricken shanty towns, which stood in stark contrast to the city's expensive suburbs, previously the preserve of the white colonial élite, into which a new black élite was now quickly moving. Patrick could picture a liberated South Africa going the same divisive way and hoped it would not be so.

They left Nairobi on 6 April and after two days of difficult hitchhiking through Kenya and across newly independent Tanganyika they arrived in the Tanganyikan capital, Dar es Salaam.[21] The Salvation Army Hostel in which Patrick and Liz stayed was simple but charming – a collection of small thatched huts surrounding a restaurant, where, on their first evening, they met Joan Wicken, the British Fabian socialist who was Julius Nyerere's personal assistant. She had held this privileged position from 1960 and would continue to do so through all his years as president, and afterwards, until his death, in 1999. She was said to have known Nyerere's political thinking better than anyone – indeed, some argued that she *shaped* his thinking.

According to the political economist Lionel Cliffe, Joan Wicken was 'the organiser of Nyerere's schedule, drafter of his speeches and policy statements, she tuned into his wavelength, and gave detailed expression to his ideas'.[22] Despite her exalted position she chose to stay in a simple bedsit (one-roomed home) in the Salvation Army compound.

She invited Patrick and Liz for a meal in a Chinese restaurant and talked of development in an emerging country. They did not meet Nyerere on this visit to Dar es Salaam, but, according to Liz, 'I think we always thought that our fortuitous meeting and discussions with Joan Wicken at that particular moment almost amounted to the next best thing!'[23]

Joan put them in touch with Michael Scott, who was in Dar es Salaam campaigning to prevent French nuclear testing in the Algerian

Sahara. Scott provided Patrick with many useful contacts and, while Liz helped Scott address envelopes for his campaign, Patrick met numerous people with whom he discussed subjects as diverse as world peace, South African sanctions, and educational and rural development policies and projects.

They thoroughly enjoyed their two-week stay in the city, and when Patrick was not meeting people they trudged the streets of the old town and swam in the Indian Ocean. They were tempted to stay longer, but they were a long way from Patrick's homeland and it was time to move on.[24]

***

They headed south on the next stage of their journey, elated by the possibilities of the *uhuru* (Kiswahili for 'freedom') they had glimpsed in Nyerere's Tanganyika. Their journey thus far had been transformative. When Patrick had left London in January he had had little clear idea of what kind of school he wanted to set up in Bechuanaland.

At the All-African Conference in Tunis in January 1960 he had fantasised about red-brick, ivy-covered walls such as he had seen in the élite private schools of England. Then he had imagined he would set up his own élite school in one of the protectorates, but it would be multiracial, as an example – and a challenge – to South Africa.

Something along those lines would be set up at Waterford in Swaziland in 1963 by Michael Stern, the former headmaster who had offered Patrick a job at St Martin's in Johannesburg in 1959. In due course, among Waterford's alumni would be 'children of anti-apartheid leaders like Nelson Mandela, Walter Sisulu and Desmond Tutu' and Seretse Khama's eldest son, Ian, who went on to become president of Botswana.[25]

If Patrick had not been entirely weaned from élitism as he packed his tropical white suit in his colonial-style tin trunk in London in January 1962, by the time he and Liz reached East Africa the trunk was long gone and the white suit given away as totally unsuitable for the vision that was clarifying in his mind during the long months of travel through newly emerging independent Africa.

Travelling third class on buses, boats and trains and hitchhiking at the roadside, they had mixed with rich and poor and people of different cultures in rural communities as well as cities. The experience had utterly changed Patrick's perspective and priorities. He had seen the urban slums of Nairobi and the élitist ambitions of Kenya's emerging African middle class and he knew that was not the kind of 'development' worth fighting for.

In Tanganyika, both Patrick and Liz had been enormously impressed by the humility of Joan Wicken, living and eating at the hostel despite her exalted position as PA to the president. President Nyerere himself had no pretensions to grandeur: not for him the presidential cavalcade – he drove himself around Dar es Salaam in his Volkswagen 'Beetle'.

Joan Wicken had opened Patrick's eyes to the real prospect of non-élitist development, especially rural development, combined with self-reliance. Ever since leaving South Africa in March 1960, Patrick had been absorbing ideas about what he might do that would be useful for the cause of Southern African liberation. As Liz recalls:

> He was always gathering information, reading local newspapers and talking to all kinds of people in a very open-minded way – always hoping to learn something new. He had this way of storing information, and turning it over and over in his mind – and then using it later in creative and unusual ways to transform seemingly insoluble situations.
>
> Looking back, I think that by the time we came to leave Tanganyika, he probably had already decided to build the school if we were given permission to do so and he had a rough idea of what it might look like (it certainly wouldn't be ivy-clad red brick), but it was mostly all in his head at the time – he didn't describe it in any great detail.[26]

Patrick still felt a strong pull towards South Africa, but he had not yet contacted his Liberal Party friends there and Liz and he were agreed – they would start the school in Bechuanaland before making any decisions about South Africa. The past two months had consolidated their relationship and they looked forward to getting married as soon as they were settled.

They left the *uhuru* of Tanganyika for the settler-dominated Central African Federation on 24 April.[27] They were viewed with suspicion at the

Northern Rhodesia border post – a young white couple, destination a remote village in Bechuanaland – but they were eventually allowed through.[28] Hitchhiking for four days got them down the long and dusty 'Great North Road' to Lusaka and on to Southern Rhodesia and Salisbury. Here they were able to stay for three days with the soon-to-be parents-in-law of Polly Loxton.

The previous year Patrick Duncan had recommended that when they got to Southern Rhodesia they should get in touch with Guy and Molly Clutton-Brock, who, in the 1950s, had helped set up and run a multiracial farming co-operative on a mission-owned farm known as St Faith's, not far from Salisbury. During the 'state of emergency' of 1959 St Faith's, considered to be a hotbed of subversion and contrary to the spirit of colonial land policy, had been closed, and Guy had been imprisoned for a month.

On his release he and Molly had moved to a small rondavel on the farm of their like-minded South African friends Mike and Eileen Haddon, who had renounced their South African affiliation for Southern Rhodesian soon after the National Party had come to power in 1948. Their small agricultural property, also not far from Salisbury, was called 'Cold Comfort Farm' and there the Clutton-Brocks helped set up another multiracial farming co-operative, along similar lines to that at St Faith's.[29]

The fame of St Faith's and Cold Comfort Farm spread and Tshekedi Khama, who had visited St Faith's in 1958, invited the Clutton-Brocks to Bechuanaland to help set up a similar co-operative farming venture there. They promised to do so but were not able to fulfil their promise until 1961, by which time Tshekedi had been dead for two years.

They were allocated some land for a 'communal development farm' at Radisele, an area of bush at the foot of some rocky hills near the 'line of rail' south-east of Serowe. It had a water point in a nearby ravine which was close to Pilikwe, the village of the late Tshekedi Khama. 'A committee was formed which ambitiously became the Bamangwato Development Association (BDA) with the motto *Ipelegeng*, meaning "Let us go forward together".'[30]

And together they went. Guy demonstrated the principles of dry-land farming through rotational cultivation of sorghum, beans and groundnuts, combined with fallow pasture and controlled grazing. They got financial support from contacts in Britain and the assistance of a handful of expatriate aid volunteers, including Arthur and Deirdre Stanley and, later, Vernon and Tineke Gibberd.

The Radisele community continued to grow through the early 1960s and its ideas spread, showing the possibilities of rural communal development – modern agricultural principles and a small tractor, harnessed to traditional technology. Guy was driven by the principle that the local people should be able to grow their own food, even in the dry and environmentally hostile conditions of Bechuanaland.[31]

Once the community was up and running the Clutton-Brocks divided their time between Radisele and Cold Comfort Farm.[32] They were in Bechuanaland when Patrick and Liz arrived in Salisbury in April 1962. After a couple of days' rest in the settler capital the travellers were eager to leave its surreal atmosphere, but before continuing their journey south they were invited to visit a white-owned cattle ranch in the eastern district.

The ranch was fenced off into large paddocks for rotational grazing, involving periods of fallow and cultivation of lucerne (alfalfa) for forage during the long dry season. The cattle, a mix of indigenous and imported breeds, were of high quality. Patrick was impressed and mentally stored what he had learned for future reference.

They hitchhiked their way south, through Bulawayo, as far as the border town of Plumtree, where they boarded the next south-bound train, thankful to be leaving the settler tensions of Rhodesia. They arrived at the 'frontier-like town' of Francistown late that afternoon, and as they took tea on the veranda of the Tati Hotel near the railway station they were accosted by a plain-clothes police officer who knew exactly who they were.

It reminded Patrick of his experience in Swaziland, where the protectorate police were in regular touch with their counterparts in South Africa. The man did not believe Patrick's story about building a school, and the veiled threat in the manner of his interrogation made it clear that the pair would be under close observation. It eventually emerged that the police had received a telegram from Patrick Duncan, who had requested that Patrick and Liz be allowed to enter Bechuanaland and proceed to the Bamangwato Development Association at Radisele.

Duncan had visited Serowe and stayed with Ronald and Theresa Watts in May 1961.[33] He had at that time been trying to buy land that could be used as a base for military training for the PAC, with whom he had become closely affiliated. The protectorate's intelligence report recorded his visit under the heading 'SUBVERSIVE ACTIVITIES'.[34]

Patrick van Rensburg's connection to Duncan meant that from the moment he entered Bechuanaland in 1962 he was regarded with suspicion by the colonial authorities. His association with Clutton-Brock did not improve matters as far as the administration was concerned. An intelligence report of August 1960 had referred to Guy as 'an alleged "missionary-farmer"', who had contact with Michael Scott and 'known communists'.[35]

Patrick and Liz spent the night at the Tati Hotel and early next morning got a lift down the main, untarred north–south road as far as Shashe River, about 30 kilometres south of Francistown. After several hours with no further lift they boarded the slow mixed-goods train and arrived at about midday in Palapye, where the road to Serowe, 50 kilometres to the west, joins 'the line of rail'.

A bus was about to leave in that direction, and they decided they should take it into Serowe to try to make contact with Seretse Khama. If they could win his support for their school project it would be a very good start. After a journey of nearly two hours down an unpaved, rutted and potholed road they arrived in Serowe, to find that Seretse was away from home. His wife, Ruth, seemed sceptical about whether the bedraggled pair before her were up to the task they had set themselves.

Somewhat dispirited, they hitched back to Palapye, intending to spend the night at the Palapye Hotel, but one look at the clientele of 'threatening racist "Rhodies [Rhodesians]", whose sick-humoured malice simmered so close to the surface',[36] was enough to make them change their minds. They set off on the road to Radisele in the gathering dusk. They were resigned to spending the night in the shelter of a tree, when, out of the darkness, came a small bus with lights blazing. The driver said he would take them directly to Radisele.

Some 50 kilometres later he proudly announced, 'The Bamangwato Development Association', and there in the darkness to the right of the road was Radisele, a collection of dimly lit rondavels and a caravan. It was Wednesday 2 May. Three months and five days after leaving London Patrick and Liz had arrived at their destination.[37]

9 | The Founding of Swaneng Hill School, 1962–1963

Patrick Duncan had written ahead to the Clutton-Brocks at Radisele and Patrick and Liz were expected. They were welcomed that night by Arthur and Deirdre Stanley, who showed them to the guest rondavel and offered them a meal. Guy and Molly were away for a few days and in the interim they got to know the Stanleys and the work of the Bamangwato Development Association.

The Stanleys were in charge of the overall management of the settlement and seemed fairly fluent in Setswana. Liz made a start on trying to teach herself the language, while Patrick, not expecting to stay in Bechuanaland for more than a year or two, declined to make the effort. It was something he was to regret later. In due course he developed some understanding of the language, but never spoke it fluently.

Guy returned at harvest time and went out each day to work with the men and women of the community. Patrick joined them in the 'tedious and tiring work of harvesting and threshing a sadly meagre crop'.[1] In the evening they would gather round an open fire and the fifty-six-year-old Guy would talk of his experiences and how he had come to respect the African decision-making process, where the people 'sit in the shade under a tree and talk until they agree'.

He was something of a father figure to this pair of young idealists keen to become involved in African development, and he offered Patrick and Liz two pieces of invaluable advice. He said it would be a pity if they founded 'just a school', insisting that it would be 'so much more useful to Bechuanaland if it could be a farm-school – or at least productive in some way'. This was very much in line with the ideas and images that had been freewheeling in Patrick's mind since he and Liz had left Cairo in February.

Guy went on to recommend that they start by teaching in a local primary school in Serowe for some months. This would give them the chance to understand the pupils as well as the teachers and the system of primary education in the country. Patrick was grateful for this wise advice, 'and took it all on board'.[2]

Following his experience with the colonial police on his arrival in Francistown, Patrick steered clear of the colonial authorities and made a point of avoiding David 'Robbie' Robinson, the local district commissioner (DC). Robinson, of course, knew of this white South African exile, who, together with his British partner, was staying at Radisele, and he sought him out.

Arthur and Deirdre Stanley 'were amused to see Pat dive under a table when Robbie drew up at Radisele in his Chevy truck'. And when Patrick crawled out from under the table he was 'surprised to be introduced to a tall liberal-minded Oxford graduate with a crew cut, looking more American astronaut than British official'.[3]

Robinson would have been pleased to learn that Patrick and Liz were hoping to set up a school. He confirmed that there was a need for a day secondary school in Serowe that emphasised the practical and assured Patrick that such a school, with a farm attached, would have his full support.[4]

Patrick and Liz made several trips to Serowe in the coming weeks to discuss their plans with the local Bamangwato authorities. On one of their first visits they got a lift from Peto Sekgoma, a second cousin of Seretse Khama, and his son, Mokhutshwane Sekgoma. Peto Sekgoma was supportive of Patrick's desire to start a secondary school and introduced him to a number of the key individuals who made up the African authorities in Serowe.[5]

The situation was complicated. Although DC Robinson was officially in overall charge of the district, he and his predecessors had learned through bitter experience that they could only rule with the full cooperation of the local African authorities. And there were two African authorities in Serowe. For decades the British had been trying to 'modernise' the system of chiefly control, which traced its origins back to pre-colonial times.

The traditional system centred on the *kgotla*, the chief's court. This was an open space in the centre of town in the shade of a large thorn tree and surrounded by a palisade of wooden posts. It was here, close to the chief's house and the office of what the colonial administration called the 'Tribal Authority', that the men of the community – mostly elders and headmen of the wards – met to discuss and settle important issues.

It was to the *kgotla*, for example, that Seretse Khama had had to appeal for acceptance of his marriage to Ruth Williams. The *kgotla* was an important symbol of Setswana culture and of the chief's ancestral authority, independent of the colonial administration, and for that reason the traditionalist elders of the community were jealous of any perceived attempts to weaken its significance.

In 1957 the protectorate administration set up a modern 'Tribal Council', largely at the initiative of Seretse Khama, who had returned from exile the previous year. From 1959 Seretse had served as secretary of the new tribal council.

The designated acting *kgosi* (chief) of the Bamangwato was Rasebolai Kgamane, appointed by the British in 1953 after the Bamangwato had refused to elect anybody other than Seretse. Rasebolai, an impassive administrator and cautious traditionalist, was slow to embrace change. As acting *kgosi* he was both the tribal authority and chairman of the new tribal council.[6]

Seretse Khama and DC Robinson had a good working relationship – they had been students together at Balliol College, Oxford, in the late 1940s – and when Patrick and Liz eventually met Seretse he gave their school scheme his personal blessing. Gaining the approval of both the tribal council and the tribal authority, however, was another matter. Both institutions comprised most of the important Serowe elders, many of whom were deeply conservative and understandably suspicious of change, especially when it was proposed by an outsider.

Patrick was fortunate that when asked for two testimonials from reputable people he was able to call upon Michael Scott and Canon Collins, both of whom were well known by reputation in Serowe, having been supporters of the late Tshekedi Khama and of Seretse.

The exchange of letters took a month and the council then referred Patrick to the protectorate's director of education, Jack Hunter, whose office was across the South African border in Mafikeng's 'Imperial Reserve'. South Africa was forbidden ground for Patrick, but protectorate officials regularly visited the small south-eastern town of Lobatse, where the High Court was located and meetings of the newly established legislative council were held.

He arranged an appointment with Jack Hunter in Lobatse to discuss the school project and, following Guy's advice, to seek permission for him and Liz to teach in the meantime in one of Serowe's primary schools. This would not only give them a salary, to conserve their 'dwindling reserves',[7] but would also demonstrate the seriousness of their commitment to education in Serowe.

In its nearly seventy years of existence the British administration had done nothing to develop secondary education in the protectorate, assuming that the territory would in due course become the responsibility of South Africa. Those from better-off families seeking secondary education went to the mission-founded Tiger Kloof Institute in the north of the Cape province of South Africa, or to a mission school in Rhodesia.

The British had left secondary schooling in the protectorate to foreign missionaries and to local initiatives by Batswana. Hunter's main concern was how Patrick and Liz would fund their school; perhaps he was fearful that the costs would ultimately have to be covered by the protectorate's limited budget.

Patrick explained that they planned to start with a small intake of just one class. He and Liz, drawing only small salaries, would do all the teaching apart from Setswana, for which a local person would be employed. He believed they could raise enough money initially to build a single classroom and a small rondavel for their accommodation and be ready to start at the beginning of the school year in February 1963.

Hunter seemed satisfied and accepted Patrick's assurance that they could raise more money once the school got started. He accepted them onto the protectorate's primary teachers' roll but, since their degree certificates indicated that neither of them had studied more than two of the subjects they were to teach, they would not be paid as graduate teachers. Patrick would receive R24 a month, the same amount he had received in his very first job at the age of seventeen.[8] Since there was no equal pay for women in this colonial backwater, Liz would receive just R18.[9]

Through the month of June Patrick and Liz made numerous visits to Serowe to organise their future life there. Pressed by Guy, a devout Anglican, they posted the banns for their marriage and set the date for 29 June; the ceremony was to be performed by David Robinson.

They visited Simon Ratshosa Primary School, where they were to teach. The headmaster, Mr K. K. Baruti, who was to become a key supporter of Patrick and his ideas in the years ahead, allocated them the two most senior classes, Standards 5 and 6,[10] and it was agreed they would start in July and teach until the end of the school year at the beginning of December. Stephen Sello, who had looked after the refugees' accommodation in 1960, introduced them to Mr J. T. (Job) Mataboge, a fellow South African, who had built a house for himself in what was then just beyond the eastern edge of the main Serowe settlement.

He ran a small store and his wife ran a local bakery. They had a small, rectangular, mud-plastered, tin-roofed structure that they were not using, and they let Patrick and Liz have it as a bedsit for a nominal rent. All that remained was to open an account at Watson's General Dealers and order two bicycles, for it was 6 kilometres from Mataboge's home to the primary school.

On the day of their wedding, 29 June, Liz was suffering from tick-bite fever, but nothing would stop her going through with the service. Guy drove them from Radisele to Serowe together with Arthur and Deirdre Stanley and two of their Batswana friends from the BDA community. The ceremony only took five minutes, then it was back to Radisele for a party. Molly had been to Bulawayo and bought a large wedding cake, while the BDA community had slaughtered a goat and brewed some sorghum beer (*bojalwa*). As Patrick remembered it:

We danced in the dusk and the dust to a radio playing popular music of the day and ate goat stew and drank Guy's brandy and draughts of thick Tswana beer. Guy remarked on the quality of social relationships and of mutual caring that still existed here, which people of the northern world had largely lost, and we both agreed with that.[11]

Figure 9.1: Patrick and Liz (already aboard the truck) hitch a lift from Palapye to Serowe, 30 June 1962. (Van Rensburg family collection; photographer: the late Arthur Stanley)

The next day Patrick and Liz got a lift to Serowe in the back of a truck that dropped them off at *Rra* ('Mr') Mataboge's yard. They picked up their Hercules bicycles from Watson's store and ordered kitchen equipment – Aladdin lamp, Primus stove, paraffin, pots and pans, cutlery, enamel mugs and plates – and some food to get them started. By midday these had been delivered to their new home and they had made their room habitable.

Liz, 'whose tick-bite fever [was taking] its aching hold again', was able to rest on the mattress on the floor, lent to them by the ever-helpful *Rra* Mataboge, while *Mma* ('Mrs') Mataboge helped tend to Liz's fever.[12]

It was Saturday 30 June 1962 and they were embarking on a major new chapter in their lives.

* * *

Patrick and Liz van Rensburg (as she was now) soon settled into a daily routine, setting off for Simon Ratshosa Primary soon after dawn and returning in the early afternoon. They cycled to and fro along the dusty paths that criss-crossed Serowe and soon learned the geography of the sprawling town. They became adept at repairing punctures as their tyres fell victim to the ubiquitous thorns that littered the countryside beyond the perimeters of the neatly swept homesteads.

It was winter when they started work at the school and, with dawn temperatures sometimes not far off freezing, they cycled to work wearing thick sweaters, thankfully removing them in the warm sun of the return journey.

Patrick had no prior experience or formal training in teaching, but he knew that the keys to successful learning were an enquiring mind and enthusiasm for the subject. He had no time for what the Brazilian educator Paulo Freire was to describe as 'the banking style' of teaching, in which students are regarded as empty vessels to be filled with knowledge.[13]

He had worked out for himself that this method, widely practised in Botswana's primary schools, ended with little knowledge actually understood and therefore little usefully remembered. He based his teaching on questions and answers, stimulating discussion and never belittling a student's efforts to formulate an opinion.

In this way he built up trust and enthusiasm among his students and it was no surprise that those same primary students developed intellectual self-confidence and a sense of responsibility when they moved up into the secondary school that he was to establish. It was only some years later that Patrick was to receive theoretical support for his methods when he actually read Freire's works.[14]

Meanwhile, he and Liz continued to wait for a decision to be made about their secondary-school project. They had satisfied the education department and the tribal council seemed in favour. All that remained was for the tribal authority, and that basically meant *Kgosi* Rasebolai, to decide on the allocation of a piece of land.

Patrick had asked Stephen Sello to recommend some people to form a provisional governing committee for the school and he had gathered a selection with both traditional and modernising tendencies. They began having regular meetings, conducted in English, Patrick having been advised that if Setswana was used, the discussions would be interminable.

It was not in Patrick's nature to be conspicuously dominant at meetings and many who worked with him in the coming years were struck by his quiet manner. But there was a rare determination beneath the calm exterior. Arthur Stanley was to describe him as 'quiet, driven and fanatical',[15] and Patrick's soft-spoken certainty and passion for his subject were often sufficient for a consensus to develop around his ideas; but there was still not a word about the allocation of land for the school.

The committee managed to establish that a suitable piece of land on the eastern edge of the town had no claims on it and might be large enough for a small school farm. But it was just 'not done' to push the chief into a decision.

Figure 9.2: *Left to right, front*: Seretse Khama (uncrowned chief), Sekgoma Khama (future acting chief) and Rasebolai Kgamane (acting chief), Serowe, late 1950s. (By kind permission of the Khama Memorial Museum, Serowe)

From *Kgosi* Rasebolai's point of view, this young white couple might have been enthused with the concept of 'development', but they had no money; nor did they represent an organised aid donor. They simply wanted to start a school. As *kgosi* he knew that Serowe needed a local secondary school, but were these the people to provide it? Was it wise to trust a white South African, especially an Afrikaner?

The couple had the backing of Seretse Khama and the approval of the colonial administration, but, as the *kgosi*, Rasebolai would be held responsible if the whole project fizzled out. Better to procrastinate; put them off and see what happened.

The months slipped by and in the dry oppressive heat of late September Patrick's patience ran out. There was much to be organised if the school was to have any hope of opening in February. Overriding the hesitancy of the committee, he decided to speak up at the next meeting of the *kgotla*. The meeting assembled on Saturday 13 October and Patrick laid down an ultimatum: 'We are not beggars. We are not asking for land for *ourselves*. If you cannot decide today, we will have to make plans to quit Bechuanaland at the end of the school year.'[16]

Rasebolai sensed that he meant every word. After the meeting he went into an inner room and came out with Lenyeletse Seretse, a cousin of Seretse Khama, whom Patrick had previously met. Lenyeletse drove Patrick to the eastern edge of town and together they spent the best part of an hour 'walking over the hard, brown, grassless ground', with 'Lennie' notching the trees with an axe to mark the boundaries.[17] And that was it. Their land grant was allocated.

That evening Patrick and Liz stood on the western boundary of their land allocation, which happened to be just next to Job Mataboge's plot. They gazed across the site of their future school and home and were struck by the primeval silence as they watched a golden full moon rise from behind the larger of two hills that dominated the skyline on the eastern horizon.[18]

They were deeply moved by the scene and very aware of the heavy responsibility they were about to undertake. Their immediate instinct was to name the school after the hill over which the moon had risen and learned the next day that the pair of hills was considered male and female: *Rra* (which can also mean 'father') Swaneng for the larger and *Mma* (which can also mean 'mother') Swaneng for the smaller one, which had two humps. That decided them on the name: 'Swaneng Hill School', subject to the approval of the provisional committee.

* * *

The Van Rensburgs had arrived in Bechuanaland at the very start of the protectorate's development into a modern state. Hitherto, colonial over-rule had been exercised with a light touch – economically as well as polit-ically. There had been some small attempt to assist the cattle owners with boreholes and an ineffective attempt at co-operative cattle marketing; but at best this only assisted the concentration of cattle in fewer hands.

By the early 1960s a third of the families in the country had no cattle at all and a further 20 per cent had only a handful. The British had no clear policy for any wider rural development. The main sources of wage employment were perceived to be over the border, down the mines, in the industrial cities and on the farms of South Africa. The WNLA base in Francistown was indicative of impoverished Bechuanaland's dependence on its position as a 'labour reserve' for its powerful neighbour.

Just as 1960 marked a political watershed in South Africa, it was also a watershed year for Bechuanaland. It had become increasingly clear through the 1950s that incorporation of the protectorate into apartheid South Africa was no longer an option; but it was not until 1960 that the British Colonial Office woke up to the need to prepare the territory for internal self-government. As though symbolic of this change, the first sit-ting of a partially elected legislative council in Bechuanaland took place in June 1961, one month after South Africa became a republic and left the Commonwealth.

By this time the political initiative in Bechuanaland was already pass-ing into the hands of the country's African population, with the founding of two main political parties between 1959 and 1961. The leadership of the radical Bechuanaland People's Party (BPP), which had served its political apprenticeship with the ANC in South Africa, demanded immediate inde-pendence. In contrast, the Bechuanaland Democratic Party (BDP), founded as a more cautious and conciliatory alternative to the BPP, indicated its preparedness to work with the British administration to fashion a smooth transition of power.

The BDP was led by Seretse Khama and some of his key allies and relatives in Serowe. As something of a balance against the perception of Bamangwato domination, Quett Masire, a progressive farmer and cattle owner from the southern (Bangwaketse) town of Kanye, was appointed party organiser.[19] Despite Masire's energy in organising rallies around the country, his presence did little to dilute the perception that the BDP was the party of the Bamangwato royals. In the course of 1962 the radical BPP fell apart in personal faction fighting and the BDP became the dominant political force in the country, despite not yet having any clear programme for development.

In terms of social, economic and cultural development, that left the field wide open for Patrick van Rensburg – a man with imagination, commitment and drive, accompanied by a conviction that there was an egalitarian solution to Africa's development problems: he would find it and prove that it worked.

He was no longer simply starting a school while staying in Bechuanaland en route to South Africa. He had seen Radisele's Bamangwato Development Association at work and approved its principles and methods, but they were on a small, local scale and confined to agriculture. Patrick's dream, which he had not yet clearly formulated, was to find a path to broader development that would benefit the wider Bamangwato territory (*Gamangwato*)[20] and could become a model for the development of the whole country. He would start with the founding of this school that would teach his developmental principles – when he had worked out more clearly what these were – by combining the practical with the academic.

* * *

As they had requested, the land grant was large enough for a small school farm, a total of about 40 hectares (100 acres).[21] It was bounded on the south by the Palapye road, close to Patrick and Liz's home at Job Mataboge's, and rose slightly to the north, where the boundary was a line of hills. The ground sloped away towards the east and was cut by two sharp gullies that had been 'gouged out by surging run-off water from past rains'.[22] There was also an old disused dam that had been breached by flood waters long before. There were substantial numbers of thorn trees on the hills and a few on the lower ground, which was mostly dotted with thorn scrub. Overgrazing by free-roaming cattle had ensured that there was precious little grass.

On the Monday morning Patrick told his class of his plan to build a secondary school and invited them to join him in the afternoons and at weekends, working to prepare the site. Volunteering labour for the benefit of the community was nothing new in Setswana culture,[23] and Patrick was able to draw unwittingly upon these traditions, combining custom with the desire on the part of the volunteers to gain a much-coveted place in a local secondary school.

At this stage Patrick could make no promises of admission, but, in case some of the volunteers did not get a place in the new school, he offered them 5 cents each for an afternoon's work, paid for out of his and Liz's wages.

The initial tasks were twofold: to clear a roadway through the thorn scrub from the site to the Palapye road and to halt soil erosion caused by the annual heavy storms, which were expected within the next month or so. Trees were uprooted and thorn scrub and branches were thrown into the gullies, along with some of the larger stones, while the smaller stones were laid in rows along the contour lines across the low-lying ground. The workers' efforts were rewarded when the first heavy rainstorm broke the blistering heat in late November. The run-off was dramatically slowed and deep muddy silt collected along the contour lines and in the gullies.[24]

It was one thing to prepare the land, but constructing classrooms and accommodation required serious funding. Thus, every evening through October and November, after completing their preparation for the next day's lessons, Patrick and Liz worked late into the night writing letters in long-hand 'to all the people [they had] ever met, asking for funds for the school'.[25]

Once it could be seen that the project had started, help came from many quarters. The store owner, Benjamin Steinberg, dug a borehole for the site for no charge.[26]

Job Mataboge helped them with lifts and his wife, Maria, baked them bread or cakes and brought them mugs of tea. Stephen Sello lent Liz an old typewriter, which made their fundraising letters look more official, and before too long their late-night work began to pay off. They received their first cheque, for £750, from the British Humanist Association, whose founder, Harold Blackham, happened to be Liz's uncle. Liz had also appealed to the Olympia Typewriter Company and they had donated a brand-new typewriter.

Visitors began to arrive from South Africa, most of them friends and contacts from the Liberal Party. Among them were Alan Paton, Robin Farquharson and John Harris. They brought light relief, humour and some welcome beer for the partying that Patrick enjoyed so much.

Jean van Riet, branch chairman of the Liberal Party in the Orange Free State, arrived on an unexpected mission. He had been sent by Patrick Duncan to pick up the Van Rensburgs and convey them to Basutoland, where Duncan had gone into exile on 3 May 1962, coincidentally just one day after Patrick and Liz had arrived in Bechuanaland.

He hoped to set up a safe haven for South African refugees in Basutoland, in due course providing a base for anti-apartheid activities back in South Africa. He also thought he might publish *Contact* there, for the critical news review was in imminent danger of being banned in South Africa. Presumably Duncan saw Van Rensburg as the ideal colleague to help him in these activities. The plan was for Van Riet to smuggle Patrick and Liz through South Africa, crossing the borders hidden in the boot of his car.[27]

It sounded like a hare-brained scheme and Patrick declined. He was too deeply committed to his school project, which was picking up momentum. In December they began digging foundation trenches for 'Swaneng Hill School'. The provisional committee had approved the name. They would start with just one classroom and a rondavel for Patrick and Liz to live in and continue building for expansion as they went along.

Patrick contacted Frank Krawolitski and, in the last week of December, a group of twenty young volunteers, mostly students, arrived from the South African Work Camps Association (SAWCA). They stayed for a few weeks, camped in tents. What they lacked in building skills they made up for in enthusiasm.

From his days working with Eric Francis in Durban, Patrick had the knowledge, practice and confidence to plan, set out and supervise the construction of the buildings. He hired two local artisans and the work campers joined the primary school volunteers in providing the labour. Neil Parsons, who was a volunteer teacher for the British charity Voluntary Service Overseas (VSO) at Moeng, joined them for ten days at the beginning of January.

The scene appeared to him to be fairly chaotic, with Patrick directing and throwing himself into the physical side of things; but a remarkable amount of work got done.[28] It was Liz who impressed Parsons most; she quietly and calmly organised the logistics, including, in particular, food and water. She had had the experience of work camps in her teenage years in continental Europe, fruit picking or on building projects, and she knew how a work camp should be run.[29]

Patrick and Liz would join the volunteers around a huge fire in the evenings and the singing would be led by camper Liz Malaza, 'with her powerful and resonant voice'. On one occasion, after Patrick and Liz had retired to bed, or to write more fundraising letters, the campers were joined by Seretse and his cousin Sekgoma Khama, who swept in in their cars and spent a couple of hours around the fire.[30]

When the campers left Patrick hired some local labour to support the two artisans and, with the primary school students 'still fully engaged', they reached their target. The buildings were completed in the first week of February and a start had already been made on the foundations for further buildings. Although desks and set books had not yet arrived, the school would open in time for the start of the new school year on Monday 11 February 1963.

* * *

Liz was six weeks pregnant and they would start the year sharing the teaching. They planned to offer English Language and Literature, History, Geography, Mathematics and Science. During the course of the year Patrick developed more ambitious plans to offer Bookkeeping, Economics, French and Latin; but for the moment this was all that he and Liz could manage. Setswana would be taught by Peto Sekgoma's son, Mokhutshwane Sekgoma, who had just passed his Form V Cambridge School Certificate examinations.

On the evening before opening day they had an unexpected visit from *Kgosi* Rasebolai Kgamane, who was visiting the site for the first time. Rasebolai had thus far doubted that these two impoverished *makgowa* (white people) would ever live up to their commitment, but they had had support from within the community and they had Seretse Khama and a few other key modernising allies to thank for ensuring that no obstacles had been placed in their way.

Rasebolai was to step down as *kgosi* during the course of 1963.[31] His place was taken by the eldest son of Tshekedi, the convivial Leapeetswe Khama, affectionately known as 'Peachy', a nickname acquired during his studies in Ireland. He and his brother Sekgoma 'Secky' Khama, who took over as acting chief in 1970, were both to prove more amenable to Patrick's various developmental ideas than the more austere Rasebolai.

That Rasebolai visited the school at all that evening was probably thanks to a request from the man who accompanied him, who had asked to be shown the project. The guest was Bereng Constantine Seeiso, whom Patrick had met in England during the boycott campaign. Then he had been a student at Oxford and crown prince of Basutoland. Now he was paramount chief and, when Lesotho became independent in 1966, he would become King Moshoeshoe II. Although in principle far from being a royalist, Patrick was thrilled that 'His Royal Highness' should be Swaneng Hill School's first official visitor, and it was a contact he was able to draw on years later when he was looking to expand his concept of 'Education with Production'.

10 | Challenging 'The Ladder to Privilege', 1963–1965

Accurate figures are hard to come by, but, in the early 1960s, it seems that of the two-thirds of school-age children who entered primary school in Bechuanaland more than half dropped out along the way, for a whole variety of reasons, and those who remained faced a competitive examination which barred the vast majority from secondary education. Only a small minority gained admission to one of the country's six secondary schools and these, in turn, would be further weeded out by the Junior Certificate (JC) examination at the end of their third year.

In 1963 there were only three secondary schools in the country that took students up to Form Five and the Cambridge Overseas School Certificate ('O' level). Although that number would increase in the next few years, the whole system, as Patrick perceived it, was directed towards the creation of an élite, who, like the colonial administration itself, would care little about the fortunes of those they left behind.

In a direct challenge to the system – the first of many to come – Patrick had offered places on a first-come-first-served basis. And for this first year he restricted the intake to one class of twenty-eight, among whom were two unmarried mothers. The Swaneng governing committee and several of Serowe's elders were opposed to the admission of these girls but, in his own words, Patrick 'took a strong stand against their position, on the grounds that these girls needed education even more than others, to be forearmed against impregnation in future and to be able better to care for their children'.[1] The target intake of twenty-eight students, several of them of South African origin, was quickly signed up.

Patrick held his first assembly, outdoors, in the manner that he was determined to continue, with two minutes' silence for personal reflection rather than the customary religious prayer or hymn. He then took the students into his confidence, explaining the financial constraints the school was under and that it would only survive with the willing cooperation and hard work of everyone – students and staff.

They would begin with the students electing a head boy and head girl and, fulfilling the dream he had had at Glenwood High, he asked them to elect three additional students who would serve with them on a school council. The council would be advisory, but he promised to take its advice seriously.

The first request from the council was for a sportsfield. When Patrick pointed out that the school could not afford the labour, the head boy, Otsogile 'Oats' Pitso, said the students would do the work themselves. They began that first Saturday morning, cutting and uprooting trees, clearing thorn scrub and levelling the ground. Patrick and Mokhutshwane joined them, and thus began an important custom that was to become a cornerstone of the Swaneng philosophy: Saturday morning voluntary labour, by staff as well as students, for the benefit of Swaneng Hill School and, in due course, the wider local community.

The commitment of Oats Pitso and the founding intake of students was crucial to the consolidation of the voluntary-work principle. Indeed, it could be said to have been initiated by them. Besides Saturday mornings they worked for an hour each evening until the sportsfield was completed. Thereafter, Saturday mornings were dedicated to other tasks around the school and, later, in the community.

There was always plenty to be done, for the school was a permanent building site. A couple of local artisans and a handful of labourers were employed full-time on the work. The foundations had already been laid for further classrooms, a common-room block and a library with a small office attached. Additional rondavels would be needed to accommodate expatriate volunteer teachers, who were expected before the end of the year.

In the same spirit, from the beginning the students willingly agreed to establish a rota for cooking their own meals, twice a day – early morning and late afternoon – coming to school early and leaving late to do so, and would do their own cleaning. It fulfilled an important principle for Patrick, who did not want a culture to develop which suggested that anybody was above such menial tasks. A midday meal was prepared for the students by two local women who were employed for the task. They also, in due course, did some cooking for the staff, who ate communally in the common room once it was completed.

The acceptance and success of the voluntary principle among students and staff in this first year of Swaneng Hill School inspired Patrick, so much so that it became a major part of the foundation of his evolving educational philosophy. He saw voluntarism as a fundamental self-reliant solution to the problems of rural development in a poor underdeveloped country such as Botswana.

The voluntary spirit was alive not only in Serowe but in a far wider world. In the 1960s, the decade in which Patrick began his educational work, the old certainties of the post-war world were being challenged both in the emerging post-colonial nations of Africa, Asia, the Caribbean and Latin America and in the former colonial metropoles and the industrial nations of the developed world.

Despite, or perhaps because of, the dark shadow of the Cold War and the very real threat of nuclear annihilation, the decade was full of positive hope for the future. It stemmed from a belief that a better, more humane world was on the horizon. 'Third World Development', in which the earth's resources would be shared more fairly, was seen as an achievable goal. Perhaps, even without realising it at first, Patrick was tapping into the *zeitgeist* of the 1960s and, by adding his as yet unclarified vision of an alternative, more all-inclusive approach to education, he was able to play his part in the search for a better future for all in the developing world of the post-colonial era.

* * *

Patrick let it be known that a formal board of governors would be established for the school, its members elected by the parents. Although accepted by the provisional committee, such democratic accountability caused anxiety and raised eyebrows among many Bamangwato officials, tied as they were to a quasi-feudal hierarchical society that the colonial administration had so far done little to unwind; but Patrick was undeterred.

He called a meeting of parents, who elected a twelve-member board. A majority were parents, while others were primary school teachers or elders in the community. In addition, there were three ex officio members: Archie Mogwe, local education officer appointed by the Department of Education; Mokhutshwane's father, Peto Sekgoma, representing the 'Tribal Authority'; and Patrick, as school principal and project organiser.[2]

Patrick had already drawn up a constitution for the board and he presented this and an outline of educational policy to its first meeting. He had been thinking of this moment at least since Dar es Salaam and, following Nyerere, he believed that a limited competitive secondary system was in danger of creating an élite of individuals, concerned primarily with their own careers and privilege.

He was determined to demonstrate an alternative model that could be replicated throughout the country and beyond. The students and work-camp volunteers had shown what could be achieved with limited funds, through self-reliance. This had been born out of practical necessity, but he did not see why it could not become a guiding principle. The students would be taught about development. Combined with a spirit of voluntarism, when his students finished their schooling at Swaneng

> they will consciously recognise their role as agents of progress. Most of all, we would like them to feel under some compulsion to fight hunger, poverty and ignorance in their country. At Swaneng Hill School, we will certainly discourage any notion that education is just a ladder on which ambition climbs to privilege.[3]

He was not yet clear how he would achieve this, but the board members, only too aware of the need for some form of broader rural development, were happy to go along with these guiding principles.

The board was also gradually won over to Patrick's attitude of refusing to expel any female student who became pregnant. Ironically, he was supported in this decision by Peto Sekgoma, the father of the school's Setswana teacher, Mokhutshwane.

Peto Sekgoma, who was very much a traditionalist, had opposed Patrick's stand on this issue, until his daughter Valerie became pregnant and dropped out of school. When Patrick wanted to readmit her after she had given birth, he had Sekgoma's support and, between the two of them, they managed to persuade the board to accept Patrick's stand.[4]

It was to be many years before any other school in the country followed suit, but the decision benefited many young women who were able to further their education and lead fulfilling and productive lives.

In 1968 Julia Majaha-Jartby, a Form IV student at the strict Catholic mission school of St Joseph's, near the present city of Gaborone, was expelled when she fell pregnant. The previous year she had attended a debate exchange at Swaneng Hill School and been impressed by the liberties she had observed there.

Three or four of the students had children, including Pelonomi Venson, who went on to become a senior minister in the Botswana government. Julia's family lived near Francistown and, after she gave birth in December, she applied to Swaneng, was interviewed by Patrick and was admitted to Form IV in January 1969.

She fell pregnant again in 1970 and left the school in March, returning to Swaneng that October in time to sit her Form V Cambridge exam in November, having left her two children with her mother. She was one of five to gain a second-class pass and went on to the new University College of Botswana. In due course she rose to a very senior position at the International Monetary Fund in Washington, DC. She believes that had it not been for Patrick she would have struggled in poverty as a partially educated rural mother and grandmother.[5]

Patrick followed government policy in charging a small annual fee for admission to the school, but he refrained from imposing the extra financial burden of a school uniform. Perhaps recalling his own feelings of pride and superiority as he moved up to secondary school and, for the first time, put on his new school uniform, Patrick viewed uniforms as a status symbol.

The secondary-school students of Bechuanaland were already a privileged group and Patrick was determined to inculcate in them an egalitarian attitude towards their less fortunate fellows. The students should thus simply be dressed as smartly as they were able, as he himself was.

To demonstrate their commitment to egalitarian self-reliance Patrick and Liz set themselves two rules: to share in the menial and manual work they expected their students to perform and to maintain a modest lifestyle. The latter was a financial necessity, but also, as they cycled around Serowe, begged lifts or took local buses, they were demonstrating solidarity with the local people. The white trading community might ridicule them, but they drew strength from the way they lived and felt better able to ask others to follow their example.[6]

* * *

Not long after the school opened it underwent an inspection by Mr Hunter and two of his education officers, Gaositwe K. T. Chiepe and Archie Mogwe. Chiepe was a local Serowe woman, and both she and Mogwe had attended the Tiger Kloof Institute in South Africa in the days before the Bantu Education Act of 1953 had led to its closure.

They expected similar high standards from any new secondary school in their home country.[7] Swaneng Hill School passed inspection in all educational matters. The only criticism was the lack of school uniform and the worn-out appearance of some of the pupils' shoes, factors that reflected the priorities of Patrick and Liz van Rensburg.

The next school visit of significance was that of *Kgosi* Linchwe II Kgafela. He was soon to be formally installed as chief of the Bakgatla, whose traditional town, Mochudi, lies in the south-east of the country, close to the 'line of rail', about 40 kilometres north of what is now Gaborone.[8]

He was staying with *Kgosi* Rasebolai and brought with him as his friend and guest the prolific Scottish writer and Labour Party politician Naomi Mitchison. Patrick developed an easy rapport with Linchwe, who was impressed by the spirit of volunteerism that was such an important part of the school ethos. Naomi spent a couple of hours speaking with the students and answering their questions. Drawing on her Scottish experience, she stressed the importance of development that uplifted the neediest in society.

Patrick and Liz entertained the pair to dinner and Naomi later wrote of the humble simplicity of the small rondavel home.[9]

On his return to Mochudi, Linchwe sent a cheque to the value of R500 for the general fund of the school, and over Easter 1963 a truck arrived to convey Patrick and Liz and fifteen students to Mochudi for a most enjoyable two-week volunteer work camp, helping to build a community and refugee centre in the town.

There followed a steady flow of visitors from South Africa, most of them friends of Patrick from the Liberal Party. Robin Farquharson was probably the most regular and his support was invaluable. He became Patrick's 'unofficial buying agent' for all sorts of goods from Johannesburg.[10] Dr Cato Aal, a Norwegian, in the country to help arrange the regular passage of South African refugees through Bechuanaland, was impressed by what Patrick and Liz were achieving at Swaneng and promised to try to find them some regular source of funding.[11]

In due course volunteer teachers began to arrive, starting with young school-leaver Chris Gore-Booth, son of Sir Paul Gore-Booth, British high commissioner in India, and great nephew of the Irish revolutionary Constance Gore-Booth, the Countess Markievicz.[12]

Chris spent three months at the school, from June to August, before returning to Britain overland, following Patrick and Liz's route in reverse. Although he came from a privileged background he had been educated at Eton and was unfazed by the spartan living conditions. He introduced the music of the Beatles to Serowe and was welcome company for Patrick and Liz, who, until his arrival, had been the only people living on the school site.

He took on some of Patrick's teaching load, leaving him more time for fundraising and supervision of the ongoing building work. Chris was followed by two Maths teachers, Don Baker (and family), sponsored by the British Humanist Association, and Mike Hawkes, from the British International Voluntary Service (IVS).[13]

The ebb and flow of expatriate volunteers had begun. The volunteer agency would pay for flights and a small cash allowance of a few rands per month, while the school provided accommodation and communal meals. Patrick believed that expatriates should not be visibly better off than local Batswana in a similar work position. Unsurprisingly, the bulk of the expatriate volunteers who came over the next decade and a half were leftward-leaning in a political sense, which suited Patrick's developing political thought.

Figure 10.1: Swaneng staff quarters: British volunteer Mike Hawkes at his rondavel, with staffroom and offices to the left, 1963/1964. (By kind permission of Mike Hawkes)

Patrick worried about the geopolitical future of Bechuanaland, to which he was becoming increasingly committed. Construction of a new capital at Gaborone had begun in 1963: the British colonial administration was clearly preparing to leave. Patrick saw Bechuanaland as a large, impoverished, semi-desert state with a small population, surrounded by hostile, white-ruled neighbours, and he wondered whether it could ever stand alone as an independent nation.

In August 1963 Harold Wolpe and Arthur Goldreich, two of those charged alongside Nelson Mandela and others in what was to become known as the 'Rivonia Trial', escaped from prison before the trial began and crossed into Bechuanaland dressed as priests. In the wake of this highly publicised event and the large number of other South African refugees passing through Bechuanaland, Prime Minister Verwoerd made a final bid to absorb the three High Commission Territories into South Africa.[14]

The move was, of course, rejected out of hand by both the British government and the emerging African political leaders in the protectorates. But it prompted Patrick to give expression to an idea that had been evolving in his mind for some time – namely, the amalgamation of Bechuanaland with Northern Rhodesia.

Bechuanaland, as Patrick saw it, was entirely surrounded by white-ruled states: Southern Rhodesia, South Africa, South West Africa (Namibia) and, in the north, just across the Caprivi Strip, lay Portuguese-ruled Angola. What chance would half a million Batswana in their drought-stricken country stand against the hostile intentions of these white-ruled neighbours?

A previous South African prime minister had threatened to seize the protectorate during the Seretse Khama marriage crisis. What was to stop the current prime minister from carrying out that threat? On the other hand, with the imminent breakup of the Central African Federation, Northern Rhodesia was likely to gain its independence (as the Republic of Zambia) the following year. It had a thriving copper-mining industry and, compared with semi-desert Bechuanaland, almost limitless agricultural resources. Quite apart from the development opportunities, amalgamation would strengthen a future independent Bechuanaland's security vis-à-vis its hostile white neighbours.[15]

It may seem an unlikely scenario, the only direct connection between the two countries being a ferry crossing and a theoretical pinpoint border shared among four states in the middle of the Zambezi River. But a number of African countries were experimenting with political unions, and when Patrick put the idea to Seretse Khama he agreed it was worth seeing what Zambia's 'president-in-waiting', Kenneth Kaunda, thought of it.[16] Patrick would be regarded as a neutral party and his approach to Kaunda would not commit Seretse to anything.

In the first week of September a meeting was arranged with Kaunda in Lusaka for Saturday 7 September, the day before Liz was due to go into labour with her firstborn. The Serowe doctor assured Patrick that first babies rarely arrived early or on their due date and if he went immediately he should be back in Serowe in plenty of time for the birth.

Patrick must have been excited by the prospect of a real diplomatic mission, something he had never actually undertaken during his years as a South African diplomat. He left by train via Bulawayo and Livingstone, on the twenty-four-hour journey to Lusaka. Kaunda had initially been hesitant about meeting this white Afrikaner, but he had checked him out and agreed to the meeting.

Their discussion was short and non-committal. Kaunda was about to see the dissolution of one federation and was not about to rush into another. But he left Patrick with the assurance that he was open to discussion on a possible link between the two countries, although only if a firm proposal came from the African leaders of an independent Bechuanaland.

There was no more that Patrick could achieve in Lusaka. The ball was now firmly in Seretse's court. Seretse, however, intent on negotiating a way to his country's independence, did not pursue Patrick's initiative at the time.

As on so many other issues, Patrick's thinking was ahead of its time. From 1973, however, as the Rhodesian liberation war began to spill across the border of independent Botswana, President Seretse Khama was a key figure in the formation of the 'Front Line States' grouping of Botswana, Zambia, Tanzania, and (from 1975) Angola and Mozambique. In due course this informal grouping would lead in the 1980s and 1990s to the Southern African Development Community (SADC).

His brief mission in Lusaka completed, Patrick hurried home to Serowe. He arrived on the evening of Sunday 8 September to find that his firstborn had indeed been delivered on the due date. That morning Liz had been rushed to Sekgoma Memorial Hospital in the little black Austin car donated by Cato Aal and had already given birth to their son, Thomas Masego van Rensburg.

Thereafter, the new parents were granted Setswana monikers, being named, according to tradition, after their firstborn: Rra Masego and Mma Masego. Clearly Patrick and Liz were becoming an integral part of the Serowe community.[17]

* * *

At the end of that first academic year Swaneng Hill had a second classroom, a common room, an office with adjoining double bedroom into which the Van Rensburg family had moved, and two further staff rondavels. Over the summer break Mokhutshwane Sekgoma organised a work camp at Swaneng for fifth formers from around the country, while they waited for their Cambridge results.[18]

There was a good response and they made a start on the foundations of an eight-classroom block. It had been designed according to Patrick's plan by a visiting architect, Lawrence Isaacson, who had not charged for the job.

Hitherto, buildings had simply been laid out by Patrick and details like windows and doors discussed with the builders as they went along. This classroom block was designed around a courtyard in which morning assembly could be held. Initially the classrooms were open-sided onto the courtyard, which provided a sense of community and had a good effect on classroom behaviour. The work camp also made a start on the foundations of a Science lab, which the Swaneng students were to complete themselves over the next sixteen months.[19]

When he was not teaching, Patrick would be in the office ordering goods and equipment, corresponding with existing or potential donors and planning the next building work, or rushing into Serowe to buy some emergency item from one of the local white-owned trading stores. Between any or all of these, he would most often be found around the building site, supervising the work and listening to any problems expressed by the labourers, his employees.

He was a good listener, even with his limited understanding of Setswana, and with some translation from those with a little English he learned that their greatest complaint was the price of food and basic essentials at the local trading stores. Patrick understood the problem only too well. He had an account and even a credit facility at Watson's store, but he made all his bulk purchases in Rhodesia or South Africa. He was a great believer in the old adage that there were no problems, only solutions. And his solution here was to start a consumers' co-operative.

Drawing some of his inspiration from the Co-operative Society in England, which had been so good at raising money for the Boycott Movement, he gathered the workers together one afternoon. He explained to them about consumers' co-operatives and how they worked, and suggested they might start one in Serowe.

After holding a couple of meetings at the school on Saturday afternoons he gathered considerable support from within the local community. He explained that the capital for building a store would have to come from the members themselves by way of membership fees and, in the meantime, he started a bulk-buying scheme from a wholesaler in Mafikeng. He delegated the role of keeping the books to newly arrived Mike Hawkes, who kept the accounts in a school exercise book and doled out the pre-ordered and pre-paid goods from the office window on Saturday afternoons.[20]

At first the scheme worked well, but there was soon opposition from what Patrick called 'the all-White Serowe Chamber of Commerce'.[21] He received a letter from the new district commissioner calling on him to cease trading or risk losing his residence permit for going beyond his education remit.

Patrick applied for a trading licence at a licensing tribunal in Palapye. In the view of the 'Serowe Chamber of Commerce', which was well represented at the tribunal, he should stick to education and keep his nose out of other people's business. The DC agreed and Patrick's application was turned down.[22]

On returning to Serowe Patrick realised he had better suspend the bulk-ordering scheme, while at the same time going over the head of the DC. He prepared a petition to present publicly in the *kgotla* to the resident commissioner (Bechuanaland's most senior colonial official), who was due to visit Serowe in the near future. In this he had the support of Seretse Khama, who, by now, was in full political-party mode.

The opposition of the traders and the DC had galvanised the public in Serowe in favour of the consumers' co-operative and the membership swelled considerably. Seretse himself became a member, for form's sake.

The issue was finally resolved in the consumers' favour, following the British administration's appointment of Trevor Bottomley as registrar of co-operative societies. Bottomley, formerly national education officer at Stanford Hall Co-operative College in the UK, was a dedicated supporter of the co-operative principle.[23] The Serowe Consumers' Co-operative Society that he registered in 1964 was the first of many co-operatives he would register in the country in the next six years.

With Bottomley's official registration, and clearance from the tribal authority, the members of the Serowe consumers' co-op were able to start building their store in the heart of the town. Members offered their labour free, or at minimal cost, helped by a two-week student work camp. The headmaster of Simon Ratshosa Primary School and a key supporter of Patrick's ideas, Mr K. K. Baruti, was chairman of the co-operative committee.

At this point Patrick's position in Bechuanaland was nearly put in jeopardy by the actions of a former Liberal Party colleague, John Harris.[24]

Through 1963 and 1964 the South African government had clamped down on Liberal Party activists, placing most of them under banning orders at one time or another. Visits to Patrick were less frequent and several of those were made en route to the safety of exile in the UK. Some within the much harassed party, including John Harris and, possibly, Robin Farquharson, both of whom had visited Patrick in 1962, joined the African Resistance Movement, which was made up mostly of white liberals who were prepared to engage in acts of sabotage.

Towards the end of July 1964, with the new co-operative store about to be opened in Serowe, news came through that a bomb had gone off in Johannesburg's central station, killing one person and injuring several others. John Harris was arrested for placing the bomb and charged with murder. It turned out that he had phoned the police to clear the station, but they had failed to respond to the warning.

In Bechuanaland the explosion merely compounded the suspicions of colonial officials that Patrick van Rensburg was not a man to be trusted. In what can only be seen as an attempt to discredit him, they let it be known that Harris had visited Patrick.

Patrick, however, stayed on, helped in no small manner in Serowe by the young district officer John Harlow, who was very supportive of his school and co-op projects. Patrick credited him with allaying some of the suspicions of his more conservative colonial colleagues.[25]

The co-op store was officially opened in August 1964 by Trevor Bottomley. Seretse Khama was away from home, but was represented by Ruth, who came with her twin boys. John Harlow represented the district commissioner, who had turned down Patrick's original application. The DC discreetly stayed away from the opening ceremony – he was said to have been lunching with the white traders.[26]

* * *

Patrick absorbed a number of lessons from the first year of Swaneng Hill School. Perhaps the most significant and long lasting was on a personal level. He was to write a couple of years later, in a publication intended for international consumption:

… my work at Swaneng Hill School has cleared from the dark corners of my mind any racial prejudices that may still have lurked there after an upbringing in the *most* bigoted land on earth. Taken as a group, Botswana schoolboys and schoolgirls are not basically different from the schoolboys and schoolgirls whom my wife and I went to school with in Britain and South Africa, respectively. And the Botswana people, as human beings, are on the whole basically the same as any other I have known. There are, of course, differences, but I am convinced that these are superficial and transient, and can be explained by differences of time and place.[27]

He learned professional and practical lessons too. Having experienced the problems of teaching the first intake, with their very mixed abilities, he decided he would no longer accept students on a first-come-first-served basis but would determine admission by a combination of primary-leaving results and interviews. In contrast to all other secondary schools in the country, however, he extended acceptance to third-class primary passes.

The interview would enable him to assess the student's willingness to accept the school's voluntary work ethos. He also decided to restrict class size to just twenty pupils, half the government's maximum limit. This would help the school maintain standards among its mixed-ability intake and, most importantly, develop effective student–teacher interaction.

He realised that the spirit of voluntarism must not be squandered by using it as a source of unskilled labour. If his students were to fulfil his dream of becoming the committed drivers of their country's meaningful development, they must be trained, not just academically, but also in practical skills.

With this in mind, he recruited Martin Kibblewhite, a qualified teacher with additional skills in building. Kibblewhite arrived in 1964 and, besides teaching English and French, took on both the day-to-day supervision of the building work and the classroom teaching of the theory and practice of building and construction, two periods a week for each class.[28]

Patrick's attention had been drawn to the importance of offering French by the experience of Education Officer Chiepe, who had spoken of her embarrassment at a West African conference when she had had to rely on a white man to translate for her from the French, which was the language of education in more African countries than English.[29]

Figure 10.2: Saturday morning voluntary work: Patrick leads the trench digging. (Van Rensburg family collection; photographer unknown)

Kibblewhite's presence set Patrick free to undertake research into a new subject that would in due course become known as 'Development Studies', although he would initially call it 'Civics'. It would involve learning about the origins of the 'developed' world and its industrialisation and the lessons to be learned for an underdeveloped country like Bechuanaland. 'Civics' was already on the approved school curriculum and he would simply adapt that syllabus as he saw fit.

As was his practice in those early years, he started by discussing these issues with the students and envisaged his new course as a formalisation of those discussions.[30] He knew he would need professional help to turn his and their ideas into a formal curriculum, but, in the meantime, he and a couple of other teachers would simply incorporate some of the ideas into the standard Civics course that would be taught from the beginning of the 1965 school year.

Another lesson Patrick drew from the first year grew out of the struggle to set up the consumers' co-operative: the crying need for some form of adult education among the wider Serowe community. At the request of the tribal authority he set up a secondary-level night school, starting in 1964 and taught by the Swaneng teachers on a rota basis. They offered a range of subjects in a four-year course, leading to the JC examination.

* * *

With most expatriate volunteers staying for one or, at the most, two years, Patrick needed a reliable source of volunteer teachers. In this he was fortunate to have established contact with Frank Judd of Britain's IVS. Frank had already sent out several volunteers to Swaneng Hill and in June 1964 he visited Serowe to see the project for himself. Patrick and Liz put him up in one of the bachelor rondavels. He remembers enjoying the sight and smell of the high rafters and neat new thatch, though, as it was midwinter, the nights were bitterly cold.

He ate in the staff common room with Patrick and Liz, and during the day Patrick did what he did best – showed his visitor round the school.[31] It was largely a building site, which gave Patrick plenty of scope for expounding on the achievements to date and explaining his vision for future growth. It would, he explained, be both a local educational project and an inspiration for wider co-operative development.

From his various interchanges with visitors – which fed into his funding appeals and, in due course, his lectures – Patrick had learned that what impressed them most was what continually inspired him: namely, the knowledge that right from the beginning the students were willing volunteers, actively involved in building their own classrooms on Saturday mornings and during holiday work camps. It was the self-help element that raised the most money and captured the *zeitgeist* of the 1960s. It brought in enthusiastic young volunteer teachers, mainly from Europe and America, but also some from South Africa.

As the large, red-bearded principal of Swaneng Hill School strode enthusiastically around his domain, Frank had difficulty keeping up with his long stride ... and his broad vision. They were to become firm friends. As he got to know Patrick over the years, Frank judged him to be a patrician, and told him so.

He felt that Patrick behaved as though he possessed an inherent right and duty to lead; to work for the benefit of others, but never actually to be one of them. Frank did not mean this unkindly; indeed, he was proud of the support he gave to Patrick, for he believed it took an individual like him to get a project like Swaneng off the ground.[32]

Whatever the validity of Frank's judgement, Patrick was fortunate that weekend to have attracted his firm support, for the core of British colonial officers in Mafikeng did not trust him, regarding him as a 'white communist'.[33] It is probable that they did not like the idea that he had independent access to expatriate staff and international funding.

They tried to steer Judd away from Serowe, preferring that he direct IVS volunteers to the existing government-supported secondary schools. But Judd appreciated that Swaneng Hill had no financial help from the protectorate administration and he prioritised Patrick's requests.

News of Patrick's project was spreading through the network of charitable trusts in the UK, many of them making the link with the Boycott Movement and the author of *Guilty Land*, and in 1964 Swaneng received the first of a series of grants from the Rowntree Trust, which also agreed to pay for Patrick and his family to fly to the UK for a two-month holiday from December 1964 to January 1965. Much of the trip would be a fundraising working holiday for Patrick – as most of his holidays were to become – but it was a welcome break from the increasing workload of life in Serowe.

Leaving the school and building work in the capable hands of Martin Kibblewhite, on 30 November Patrick, Liz and fourteen-month-old

Tommy Masego took the train to Bulawayo and flew to Salisbury, where they caught the flight to London. On arrival they drove a hired car to York for a meeting with the Rowntree board of trustees, who agreed to give him the full grant he had applied for. They then went to Anglesey to stay for a week with Liz's parents before leaving Tommy with his grandparents and returning to London.

They had last met Joe Rogaly on the eve of their departure for their trans-African adventure. Since then he had married Sue Baring and Patrick and Liz stayed with them in their new house in London. They visited Frank Judd at IVS headquarters and met the indomitable Betty Sleath, of the charity 'War on Want'. Betty, who had made Swaneng her 'pet project', had already raised money for it through the charity's various groups around Britain.

She asked for photographs she could use for publicity and, from the many they produced, selected an unflattering one of a heavily pregnant Liz in one of Patrick's old work sweaters, reading something with Rebecca, a Motswana. Later, while travelling on a London bus, Liz saw the greatly enlarged picture on a poster near an Underground station.[34]

After they had spent Christmas in Anglesey and Oxfam had confirmed a promised grant, Liz stayed in London visiting friends while Patrick flew to Oslo as a guest of Cato Aal. Cato had arranged a number of meetings, which, as it turned out, marked the start of Patrick's relationship with a range of Scandinavian agencies that were to prove vital to his future work in Southern Africa.

He introduced Patrick to Norway's Students' and Academics' International Assistance Fund (SAIH), a solidarity organisation founded in 1961 with the motto 'education for liberation'.[35] The organisation raised money for projects and channelled funds through the Norwegian aid agency NORAD. Patrick then went to Trondheim to speak at the Cathedral School, which raised funds for development projects abroad.

At all his meetings Patrick stressed the voluntarism and self-build aspect of Swaneng Hill and that his aim was to help the students to help themselves. This went down well in Norway, particularly in Trondheim, which had a strong self-help culture. Everywhere he went Patrick was promised financial support and SAIH agreed to an immediate grant of £1 000.[36]

Before Patrick flew back to London, Cato arranged for him to go to Stockholm for an afternoon meeting with Thord Palmlund of the new Swedish International Development Cooperation Agency (Sida). Palmlund was a quiet, serious-minded man who took copious notes while Patrick spoke. When they parted he said he was very impressed by Patrick's approach and promised to visit Serowe later in the year.[37] Patrick did not realise it at the time, but this meeting would turn out to be the most significant part of the whole trip.

He flew straight back to London to find several letters from Swaneng and a telegram announcing that five of the nine students entered for the JC exam a year early had passed, two with good second-class passes. Patrick was elated. It vindicated his decision to put them forward early and proved to his satisfaction that volunteering for practical work in no way interfered with his students' academic studies. He and Liz spent a couple of weeks relaxing in London and made a trip to Anglesey to say goodbye to Liz's parents before catching a flight back to Southern Africa.

11 | The Alternative Educationist, 1965–1967

The year 1965 marked the beginning of a new life for Bechuanaland. In March the protectorate gained full internal self-government in preparation for independence the following year as the Republic of Botswana. It was also a turning point in the development of Patrick's professional life. As he was to write in 1967:

> All that I know about education I had to learn on the spot, and while teaching and building a school. I was able to judge the methods, content and purposes of education about which I was learning in the light of the needs of the people amongst whom I was working. I had also to worry about the cost of building and of running the school.[1]

In the three years from 1965 to 1967 he was to transform himself from the founder of a self-help, low-cost school and enthusiast about co-operative ventures into an alternative educationist of international renown.

It was in 1965 that Patrick started the brigades, the education and rural skills development project that was thereafter to be associated with his name. In that year, too, he began to teach his evolving Development Studies course. Experimentation with the practicalities of both these projects was to have a profound impact on the evolution of Patrick's thinking in terms of education and rural development. Together they were to form the foundation for his pioneering work in 'alternative education'. And although his ideas did not always receive the recognition in Botswana that he felt they were due, they were to receive international recognition from as early as 1967 and earn him prestigious awards in the decades to come.

* * *

Patrick and Liz arrived back 'home', as Serowe had now become, in February 1965, a week after the new school year had started. In their absence the building work had progressed, with the help of a summer work camp on the site. There were now two dormitories, one each for boys and girls, with toilets, showers and wash basins, and a small room attached to the girls' dormitory for a resident matron.

The rectangular eight-classroom block was in almost full use, for there were now seven classes in the school. On Patrick and Liz's return from Europe, however, the first thing that struck them was the barrenness of the countryside, the culmination of five years of persistent drought. There had been no significant rain during their ten-week absence and even within the fenced-off school compound the grass had withered to almost nothing. Dust was everywhere – the thorn trees were covered with it – and 'a deadening heat was sucking the last inch of water out of the dam'.[2] Swaneng's voluntary labour had repaired the dam the previous year in preparation for a 'rainy season' that failed to arrive. A month or so later the tension of overwork in the intense heat was broken when

> the rain finally appeared, after a piling up of storm clouds, nervous shifting of the wind, and a great booming and flashing in the distance like guns opening up the way for an advance. When it did come, it came in earnest, and for two days the landscape was transformed … Afterwards, on totally bare patches of ground, green shoots began to appear … The mud-caked walls of a hut would no longer be dull brown, but a vivid terra cotta … This inverted springtime [had] come too late, and the crops [had] already failed, but it … made it possible to imagine paradise.[3]

The rainstorm also breached the newly repaired dam, driving out the exit pipe in the centre. The Department of Agriculture brought in a bulldozer and labour to repair the dam but, after a few months, ran out of money and abandoned the project. Patrick managed to raise £400 from Oxfam, enough to employ thirty men with wheelbarrows to complete the task in time for the next rainy season, which once more failed to arrive.[4]

While the school, its staff and students had funding support from abroad, Patrick and Liz were acutely aware of how much more precarious life was for the vast majority in rural Bechuanaland. Martin Kibblewhite reported that when the school year had started there had been the usual queue of boys and girls, some accompanied by parents, hoping for admission. Many of them had to be turned away.

It raised an issue of concern to all the staff – what could be done about those who, having failed to gain admission because of poor primary-school leaving results, would drop out of education entirely? Patrick had been thinking about this problem during the previous year and his solution was discussed at the first staff meeting after his and Liz's return.

They were all agreed that the answer did not lie in overloading classes. Patrick proposed a scheme similar to one he had seen in Ghana, which provided a combination of simplified academic education and training in specific technical skills.[5] The students used their technical training to undertake productive work that generated an income. Such a system, Patrick explained, would help defray part of the cost of their education and training.

Building skills were the most obvious immediate need and, following the Ghanaian example, Patrick proposed calling the project the 'Builders' Brigade'. The terminology was already familiar to the Batswana through the Boys' Life Brigade, the missionary equivalent of Boy Scouts. The staff agreed to share the extra academic teaching and to prepare appropriate syllabuses.

* * *

Meanwhile, Bechuanaland was preparing for the country's first universal-franchise election, scheduled for 1 March. Seretse Khama had been campaigning vigorously for the BDP, holding a series of public meetings across the country. With his ability to portray himself as both a traditional monarchist and a member of the modern intelligentsia, his party was the favourite to win. It was evident to any observer that most of Bamangwato country was firmly in the pocket of the BDP. As Patrick recalled about Seretse's campaign meeting in Serowe: 'On his approach we literally felt the ground shake with the vibrant enthusiasm of his followers.'[6]

The turnout on 1 March was a high 75 per cent and the BDP duly won by a landslide, gaining 28 of the 31 parliamentary seats. Seretse Khama would now become prime minister.

By this stage Patrick had assessed Seretse to be a social conservative, though 'as much a democrat as a man born to be king could be'. He appreciated the important support Seretse had given to the school and the consumer co-operative, but suspected that politically it was because 'both had popular support'.[7] This seems a harsh judgement in the light of the vital support Seretse had offered from the beginning, before a general election was even in the offing. It may be that by the time Patrick came to write his memoir experience had led to political cynicism.

Although as a resident British passport holder Patrick had been entitled to vote in the election in this 'British Protectorate', he had not done so. He considered it was up to the Batswana themselves to choose their government. Seretse disagreed and at the victory party in Serowe that night he berated Patrick for being so pedantic. In his view they were on this journey together and he should have voted. After the election Prime Minister Seretse Khama moved more or less permanently to Government House (later State House) in the newly built capital, Gaborone.

* * *

Fortunately, after Seretse's departure for more important responsibilities, Patrick had the willing support in Serowe of *Kgosi* Leapeetswe, Seretse's cousin and Rasebolai's successor, and it was to him that he now took his proposal for a Builders' Brigade. The new *kgosi* valued Patrick's developmental ideas, and with his support Patrick was able to win over a large gathering in the *kgotla*. Thirty young men were selected as Builders' Brigade trainees, a site was allocated in central Serowe and, with Swaneng's artisan foreman Todd Kuhlman as instructor, they began their first practical task: building their own training centre.

It was important that the trainees were not just used as cheap labour for building the school. Their practical projects had to contribute to the cost of their training. Their first outside project was a staff rondavel at the Bamangwato Development Association at Radisele. Another was a church in Palapye. Besides their practical work, for two days a week the Swaneng teachers gave the trainees simplified lessons in English, Maths, Science and Patrick's new course, Development Studies.

Patrick involved the local community in his brigade project through the formation of the Serowe Youth Development Association (Syda), which had its inaugural meeting on 22 February 1966. Chaired by *Kgosi* Leapeetswe, with Patrick as secretary, this body had a mixture of appointed and elected local representation. The Syda oversaw the day-to-day running of the brigade and any other similar training and development projects that might arise in the future.

Patrick's version of Development Studies was very different from that intended by the government, which envisaged a course about the executive, judiciary and legislature intended to teach the role and duties of citizenship in a modern state. For his part, Patrick had no intention of teaching his students how to conform. He hoped to produce people who would question the status quo through an understanding of the underlying reasons for Bechuanaland's underdevelopment. In this way they could enter adult life sufficiently informed to play a role in directing their country along a road towards a fair and equitable development and distribution of resources.

In February 1965 Patrick had roped in two new young volunteers from the UK, Frank Randall and Alasdair McEwen, to share with him the teaching of Development Studies. The Scot, McEwen, arrived with his bagpipes and a surfeit of enthusiasm, which prompted Patrick to delegate him to draft the new Development Studies syllabus in such a way as to stress a development model based on self-help and co-operatives and intended to counter the 'university bias of the rest of the curriculum'.[8]

With the course still not clearly worked out, they started teaching it to the Form I students, with Patrick hoping that by the time this cohort reached Form III the subject would be more clearly formulated and accepted by government for the JC examination. The students, however, were confused, as much by the unfamiliarity of the title as by the purpose of the course, and were probably not helped by the unfocused way in which it was taught, on a trial-and-error and discussion basis.

Over the following several years these problems were largely overcome, as other volunteer teachers inherited the subject and contributed
to its development and clarification. But that lay in the future, and Patrick
could not wait that long. As new ideas flooded his mind he was impatient
to move on and the Development Studies course went ahead on an ad hoc
basis.

Figure 11.1: Patrick with *Kgosi* Linchwe II Kgafela, Serowe, 1960s. Linchwe was a key
supporter of Patrick's ideals. (By kind permission of Sandy Grant)

From 1965 Patrick began to develop a proactive vision of successful rural
development that could be applicable to any developing country. He saw
the secondary school as a hub of expertise, a centre for development in the
surrounding community. He believed that

> the talents and intelligence of both staff and students are an asset of
> enormous value, which should properly be utilized for development
> in a country's overall planning and development. As the school parti-
> cipates in development, it is also to carry out its function of educating

its students for development; if the students participate fully in the implementation of the school's role as a focal point for development in its area, they will thereby have an opportunity of learning both skill and commitment.[9]

From this emerged the 'Village Development' course. Patrick selected seven volunteers from Swaneng's Form IV, while Peter Wass, district officer responsible for community development, selected a handful of other Serowe volunteers who had Junior Certificates. The Village Development course would teach the students some background theory about development and co-operatives and train them in how to set up and manage a Builders' Brigade, build a dam, build classrooms and initiate a co-operative – all things Patrick had learned through practical experience in the past three years.

The expectation was that these students would become primary school teachers in various villages around the country, replicating the development policies they had seen practised at Swaneng. As Patrick saw it, Bechuanaland was a country in transition from communal ownership and family tradition to a modern society of formal employment and commercial enterprise. He was determined that the modern economy that was coming should be co-operative, not the 'grabbing kind of economic individualism'.[10]

Once again he roped in Alasdair McEwen to help and the Village Development course began to be taught in two periods a week in that first term of 1965. Looking back, Patrick believed that of the ten students who began the course only three – Otsogile Pitso, George Matiza, a student from Rhodesia, and Daniel Jankie, one of Peter Wass's selected volunteers from Ghanzi in the far west of the country – really understood and appreciated the concept of village development.[11]

Even they, however, did not fancy a future as primary school teachers, with heavy developmental responsibilities in remote rural villages. All three went on to join the staff of Swaneng and the brigades. Following the liberation of Zimbabwe in 1980, George Matiza was to play a leading role in the development of Education with Production, as principal of Rusununguko School for many years, during which time he was able to put into practice many of the ideas he had learned from the Village Development course.

The course had proved its worth by what it had taught these three, but, like many of Patrick's ideas, it was an experiment, one of several that did not work out as he had anticipated, and it was not repeated.

* * *

Towards the end of May, the weekend before the beginning of the second school term, Patrick received news that could have derailed his whole educational project. He learned from the new DC, Eustace Clark, that the administration in Gaborone was planning to build a government secondary school in Serowe. The decision would be taken in Gaborone in a few days' time. Patrick had just one day, over the weekend, in which to prepare a response.

It was clear to him that if the government built its own secondary school in Serowe, with the full backing of government funds, Swaneng Hill and all it stood for was finished. The consumers' co-operative would probably survive, though it would still need to be nurtured by somebody, but the whole alternative pattern of practical, self-help, non-élitist education that he and Liz had been striving for in the past three years would go, and, with it, Development Studies, the brigades, the night school and the Village Development course. The school would not survive the competition.

It seems likely that that was exactly the intention of the colonial officers who still dominated the administration from their new offices in Gaborone. They had never taken to Patrick or his radical educational ideas, believing him to be a dangerous South African communist. They seem to have believed that if faced with a government-funded standard school in Serowe, he would abandon Swaneng Hill and leave Bechuanaland to join other South African refugees elsewhere. But they had reckoned without the stubbornness of Patrick van Rensburg when he was fired up. He saw the government's proposal as a direct challenge to him and his ideas. His response was to fight for survival.

In a frenzy of activity that evening and late into the night he and Liz worked together on a memorandum to counter the proposal. Patrick had a remarkable ability to assemble his thoughts, some of them from way back in his memory, and then simply pour them out onto paper in logical form.

He wrote in longhand, straight off the top of his head, with few visible notes, while Liz typed, on duplicating stencils, as fast as he could write. The completed document was eleven pages of foolscap, entitled: 'Memo on the future of Swaneng Hill School, in relation to the Secondary School which the Government proposes to build in Serowe'.

He stressed that in deciding in 1962 to found a secondary school in Serowe he and his wife had been responding to a local need. In raising funds and recruiting teachers from abroad they were not trying to take the place of government but merely recognising that government was, at the time, short of funds. They had always hoped that in due course they would be able to gain financial support from the government on the same basis as all grant-aided schools in the country.

He explained in detail the facilities at the school, emphasising the degree to which the classrooms had been constructed with the voluntary labour of the students on Saturday mornings. He described the additional services that Swaneng Hill School took on for the local community – the night school, the Village Development course and the Builders' Brigade. He expected to hand over to an African principal within the next three years and, to get over any government concern about his amateur educational status, he indicated that in the meantime he hoped to hire a qualified and experienced vice-principal to run the academic side of the school.

At the same time, he was anxious to dispel the notion that he had set up the school for the benefit of South African refugees. He explained that of Swaneng's 137 pupils to date, 95 had come from the Bamangwato Reserve and 30 from elsewhere in Bechuanaland, 2 were from Rhodesia and just 10 were South African–born, most of them now resident in Bechuanaland.

Then, in what was an emotional appeal to save his school, Patrick allowed his true feelings of hurt to emerge:

If the Government builds another secondary school in Serowe at a cost of R340,000, without making a substantial grant to Swaneng Hill School, the snub that this would imply, would be interpreted as Government disfavour with Swaneng Hill School. Swaneng Hill School has come into being as a result of self-help through voluntary labour, and generally through the co-operative efforts of many people – volunteer teachers, donors of money from abroad, and pupils and their parents here in Bechuanaland. It is difficult enough to inculcate in people the idea of self-help through voluntary labour, and yet what has been achieved at Swaneng Hill School in this direction could well be destroyed. The pupils of Swaneng Hill School who have built their own laboratory, and who are building their own workshop, who made their own sportsfield and dug the foundation ditches of some of the classrooms, who helped to rebuild the old dam will be dismayed to find no reward and no incentive for their work and to see the Government building another school instead.[12]

And yet, if it was given government support Swaneng Hill could double its planned capacity to 400 students within four years at a cost to government of a quarter of that of the proposed new school. He provided a detailed financial breakdown to prove his point.

As a level of his commitment to education in Bechuanaland more generally, Patrick indicated that he hoped to set up a secondary school in Maun, the principal town in the north-west of the country, where there was currently no secondary school. It would, he proposed, be established on the same low-cost, self-help basis as Swaneng Hill. This was the first time he had openly expressed his aim to found a sister school to Swaneng and, for the moment, the Maun proposal served the purpose of show-ing that Patrick and Liz van Rensburg, with their overseas backing, their enthusiasm and their ideas, were too valuable an asset for Bechuanaland to cast aside casually.

'We hope,' he concluded, 'that we shall all be allowed to go on with our work, encouraged and substantially grant-aided by the elected government.'[13]

Patrick took the challenge of the government's proposal very person-ally and it spurred him into action. He had never applied for aid before, but the time to do so was now or never. It worked. Not only was the government school proposal dropped, the government also agreed to approve grant aid for Swaneng Hill.

Eustace Clark's support must have counted in Patrick's favour, as would any reference to the 1963 education inspectorate's report. Patrick's favourable costings for Swaneng's own expansion must have counted too, because Clark returned from the meeting in Gaborone later in the week with the promise of a government grant of R50 000. The quick climb-down suggests the alternative school proposal was the product of hostile colonial officials in the education department, who would have been happy to see Patrick leave the country.

In practice it took eighteen months for the grant to come through and when it did it had been halved to R25 000. Swaneng Hill School survived and continued to expand, but, in accepting a government grant, Patrick was taking the first step towards his eventual loss of freedom to pursue the alternative model of practical self-help schooling that he had developed since 1962.

At this stage he heard nothing more about his proposed new school for Maun and a year later, in July 1966, government indicated that its priority was to support and expand the three existing schools in the much larger 'tribal' capitals of Kanye, Mochudi and Molepolole in the south-eastern part of the country.

Keen to demonstrate the value of his alternative model of education, Patrick took a truckload of his students and staff (including Liz, Tommy and one-month-old Mothusi van Rensburg) to a weekend work camp at Kgari Sechele Secondary School in Molepolole, where they helped build new classrooms. Furthermore, he offered to send staff to help set up Development Studies and brigades in each of the three schools. Government failed to respond to that offer, but Patrick was pleased to hear that the new secondary school in Mochudi was introducing voluntary student labour, probably influenced by *Kgosi* Linchwe's links with Swaneng.

* * *

During the August school break in 1965 the Van Rensburgs went to spend a couple of weeks with friends in Lusaka. While there Patrick saw an article on the front page of the Review section of the *Observer*, just in from London. The title immediately caught his eye: 'How to Help Them Help Themselves'. It was written by the Marxist-inspired 'alternative economist' Fritz Schumacher.[14] For Patrick the article was a revelation. Here at last was the theoretical basis for what he had been working towards for the past three years. It provided all the intellectual support he had been searching for, and more.

Schumacher had been alerted to the fundamental problem of unemployment and poverty in developing countries while on an economic consultancy in Burma in 1955. He concluded in his 'Buddhist Economics' that 'production from local resources for local needs is the most rational way of economic life'.[15] His disillusionment with classical economics as a solution to the problems of the developing world was compounded by a visit to India in 1962, where he saw the destructive effect of modern technology on the traditional Indian way of life. It was this background that inspired the *Observer* article.[16]

The aid donors of the developing world, complained Schumacher, focused on 'modern sector' growth, as measured by a country's gross national product – the measure of total money flow. Taken as an indicator of 'development', this left out 80 per cent of the population in many developing countries, who were not part of the modern sector.

An urban élite might prosper, but the vast majority suffered neglect, poverty and unemployment on a scale not seen in Europe and North America since the 1930s. Growth, wrote Schumacher, should be focused on where people are living now, not just on new urban areas to which people migrate, leaving their rural homes as an economic wasteland.

The way to achieve rural growth was to use 'intermediate technology', something that was simple and cheap enough to be locally afforded and locally sustained. Foreign aid, focused on intermediate technology and delivered to the people in the places where they lived, would be fruitful, instead of destructive of local communities. What stood in the way? Schumacher asked.

> Perhaps a kind of technological snobbishness which regards with distain anything less than ultra-modern? Perhaps a certain callousness in the attitudes of privileged minorities towards the immense suffering of their homeless, jobless, miserable fellow-men? Or is it lack of imagination on the part of the planners in resplendent offices who find ratios and coefficients more significant than people?[17]

Schumacher's article was an international sensation. His focus on local 'intermediate technology' fired Patrick with the conviction that he had been on the right track all along.

Back in Swaneng, Patrick found new staff member Donald Curtis, who had arrived with his wife, full of ideas for Development Studies and the Village Development course. They were followed in October by Peter and Diane Fewster and their four children. The Fewsters, who were sponsored by War on Want, had been well briefed by Betty Sleath. Diane immediately made herself useful by taking on some of the secretarial and typing work from Liz, as well as setting up a crèche for the children of the staff, teaching First Aid to the Form I students and joining in with the Saturday morning voluntary work.

Peter Fewster, a Science teacher who had worked in Britain to raise funds to support poverty-reduction projects in villages in India, was immediately in tune with Patrick's enthusiasm for localised appropriate technology.[18] He believed in the practical application of Science and realised that Development Studies and the Village Development course needed practical projects to demonstrate the possibilities for localised development using local resources.

In addition to joining the Saturday morning voluntary work on the dam, he took a group of students into the surrounding countryside to view potential natural resources. They found a small range of limestone hills as well as some abandoned cattle hides and goatskins and collected these, together with tree roots, bark and seed pods, for possible use in treating the skins.

A Sunday excursion by the Van Rensburg and Fewster families and some students to the limestone hills in the school truck yielded a good supply of limestone. Fewster and the students of the Village Development course built a small kiln for burning the limestone. This created a fine lime powder that was used in mortar and as a limewash to paint the school buildings and the mud walls of houses to protect them from damage in heavy rainstorms. Limewash also removed the hair from the animal skins, which were further soaked in a tannin solution of roots and seed pods to produce good-quality dark leather.[19]

In the new year of 1966 an English-medium primary school was launched on the Swaneng site. Taught by volunteer Kirsty Thomas, it was initially intended for the children of expatriate staff, but Patrick insisted that it follow the principle of 'education for all' and a number of local Batswana children were duly enrolled, with Mike Hawkes's new wife,

Jan, joining the staff.[20] Fees were charged according to the ability to pay. It attracted quite a few Batswana children, a number of them transferring from the local Newtown Primary School.[21]

***

The minister of education, B. C. Thema, was not impressed by Swaneng Hill's JC results in November 1965.[22] Only thirteen of twenty-one candidates passed. The minister, prompted by his colonial officials, blamed the poor results on the voluntary work done by the students, considering it inappropriate for a secondary education.

The Department of Education was also critical of the fact that a majority of Swaneng's expatriate teachers were unqualified volunteers who only stayed for one or two years. This, in the department's view, led to staffing instability. Patrick, however, was not at all discouraged by the results. He knew that his JC candidates had been the product of the first-come-first-served basis of his first year's intake, as opposed to the highly selective intake of Moeng College, where Minister Thema had been principal.

At the same time, he was convinced that no amount of qualification or longer contract could make up for the enthusiasm, imagination and sheer hard work of his young volunteer staff. Confident that subsequent years would show solid improvement in the JC results, he went ahead with his planned expansion of Swaneng's student numbers. By 1966 the school, with 220 students including 75 boarders, accounted for one-fifth of all secondary students in Botswana.

In anticipation of the criticism of the department, Patrick had already recruited several experienced black teachers from South Africa, two of whom became heads of department. Alie Fataar, a refugee from Cape Town, took on the English department, while Lawrence Notha, a refugee from Johannesburg, headed the Maths department.[23] To fulfil the promise made in his memorandum Patrick appealed to his various sponsors for a qualified, experienced vice-principal who would be responsible for raising academic standards. Oxfam sent him Sheila Bagnall.

Sheila arrived for the first of her eight years in the country in August 1966, just one month before the birth of the independent Republic of Botswana. One of her first tasks, in cooperation with other staff and students, was to help organise the celebrations for that great event, which included a large bonfire on the top of Rra Swaneng.[24]

With what must have been a sense of relief Patrick offloaded onto Sheila much of the day-to-day administration of the school – timetabling, ordering of stock and planning future staffing needs in the light of the high turnover of volunteer staff. Much of it was handed over without explanation, but Sheila had had wide experience and quickly learned how to cope with Patrick's unpredictability.

Her main role, however, was to raise academic standards and she did this by coaching and advising many of the young, untrained, inexperienced volunteer staff, especially on issues such as lesson preparation and class discipline. What the volunteers lacked in experience they made up for in enthusiasm and, helped by Sheila's input, their dedication and the quality of their teaching was soon noted in official circles.

* * *

Patrick first heard of the writer Bessie Head in 1964, when Robin Farquharson, the Liberal Party activist who had, by now, escaped into exile in the UK, wrote to tell him that he had heard she was teaching at a primary school in Serowe. He wrote: 'She is a very special person, she writes English like an angel and I think she is marvellous. Do find her if you haven't already.'[25] It is not clear whether Patrick got to know her in 1964, but she definitely came into his life in 1965.

Bessie Head had been born in 1937, illegitimate and of mixed race, to a white woman in a Pietermaritzburg mental institution. She was put out for fostering and was later sent to an Anglican home for 'coloured' girls. Here she endured harsh discipline, but developed a love of reading and of writing poetry and short stories. She grew up a determined, independent-minded woman.

She worked as a journalist, first in Johannesburg, then in Cape Town, where, in 1961, she met and married Harold Head, a fellow journalist and a member of the South African Liberal Party. He worked and wrote for the fortnightly news magazine *Contact*, then edited by Patrick Duncan.

Bessie had been writing poetry and short stories for a while and from 1962 these began to appear in *New African*, a monthly journal published by

Randolph Vigne, a prominent member of the Cape Liberal Party. Vigne was to become a close friend of Bessie, keeping up a regular correspondence with her in the years to come, publishing her short stories and encouraging her writing.

Her son, Howard, was born in 1962 and the following year Bessie parted from Harold and moved to Johannesburg. She came to Bechuanaland with Howard in 1964 to teach at Tshekedi Memorial School, a primary school in Serowe. She knew nothing about Bechuanaland except that it contained the Kalahari Desert, where she imagined she would have the peace to pursue her writing.[26] As a mixed-race South African, however, she did not feel welcome or accepted in Serowe, and she clashed with some of the school staff. Things came to a head in October 1965, when she abandoned the job, alleging sexual harassment by a member of staff.

Soon afterwards Patrick received a letter from Randolph Vigne asking him to befriend her and help her in any way he could. Patrick found that, having left her primary school employment, Bessie was almost destitute. He lent her money and paid off her numerous debts. He got her some money from Canon Collins's Defence and Aid Fund and gave her Swaneng's old second-hand typewriter – the first typewriter she had ever owned.

Bessie's relationship with Patrick could be fractious at times. She needed the support of a fellow South African refugee; he, often overworked, found her annoying and demanding at times. But Patrick remained loyal to her and, when needed, was always on hand to help her in any way he could.

He and Liz invited Bessie and Howard to spend Christmas 1965 with them. By then the Van Rensburgs had moved into the newly built principal's house at the top of the hill overlooking the school. Bessie met Vernon and Tineke Gibberd at the Van Rensburg Christmas gathering and accepted their invitation to come to Radisele, where Vernon was agronomist for the BDA. After some months at Radisele she moved to Francistown, where she spent several years, during which she completed her first novel, *When Rain Clouds Gather*.

The novel, like most of her subsequent work, was set in Botswana, and one of its lead characters, an agronomist from England, was based heavily on Vernon Gibberd. It was published in New York in 1968 and by Gollancz in the UK the following year. In 1969 she finally returned to settle in Serowe and once more Patrick became a significant figure in her life, featuring in more than one of her subsequent books.

* * *

In late October 1966, a month after Botswana's independence, Thord Palmlund of Sida fulfilled his promise and visited Swaneng, bringing with him Sven Hamrell, the acting director of the Scandinavian Institute of African Studies (now the Nordic Africa Institute). Since their meeting in Stockholm in January 1965 Thord had authorised two Sida grants for Swaneng Hill School, together totalling R46 000.

Patrick was clearly keen to impress his visitors. Thord stayed with the Van Rensburgs, while Sven, whom Patrick did not yet know, stayed with the Kibblewhites. They spent a few days in Serowe, Thord making copious and careful notes of everything he saw, in his quiet, non-committal way. He was not a man to show emotion or express enthusiasm easily but admitted that he was impressed by both the alternative educational model Patrick was developing and the educational support he was giving to South African refugees. He also liked the quality of the low-cost buildings at the school and the commitment of the brigade trainees.

Patrick accompanied his two guests to Gaborone, where Thord and Sven had an appointment with Hugh Murray-Hudson, the permanent secretary at the Ministry of Labour and Social Services, which included the Department of Education. Murray-Hudson, a former Rhodesian colonial official, was Patrick's nemesis at the department and after the meeting Sven told Patrick what had transpired.

As Patrick had suspected, Murray-Hudson was dismissive of the Swaneng approach to education. He considered that Patrick was lucky to have been allowed to build the school at all, claiming he was more interested in South African refugees than in teaching local Batswana students. Not only was this untrue, but Patrick's commitment to take on a small number of South African refugees accounted in large part for Scandinavian support for Swaneng Hill.

Murray-Hudson was particularly dismissive of the low-cost Swaneng school buildings, which he had not, in fact, seen, predicting they would fall down in a few years and it would cost government a lot more to rebuild them. Thord reacted strongly in Swaneng's defence and Sven reported that he had never seen him so angry. While Thord, Sven and Patrick lunched with Gaositwe Chiepe and other education officials that day, 'a heavy, gusting, drenching storm broke over the hastily-built town, lifting roofs off several new high-cost houses'.[27] The fact that Swaneng's school buildings are still standing more than fifty years later would have appealed to Patrick's strong sense of irony.

Figure 11.2: Student volunteers slaughter a goat for a party to celebrate the laying of a concrete floor for a new classroom. (By kind permission of Karl-Hermann Handwerk)

Having seen Thord off at the Gaborone airport Sven returned with Patrick to Serowe. Over the next few days the two of them consolidated what was to become a firm and fruitful friendship. As Sven left in the first week of November 1966, he extended an invitation to Patrick to undertake a lecture tour of the Nordic countries in the new year of 1967.[28]

* * *

Within days of Sven's departure Robert Oakeshott arrived at Swaneng to work as an independent volunteer. Robert was a classically trained journalist and self-taught economist who had been working for the *Financial Times* in London in 1964 when he met and befriended Kenneth Kaunda in the months before Zambian independence.

Recognising in him one of those men who could turn his hand to anything, Kaunda invited him to Zambia to draft the country's Transitional Development Plan.[29] Robert was thus working in the planning department of the government of Zambia at the time of Patrick's visit to Lusaka in August 1965. It is not clear whether they met at this time, but they had friends in common and through them Robert would have heard of Patrick's innovative development work in Serowe. As both journalist and economic planning officer he could not resist going to see for himself.

Robert visited Swaneng Hill School during the first term of 1966 and was immediately captivated by the Van Rensburg charisma, charm and vision. On his return to Lusaka he wrote an article for *The Economist* on the huge problems facing drought-stricken Bechuanaland on the eve of independence. In his opinion, however, a privately started school in Serowe provided an immensely encouraging ray of hope:

> ... even secondary schools can – given the right quality of leadership – be built partly on a self-help basis. In this case a predominantly boarding school has been built for the astonishingly low figure of £200 a place; a major achievement when one considers that Zambia's new secondary schools are costing about £550 a place.
>
> ... [But] this new Serowe school is notable in other important respects as well. There is a deliberate development emphasis in its curriculum; all boys spend two hours a week on theory and practice

of building. A consumer co-operative has been started from the school, and the policy is to use the school as a growth point in the district.[30]

Patrick would have appreciated that reference to 'the right quality of leadership'. He certainly appreciated the publicity, which brought in more donations for Swaneng through the British Humanist Association.[31] Robert had followed up the article with a cheque for £50 (the amount *The Economist* had paid him) and an offer to come and join the work at Swaneng Hill as an ordinary volunteer. Patrick jumped at the offer.

The Robert Oakeshott who arrived at Swaneng Hill School in November 1966 was no ordinary volunteer and in the years that followed he was to make a major contribution to the development and spread of Patrick's ideas. He was a live wire who proved to be an invaluable colleague and 'right-hand man'.[32] His obituarist, Charles Keen, remembered him as 'perhaps the most convivial and worst-dressed man of his generation: even men whose clothes he had borrowed and ruined remained his firm friends, relishing his intoxicating (and often intoxicated) discourse. He had a robust wit and an appetite for absurdity.'[33] This was the man who was to leave his mark on Serowe and much else besides.

Patrick knew that the Development Studies course, now in its second year, needed improvement. He showed it to Robert, who, after some discussion with Donald Curtis and others who had been involved in developing and teaching the subject, assumed responsibility for revising it. After a remarkably short time he came up with a detailed outline of a revised Development Studies syllabus that he proposed be adopted. Patrick immediately saw it as a great improvement and much more appropriate than what they had been working on thus far.[34]

Basically, Robert laid out a contrast between pre-industrial societies and modern developed societies, pointing out that even developed countries had been underdeveloped at one stage. He proposed examining the transformation process and stages that led to industrial development. The course would begin with teaching Form I about the economics of their own environment – local production, supply and demand of the market in the local stores, the consumers' co-operative and how it worked, and the role of banks in the economy.

The course would then survey the socio-economic conditions prevalent in Botswana, including examining the pre-colonial and colonial history that led to the present contrast between the small 'modern sector' and the rest of the country, which was marked by rural underdevelopment.

By Forms II and III the students would be studying the examples of development in Britain, the first to industrialise; the USSR, with its central control of production; Tanzania, as an attempt at an African alternative; and, finally, would return to Botswana to discuss the development opportunities for their own country.[35] Robert's essential point was that all societies evolve continually. Human experiences are universal; they just happen at different times in different places for identifiable reasons. What particularly appealed to Patrick was his conclusion, which comprised 'a local development plan and how to implement it, involving the school and its students'.[36]

The concept of a 'development plan' had become the norm at national level in developing countries. As noted above, Robert Oakeshott had devised Zambia's Transitional Development Plan to cover the independence period and was working in that country's planning department prior to coming to Swaneng Hill. It seemed logical to him, therefore, that if rural development was to mean anything substantial, Serowe should have its own local development plan.

Patrick agreed. He asked Robert to draft one and, as both men envisaged the school as the practical and intellectual hub of local development, it was called the 'Swaneng Development Plan'. It was based on a rough survey of Serowe and surrounding districts, their resources and economic activities, which Robert conducted with the aid of Swaneng students, as a practical exercise incorporated in their Development Studies curriculum.

The main focus of the plan was on primary-school leavers who had failed to get into secondary school. With little or no 'modern sector' employment available to them, they faced either labour migration to South Africa or 'the prospect of poverty-pinched and unsatisfying lives, subsisting on proceeds from the occasional sale of a cow'.[37]

Robert proposed that the development plan be based upon an enlarged and diversified brigade project.[38] He had already identified a number of disciplines, each of which would answer a need in Serowe. A Farmers' Brigade was, in his view, the most important, for in teaching the benefits of modern techniques in beef and dairy farming, it offered the best opportunity to 'change attitudes of young primary-school leavers to life on the land'.[39] In addition, there was scope for brigades in mechanics, carpentry, weaving and dressmaking.

Patrick was attracted to Robert as a fellow spirit with whom he could share some of the responsibility of planning and leadership. Like Patrick, he was not afraid of hard physical work and would at times 'float crazy ideas quite seriously'.[40] When Patrick told him of his dream to set up a sister school and accompanying brigades in Maun, Robert's immediate and enthusiastic response was that they could carry cement to Maun in an oxcart.

Oakeshott did not see this as a 'crazy idea' at all. During his survey of local resources he had estimated that there were approximately 500 oxwagons in and around Serowe, whereas the total amount of motorised transport – tractors, trucks and cars – was barely a tenth of that.[41] He believed, even more than Patrick, in the use of traditional technology and available resources. It was, at times, to become a source of disagreement between the two men.

12 | Expansion and Replication, 1967–1969

Patrick, Liz and the two boys left for Europe in early December 1966, spending time in the UK with Liz's family and numerous friends and supporters. Patrick did the rounds of his various sponsors, providing them with accounts of how their money had been spent and, inevitably, asking for continued support. While he was in the UK Robert Oakeshott sent him 'a full spelling out of an enlarged development brigade with fully detailed costings etc'.[1]

The part Robert was most proud of was the Farming Brigade. He thought it 'a grand project'. Eustace Clark liked it, as did Mr Atkinson at the Department of Agriculture. 'If you can get some backing for it,' he wrote in a covering letter, 'then the whole labour will have been immensely worthwhile.'[2]

In the new year of 1967 Patrick left for a month's lecture tour of Scandinavia. In Sweden he was looked after by Sven Hamrell and Olle Nordberg, Sven's close associate at the Nordic Africa Institute. Sven, who was soon to take over the directorship of the Dag Hammarskjöld Foundation (DHF), was looking for suitable projects to support. The foundation had been founded in March 1962 in memory of the second UN secretary-general, who had died in a controversial plane crash in September 1961 while on a peace mission to the Congo.[3] Meanwhile, Patrick had organised a tight schedule of meetings – lectures, interviews, dinners, lunches – in all the Nordic countries.

In Denmark Patrick met H. E. Kastoft, head of the new Danish International Development Agency (Danida). Kastoft liked Robert's brigade-expansion plan and made some constructive comments about the new Development Studies syllabus. Danida went on to become a major funder of the brigades in Serowe.

In Finland Patrick was looked after by Martti Ahtisaari of the Finnish Development Agency[4] and in Norway he met up again with Cato Aal and several of his previous contacts there. Some of those who attended his lectures knew of Patrick's anti-apartheid past, probably through *Guilty Land*, and this had attracted their attention. He remembers it as a daunting time:

> I was on new ground now and felt diffident about so strongly chal-
> lenging fixed ideas and practices in education, and the vested inter-
> ests they served, but exhilarated and stimulated too, perhaps, because
> people of influence and authority in several countries listened very
> carefully to what I had to say, and found it meaningful.[5]

By the end of the lecture tour Patrick was no longer so diffident about his authority in the field. In his lectures he promoted himself as a way of selling his ideas, which he portrayed as the results of his own hard-earned practical and physical experience. The lecture tour thus became something of an ego trip. At last he had really made it.

To a notable degree he had achieved fame, the dream of which had spurred him on since leaving school. Despite the lack of official recognition of his work in Botswana, here he was respected and listened to intently. His ideas fitted the ethos that already existed among the Scandinavian and other European aid agencies, which saw in him a man who was putting these ideas into practice.

Patrick thus found himself lauded by experts in the fields of develop-ment and education. He was no longer merely enthusing potential spon-sors who wanted to do some good in the 'Third World'. After a mere four years in the field of education, through dedicated hard work, practical experiment and vision, he had turned himself into something of an expert in the new field of 'alternative education'.

Sven asked him to write up his lectures for the Scandinavian Institute of African Studies. The resulting 48-page booklet, *Education and Development in an Emerging Country*, was published later in the year. In it

Patrick described what had brought him to Botswana, the practical origins of his educational ideas and his concern for the vast majority who failed to make it to the holy grail of academic secondary education. He referred to this majority of academic 'drop-outs', who were a common feature of most developing countries, as 'primary wastage'.

The booklet outlined his plans for the future in terms of linking education and development through the brigades and the Development Studies course, which had evolved in his mind in 1964 and had come to fruition through a series of lively discussions or seminars involving all those teaching the subject. These discussions took place fairly regularly at Patrick and Liz's house, so it was very much a joint project.

In the text of the booklet, however, Patrick makes no mention of anybody else who was involved, despite using many of Robert Oakeshott's own words to explain the brigade expansion plan. He merely portrayed the brigades and the Development Studies course as a communal effort under his leadership, which was still undergoing changes.[6] The only mention of others was in a footnote: 'Two members of our staff, Donald Curtis and Robert Oakeshott, worked with me in drafting the present outline syllabus.'[7]

When Robert saw the booklet later in the year he was hurt that his contribution had not been more fully acknowledged. Patrick defended himself by pointing out that it was a joint effort of the whole Swaneng community and that, as principal of Swaneng, he represented everyone and their contributions. It was also true that the donors to whom he appealed placed a great deal of trust in Patrick and it was therefore an essential part of his fundraising appeals that he promote himself as the leading figure in his various projects.

On reflection, Robert probably realised this. He had enormous respect for Patrick and promptly threw himself into writing a course book for Development Studies, a massive project that he worked on for the next three years. He was helped in this by those teaching the course, such as 'Lancashire lass' Alison Kirton, who had arrived at Swaneng as a Geography teacher.

The teachers reviewed and provided feedback on Robert's chapters as they progressed.[8] There were also seminars on the subject. And later, when Robert moved to set up a new school at Shashe River (see below), Patrick took groups there for further discussions. In the process of researching and writing the course book Robert broadened the subject considerably as he searched for the social origins of Britain's early industrialisation. He found it, to his satisfaction, in the period of England's seventeenth-century Civil War.[9] And on the contemporary transformation of societies he expanded the examples to include China, Cuba, Ghana, India, Mexico, Tanzania and Zambia.

By this stage Patrick was an increasing admirer of the development strategies of China and Cuba (although he did not visit either country until the mid-1980s). He had taken to the thoughts of Mao Zedong and was not averse to quoting a Maoist idea or two at morning assembly.

He felt passionately about the importance of Development Studies. The subject was still very much his baby and he was intimately involved at every stage,[10] despite the considerable input of Robert Oakeshott and others. But Patrick was not the man to write a textbook. He would never have allowed himself the time to do the research and sort out the details. His mind was too restless as he continually searched for new ways to alleviate poverty and promote self-help and sustainable development.

Towards the end of 1967 Robert turned up at Patrick's door with a bottle of whisky and a copy of Julius Nyerere's new publication, *Education for Self-Reliance*.[11] Robert was jubilant. They had got it right. Their thinking was in line with the guru of African development. That was something to celebrate. In later years, when writing his memoir, Patrick was to give Robert the acknowledgement that he knew he deserved, describing his work on Development Studies as 'a crowning achievement'.[12]

* * *

Patrick's concept of brigades had caused excitement at community level across the country. In the course of the following few years, and with the encouragement of the government, brigades were established in most of the main towns in the country. The key to their development was the commitment of local community leaders who had learned of Patrick's innovations and saw the opportunity to replicate them in their own communities.

They developed their own variations, but the central concept remained the same: the brigades provided training for primary-school leavers who had failed to gain entry to secondary school; the training, alongside some basic academic education, was tied closely to training in productive skills; and the cost of the training was, as far as possible, covered by income from production. In subsequent years brigades branched out into a whole range of craft industries, though, as we shall see in a later chapter, none as comprehensively as in Serowe under Patrick van Rensburg's leadership.[13]

The expansion and diversification in Serowe followed the Oakeshott plan. Owing to the good rapport Patrick had built up with *Kgosi* Leapeetswe and the general goodwill that his work through the consumers' co-operative and other initiatives had generated within Serowe, it was not a problem to persuade the community of the benefits of establishing training brigades for farming, mechanics and other skills.

A good-sized plot of 300 hectares near Swaneng, on the eastern side of the dam, was allocated for the dairy herd and horticulture of the Farmers' Brigade. Patrick then addressed a public meeting in the *kgotla* at which he explained the proposal to train primary-school leavers in modern farming techniques and principles. It was a well-attended gathering, with many former primary students being pushed forward by their parents.

Ditshwanelo Makwati was typical of some of those who came to the meeting to hear what Patrick had to say. His primary schooling had ended in 1965 because of a lack of finance and since then he had been 'loitering around Serowe'. His family had some land and a few cattle and he was attracted by this white man's proposal to train primary-school leavers to be good farmers. He was one of forty who signed up for that first year's intake of the Farmers' Brigade.[14]

Patrick delegated the management of the brigade to Robert Oakeshott, who regarded it as the most important of the new brigades. Robert threw himself into the challenge with his usual gusto, organising the clearing of the land and the building of an accommodation block. Tom Holzinger, a newly arrived volunteer from the USA, was commandeered with the words 'Old chap – I think you need a programme'.[15]

Nils Bodelsen, a representative of Danida, visited at the end of July. He spent a couple of nights at the school and was lavishly entertained, Serowe-style, with a party at the Van Rensburgs and dinner and a general party at the Serowe Hotel, attended by most of the staff. Sheila described

Bodelsen as 'young, slim and charming and right on the ball when it comes to appreciating Swaneng'.[16]

He was certainly seduced by the project and departed with a promise of funding to the value of £45 000.[17] Much of the money was earmarked for two Danish agronomists for the Farmers' Brigade – Carl Marstrand for the dairy and Holgar Gelting for horticulture, who arrived later in the year. The rest of the money, as it came through, was spent on fencing, livestock, an oxwagon and a donkey cart.

Ditshwanelo and other trainees appreciated the mixture of traditional and modern in the training, although some took time to adjust to the amount of outdoor practical work they had to do. They had been brought up on purely classroom learning. Now, in the Farmers' Brigade, their mornings were dedicated to practical work.

Divided into two groups, their duties alternated: two weeks dairy, two weeks horticulture. Their classroom learning – in English Language, elementary Maths and Science, Development Studies and Farming Theory – was confined to the afternoon, when the school students were not at their desks.[18]

The dairy began daily deliveries of fresh milk, by donkey cart, around the eastern wards of Serowe. Attempts to earn a higher price in Gaborone failed in the face of bulk imports from South Africa. Turning it into yoghurt, however, earned them double the price at the new copper-nickel mining complex at Selebi-Phikwe.[19]

While Patrick relied on Robert for the success of the Farmers' Brigade and gave him a free hand in its day-to-day running, the two men had their differences. Patrick worried that Robert compromised too much on the quality of the brigade dormitory; Robert felt Patrick's insistence on the construction of a large school hall at Swaneng Hill was an unnecessary expense.[20] Patrick regarded the hall as part of his concept of the school as the hub of the community. He was looking to the long-term future and saw a school hall as a facility, not merely for the school, but for the community, for meetings, films and so on.

The hall was built, on a steel frame imported from Johannesburg, with the voluntary labour of students and staff fully engaged in its construction. Regularly at weekends Patrick himself could be seen, with no safety harness or scaffolding, alongside students astride the central roof beam, fixing rafters to the steel frame.

Figure 12.1: Saturday morning voluntary work, with metal frame of the school hall in the background. (By kind permission of the Van Rensburg family collection)

Liz's sister Mary and her South African husband, Aaron Kibel, known to everyone as 'Kib', arrived in Serowe in late December 1967 with their small son, Pete. They had been in Ghana in 1963 and, after spending a couple of years in Aaron's hometown of Cape Town, they wrote to Liz and Patrick asking whether they could join them at Swaneng for a year or two.

Kib, a trained toolmaker and computer engineer, 'was generally a technical genius with wide-ranging experience'.[21] Naturally, the Kibels were welcomed and eagerly awaited. They stayed for five years. Kib took immediate charge of the Mechanical/Engineering Brigade and much else besides. The Mechanical Brigade workshop was built near that of the Builders' Brigade in central Serowe. In due course, the commercial branch of the Mechanical Brigade came to be known as Serowe Engineering.

Kgosi Leapeetswe and DC Eustace Clark were supportive of the expanding brigade complex in the centre of Serowe. A textile workshop soon followed. Lily Mapula was recruited from Johannesburg to operate the industrial sewing machines that Robert had imported and Leapeetswe's aunt, Dikeledi Montshiwa, became the spinning and weaving instructor. A Peace Corps volunteer taught spinning, weaving and silk-screen printing.

When this volunteer left after a year, Liz, who had been involved in the textile workshop from the beginning, took over her role and ran the workshop, cycling daily to and from the centre of town.[22] When, in January 1968, Liz advertised for two new recruits for the textile workshop, she had 100 applicants, which showed, as Robert observed, 'operations of this kind clearly answer to a very real demand'. A grant of £2 000 arrived towards the end of February from the UK's Dulverton Trust, for the expansion of the textile workshop.[23]

Figure 12.2: Liz and Pat in a happy mood. (By kind permission of Benny Wielandt)

* * *

In 1967 Sheila began to grow concerned about Patrick's well-being. She wrote to a friend in the UK: 'If you could see what he had created here in five years you'd think he was a magician. But at the moment he is frightfully tired and simply cannot concentrate on anything.'[24]

It appeared that the only time Patrick could unwind was at a party. In general a party would be thrown at any time of celebration, but at other times, when the stress of overwork and responsibility became too much for him, Patrick would simply say, 'Let's have a party'. At the very time that Sheila was writing the above letter a spontaneous party developed at Patrick and Liz's house. Despite the fact that the generators packed up, as Sheila wrote the following morning:

> It turned out to be a very good party indeed. We danced to the bat-tery radio and had a really gay time by candle light. Pat was terrific. Despite his bulk, he dances very well and is an excellent mimic i.e. he can mimic anyone else's dancing or mannerisms. When he relaxes, he goes down with a bang, and last night he was enormous fun.[25]

Meanwhile, the Department of Education continued to worry about the unconventional school and about Patrick's methods. Education Officer Ken Pascoe had visited Swaneng Hill in June 1967, a time when Patrick was suffering from stress and exhaustion. Sheila took charge of the 'inspection', which consisted of her spending four hours talking to Pascoe in her room, reassuring him that all was well. Pascoe did not see a single class and wrote a favourable report. Within the department, how-ever, the general feeling was that Vice-Principal Bagnall had pulled the wool over Pascoe's eyes.

In September the inspectorate returned to Swaneng in force. This time the delegation was headed by the newly promoted director of education, Gaositwe Chiepe, who had last inspected the school in a more junior capacity soon after it opened in 1963. She was accompanied by Pascoe and Education Officer Sebele.

Patrick was in good form and the inspectors were impressed by the quality of teaching, especially by the two South African heads of depart-ment, Alie Fataar and Lawrence Notha. But Chiepe reserved special praise for the untrained volunteers, who presumably had been her chief concern. Sheila Bagnall reported her as saying: 'This is teaching as it should be … Far and away better than any other school in the country. Give me a bunch of enthusiastic volunteers any time if they are all like these … You've done a fine job of staffing, Pat.'[26]

Sheila modestly did not mention her own contribution to this achievement but recognised that Chiepe's assessment was a great feather in Patrick's cap, especially considering the suspicion with which he was normally regarded in government circles. She believed these concerns stemmed partly from his South African connections, but also that there was some jealousy about the amount of foreign funding and the number of volunteer teachers who came to Swaneng.

Government appeared to feel that these should be at the disposal of the Department of Education. As Sheila observed, however, both the funding and the volunteers came specifically to Swaneng because of what Patrick was doing. Foreign aid donors liked to see the results of their donations.[27]

In November Patrick received a letter indicating that the department was considering his Maun project.[28] He was elated and started speculating that if he took a work camp to Maun in April they could get some buildings up in time to open the following September. It was an ambitious thought, especially as the building work at Swaneng Hill was slipping behind. As Patrick and Sheila looked over the list of staff to be housed in the new year and the houses available, he said to her, 'I boggle. Unboggle me.' 'Fat hope of that!' she remarked in a letter the next day.[29]

They saw off the last of the student boarders for the summer break in the first week of December and that evening Patrick came to Sheila's room and they talked into the early hours. As she recalled in a letter the following evening:

> What a relief it is to have someone like Pat at the head of things. I know that my account of things here often gives the impression of chaos and this is often true of the peripheral things, but the solid core of education and development goes on in the middle. I really felt, last night, that Pat is a great man. He talked so reasonably yet excitedly about his ideas.[30]

The 1967 end-of-year Junior Certificate results were a cause of great celebration: thirty-one of the thirty-four who had sat the exam passed. As Patrick recalled, 'and celebrate we did – wildly'.[31] The end of year, in fact the end of every term, was party time and parties were often the only time

Patrick really let his hair down, relaxed and talked of trivialities. But the end-of-term parties were also tinged with sadness as it was a time when some of the staff left: most were on short contracts of only a year or two.

Bishi Mmusi, who was a student at Swaneng Hill from 1965 to 1969, observed that on these occasions Patrick could be seen wandering off on his own with head bowed. He was clearly troubled. Each term he lost staff he had got to know and value just when, after a year or two in the country, they were at their most productive and most imaginative. And each time, with their departure, their special innovative skills and projects were lost to the school and the community.

New staff would be coming to replace them, but he would have to start all over again, explaining his concepts and inspiring them with 'the spirit of Swaneng'. Patrick was, thought Mmusi, 'a victim of his own ideas'. He took too much upon himself and had no project team with whom to share some of the responsibility and new ideas.[32]

* * *

Patrick and Liz flew via Francistown and Livingstone to Chobe with their two young sons for a few days' holiday in early 1968, returning to Swaneng to receive the news that the government had changed its mind and wanted him to open a new school at Tonota instead of Maun.[33]

Patrick concurred, simply shifting his Maun plan to Tonota, a small town along the 'line of rail' about 120 kilometres north of Palapye and 30 kilometres south of Francistown. With barely time to draw breath he instructed Sheila to admit 80 extra students to Swaneng for Form I in 1968, for transfer to Tonota as Form IIs when the new school opened in January 1969. He declared that Swaneng would provide a work camp to prepare the new site during the April school break.

Land allocation at Tonota was in the gift of the Serowe-based Central District Council, so there was no problem identifying a suitable site near the Shashe River and it was decided to name the school after the river. In addition to its position near a water supply, the Shashe River School was not far from a sizeable population in Francistown, from which it could hope to draw trainees for its brigades. This time, unlike in Swaneng in 1962–1963, Patrick already had the whole concept clear in his mind. The new project would benefit from the mistakes made at Swaneng. In particular, the school and the brigades would be closely aligned, to provide two tiers of education within the one school.

Robert Oakeshott was the obvious first choice to head the new school. By March, however, it was clear that Patrick's ideas for the new institution and Robert's were starting to diverge. Where cost-cutting was concerned Patrick was not going to be nearly as radical as Robert would have assumed, and he suspected that Patrick was under pressure from government.

Patrick proposed having a school hall and virtually insisted on special offices for heads of department. Robert regarded both of these as a waste of money. Patrick also thought that the principal's office should be big enough for meetings of the school board, which Robert felt could be perfectly adequately held in a classroom.[34] Patrick's vision had not reverted to the ivy-clad brick buildings of English private schools, but he was clearly looking to the future, when Shashe River School would be a major institution, of which its students and staff would be proud.

He wanted quality staff housing that would attract the local Batswana teachers of the future. It had been with this in mind that he had built the Swaneng principal's house on the hill overlooking the school. He also understood only too well that government's request for him to found a school at Tonota was not the result of any newfound enthusiasm for his innovative ideas; the attraction was his ability to raise foreign aid and staff the school without recourse to hard-pressed government funds.

For the best part of six months Patrick prevaricated about whether or not Robert would be the best choice to take on the new school, and Robert consoled himself with the thought that since the school plans were being 'sharply modified' and the confidence between himself and Patrick was not what it had been, he would probably be better off out of it. As he explained in a letter home, he had commitments until the end of August and would possibly stay until the end of the year, but then he would return to the UK.[35]

With the headship of the new school still in abeyance, a site engineer was appointed, local labour was hired to clear the site and the work camp from Swaneng Hill went ahead in April. On the day school broke up that month, four trucks conveyed '120 students, ten members of staff, an electricity generator, wheelbarrows, picks, shovels, food for everyone, axes for chopping wood and portable latrines' to the Shashe River site.[36] Patrick spent most of the month at Shashe, with Sheila left behind to carry on with 'normal' work at Swaneng. Later in the month Patrick came back and collected Liz and the two boys.

Figure 12.3: A work camp at Shashe River School in 1969, with Robert Oakeshott (*back row, second from left*). Standing (*back row, extreme right*) is Oats Pitso (by then on the Swaneng staff). Robert and Oats were key to the success of Patrick's projects at this stage. (By kind permission of Karl-Hermann Handwerk)

Despite the hostile attitude of many within the Department of Education, the depth of support for Patrick's efforts at the very top of government was revealed by the arrival at Shashe for a long weekend of Quett Masire, now vice-president, minister of finance and minister for rural development. He brought with him Quill Hermans, head of development planning in the Ministry of Finance. More surprising was the presence of Hugh Murray-Hudson from the education department, who had been so scathing about the quality of building at Swaneng, despite not having inspected it.

Perhaps Masire had deliberately invited him, knowing it was an invitation Murray-Hudson could not turn down. Nearly fifty years later Masire, by then former president of Botswana, recalled vividly a most enjoyable weekend of physical labour at Shashe, during which he had helped staff and students build a lime kiln to render the abundance of limestone in the area.[37]

The enthusiasm of the vice-president for Patrick's self-help and voluntary labour principles may have been obvious, but Masire has revealed that, apart from Patrick's critics in the Department of Education, there were many within the Cabinet who did not trust him.[38] Most of them had been through the Tiger Kloof Institute and were acutely aware of South Africa's divisive education system, which had led to the closure of that worthy institution.

The apartheid Bantu Education Act of 1953, aimed at training black people for manual and menial tasks, deprived them of access to the high-quality academic schooling offered to whites. Now here was an Afrikaner, who had come to Botswana as a refugee, saying that an education with a strong emphasis on practical training and manual tasks was more suitable for Botswana's students than a high-level academic education. Was Van Rensburg trying to replicate the South African system in Botswana? Besides this, he was challenging their perceptions of what entailed 'a good education'.[39]

Despite Masire's obvious show of support, every time Patrick went to Gaborone he could perceive that government thinking on secondary schooling was leaning increasingly towards the academic and, as he saw it, élitism.[40] Nevertheless, he was convinced that he was on the right track and, while he became increasingly despondent about the future of Swaneng, he was offered the opportunity to share his ideas at a regional conference on 'Education in Predominantly Rural Countries'.

The conference, scheduled for the last week of June, was hosted by the University of Botswana, Lesotho and Swaziland (UBLS) at its campus in Roma, outside Maseru, the capital of Lesotho. The government of Botswana might not have been entirely favourably disposed towards Patrick, but there was a growing international awareness that he was onto something in Serowe and he was invited to explain his ideas to the conference. He was not able to attend in person as it would have entailed a journey through South Africa, but Sheila Bagnall went in his place and read his paper.

Patrick's ideas had advanced considerably in the five and a half years since the founding of Swaneng Hill School. He recommended that the widespread establishment of multiple secondary schools with academic focus should be abandoned and replaced by large post-primary institutions that covered all aspects of learning and training. He argued that

> technical and academic subjects ought not to be taught in separate institutions, in isolation from each other, but in the same institution, and that students specialising in either should take subjects in the other. Administrators, teachers, community developers and bankers all need to know what technology is about; technologists, artisans and scientists need education in the humanities.[41]

Sheila Bagnall reflected that Patrick's paper was primarily about 'not producing an elitist class'. She believed the message 'really struck home' at the conference, although she was sceptical about whether, in reality, any more than lip service would be paid to his ideas.[42] In fact, the paper was about a lot more than a critique of élitism. He was passionate about rural development and was convinced that a focus on academic secondary schooling, with limited practical training for the less able, not only bred an élite but abandoned the vast majority to a life of rural poverty and underemployment.

A developing country, in particular, needed a well-trained workforce, with a combination of academic, practical and manual skills.[43] Tellingly, the government-produced *Botswana Daily News*, which named the Gaborone civil servants who attended the conference, did not mention Patrick's paper.[44]

On Sheila's return to Serowe she found Patrick even more despondent than when she had left. He confided that he was fed up with running a school, insisting that he was 'an innovator and not a consolidator'. Sheila reflected that she would like to be more of an innovator herself, but she was too busy running around trying to consolidate Patrick's innovations.[45]

A few days later there was an opportunity to show off Patrick's latest innovation, a local newspaper. It was first published on the day of the Serowe Agricultural Show, Saturday 6 July 1968. An independent local newspaper was something Patrick felt was an essential part of community education and for that reason the early editions were written entirely in Setswana, to reach the largest possible audience. Although initially aimed at a local Serowe audience, the paper, called *Mmegi wa Dikgang* ('The Reporter'), was Botswana's first independent newspaper.

Produced by the students of the Printers' Brigade, initially under the supervision of Aaron Kibel, the paper contained mostly local Serowe news and letters to the editor. Typed in double column, it sold for one cent and consisted of several single sheets that could be posted on walls or pinned to trees for maximum readership. Although very simple, the production was of higher quality at the time than the government's cyclostyled *Daily News*.[46]

A second edition came out the following month, but then the paper suffered the perennial Swaneng problem of transient staff. Aaron Kibel transferred to run the Mechanical Brigade and there was a gap of two and a half years in the production of the newspaper.

* * *

Patrick continued to overwork himself. He admitted to Sheila in September that he was 'exhausted and hate[d] schools'. She feared he might be heading for a breakdown and wished he would go abroad for a while to raise funds, or even just to Shashe for a week and lose himself in physical construction work, which he always seemed to find relaxing.[47]

It was hardly surprising that he was so exhausted, with all his responsibilities in Serowe – school, brigades, consumers' co-operative, as well as the construction work at Shashe and trips to Gaborone to negotiate various issues with government. The opening of a flight connection by the newly established Botswana Airways that took in Serowe on the regular Gaborone–Francistown route greatly eased the connection between Serowe and the capital before the tarred road was completed. Patrick and Seretse Khama were among its most frequent users.[48]

As Vernon Gibberd, who took over the Farmers' Brigade from Robert Oakeshott in 1968, has remarked: 'Patrick was like a juggler – except that if he dropped one skittle, he would bend down and pick up two more.'[49] By the end of October he had managed to raise enough pledged funding for Shashe River School – most of it from Sweden's Sida – to last for seven years, and all of that in just ten months since the project had first been mooted.[50]

At the same time, he managed to persuade the government to promise a grant of R50 000 to start his long-planned school at Maun. It was only then that the impracticality of trying to set up a third school 700 kilometres away by road, on top of his responsibilities in Serowe, began to hit home.[51] A few months later he told Sheila he had given up on Maun, admitting it was 'a romantic dream' for which the problem of transport was too great. Instead, he turned his attention to Mahalapye, the next town, 70 kilometres down the 'line of rail' from Palapye.[52]

Meanwhile, time was running out for the appointment of a principal for Shashe River School – 1 160 students were due to arrive at the end of January 1969, 80 of them transferring from Swaneng Hill, where they would have completed Form I. In addition, a further 80 trainees were expected for the anticipated Builders' and Farmers' and Textile brigades. Patrick's search for a suitable African principal, Motswana or South African, had failed and at the end of October he turned once more to his original choice, Robert Oakeshott. He was prepared to offer Robert the freedom to conduct his own staff recruitment, administration and so on, with no interference from him. After a couple of days' thought Robert accepted.[53]

In mid-November Patrick, Robert and Sheila travelled to Gaborone to get government approval for Robert's appointment. Patrick argued passionately on behalf of the candidate, who had, for once, been spruced up in a new suit bought for the occasion. Even though the members of the Department of Education were, in Robert's view, 'a highly cautious & conservative bunch', Patrick won them over.[54]

In early January, after a short holiday in Europe, Robert was installed in a rondavel on the Shashe River site. His contract was for a minimum of two years, but he felt that 'so long as there [were] no disputes with Patrick' he would probably stay for three. By then the school would have reached its full size and it 'would be time … to hand over to someone with more orthodox qualifications & experience'.[55]

* * *

With Vernon Gibberd now in charge of the Farmers' Brigade in Serowe and Robert Oakeshott settled at Shashe River there was slightly less for Patrick to worry about and 1969 began on a positive note. A report by J. W. Hanson, an American academic, on the educational needs of Botswana praised the Botswana government for 'permitting, then supporting and extending, a model of educational innovation (Swaneng Hill)'.

Hanson observed that this 'spirit of innovation' was the most encouraging element in Botswana's education system. It gave the country 'its unusual professional claim to external assistance'.[56] Patrick was already aware that it

Swaneng Hill School

'Best we have had so far'

OUR results in the Cambridge Overseas School Certificate examination this year were the best we have had so far; they compare favourably with those of the other schools which presented candidates for the examination.

What is very pleasing to us is that we have been able to achieve these examination results hand in hand with many other activities. It is well-known that we are very concerned about social, cultural and economic development in Botswana, and that our students engage frequently in voluntary work. We are also anxious to make the money we can find go as far as possible. The students cook all their own meals except midday meals on week days. They clean their own dormitories and

1968/69 Matric Results

After the results of the Cambridge Matric were published earlier this year, KUTLWANO asked the principals of three of the schools to comment on these results. First, Mr. van Rensburg, of Swaneng, and then Mr. Smith of Moeding, and lastly, Mr. Russell of Gaberones.

classrooms and, of course, do all their own washing and ironing.

The money that is saved in this way is used to take in even more students and Swaneng has been able to grow so rapidly into the country's largest post-primary institution partly because of the work of

Mr. P. van Rensburg, Principal of Swaneng Hill School at Serowe, and his wife, with a view of Swaneng in the background.

PHOTO: SANDY GRANT

Figures 12.4a and b: The principals of Swaneng Hill and Moeding assess their schools' results, *Kutlwano*, June 1969. (By kind permission of Karl-Hermann Handwerk)

was his innovative approach to education that enabled him to raise funding abroad. And on this occasion the government seems to have recognised this, for soon afterwards the Department of Education gave its initial approval for his plan to set up a third secondary school and brigade complex at Mahalapye.

There was further positive news when, on the evening of 13 March 1969, Jack Smith, of the education department, rang with the Cambridge School Certificate results for 1968. Swaneng Hill had two Firsts, eight

students in the gardens, in building their own school, in maintaining it and keeping it tidy, in catering for themselves. Our students have been prepared to accept lower living standards than students in other schools on the grounds that money saved would be used to accomodate more and more students and to raise our standards of education. The good results we have had this year have now made good our claim in respect of our education standards.

There is another purpose to the work that our students do. It is important to give them as much responsibility as possible because when they leave us they must be self-reliant in addition to holding an examination certificate. And most of them appreciate this.

P. VAN RENSBURG.

Moeding School

Good, if not Outstanding, Results

MOEDING College has a record of good, if not outstanding, results in the Junior Certificate and C.O.S.C. examinations. In the December 1968 Cambridge School Certificate, Moeding obtained three passes in Division 1 and no failures out of a total entry of 20 candidates. This is very encouraging. Exam results are important because in this competitive age, they are used as a standard by which a person is selected for a particular job, or for training of some kind. Exam results are also very often used as a standard by which to judge a school. There is, however, danger in both these attitudes, and particularly the latter.

Schools are not knowledge shops where the student pays his fees and is supplied with knowledge, and the best school is the one where you get the best quality of knowledge for your money — as if knowledge was dispensed like pumpkins or second-hand cars.

Having recognised then, that exam results must be seen in their right perspective, and not magnified to look all important, it is useful to examine them and see what light they shed on the school and its methods.

The candidates who sat for the COSC exam at the end of 1968 first entered the College in January 1964 as part of an intake of 60, and 57 of them sat the Junior Certificate exam three years later. Of these 57, 1 passed in Class I, 21 in Class II, and 28 in Class III, while 7 failed. The pupil who passed in Class I, 17 of those who passed in Class II and 1 who passed in Class III and one boy from another school were admitted into Form IV in 1967. One would expect that a form with such a high proportion of good J.C. results would obtain good results in the Cambridge exam, and this proved to be the case.

This is not intended in any way to belittle the hard work put in by both pupils and teachers. But it is an important fact or when comparing Moeding's results with those from other schools, several of which were unable, for one reason or another, to apply such a rigid selection as did Moeding.

In future, Moeding, like several other schools, will be entering a larger number of candidates. This means that instead of entering one-third of those who sit the J.C. exam, the College will enter about three-quarters. This is right, because one would like to see every pupil who enters Form I given the chance of taking the Cambridge exam, but it also means that, while one hopes the good candidates will continue to get good results, there will be a larger number of average candidates whose results are unlikely to be of such a high standard.

This brings us back to the point made earlier, that an academic certificate is only one of the good things which a pupil takes away from a good school, and that academic achievements are one, but only one, of the standards by which a school should be judged.

K. M. SMITH.

9

Seconds, seven Thirds, three Passes and only three Fails – the best results it had ever achieved, and way above expectations. Not only that, but all the unmarried mothers had done well. 'A credit to them,' Sheila observed; but it was also a credit to Patrick's insistence on readmitting pregnant schoolgirls after they had given birth.

With these results Swaneng Hill had 'knocked the crack school, St. Joseph's, into a cocked hat' and were only beaten by Moeding, which Sheila dismissed as 'a missionary school which does nothing else but swat [sic]'.[57] It was party time again! Evening study was cancelled and the staff assembled at Patrick and Liz's for drinks. While the party was in full swing the minister of education, B. C. Thema, phoned from Gaborone with his congratulations. He was no longer scathing; indeed, he stressed that he was 'particularly pleased as Swaneng does so much more than just exam work'.[58] Neil Parsons believes that it must have been Gaositwe Chiepe who converted Thema to appreciate Swaneng. Parsons recalls a conversation with Thema at about this time:

> Thema (as an ex Tiger Kloof teacher in the 1930s) told me in 1969 that he was extremely impressed, after previous doubts whether PvR was a dilettante without staying power, he now saw Swaneng as reviving the original Tiger Kloof policy of prioritizing industrial trade skills together with academic skills.[59]

Sheila's worries about Patrick's mental health were temporarily washed away: 'Pat looks like the Sun – so radiant is he. And Liz is so tremendously happy, too. Millions of problems remain, but at least these academic successes help.'[60]

For Patrick, the Form V results proved that his policy of practical and voluntary work need not interfere in any way with the quality of the students' academic standards. Indeed, he believed it enhanced them, in that he was offering a more holistic education. Good results, however, carried a sting in the tail, for they attracted national attention, which resulted in applications from all over the country from students with the highest primary leaving results. This may have pleased Sheila, who saw academic standards as her responsibility, but it worried Patrick, who knew that the parents of those children expected an academic education that would be, in his words, 'a ladder to privilege', the very attitude he was hoping to change.

13 | Time of Crisis, 1969–1971

By 1969 Swaneng was a large, thriving community, with Patrick van Rensburg respected as, in effect, a new *kgosana*, or sub-chief, with his own 'ward' within Serowe. In the course of 1969, however, it became apparent that, as principal, he was not coping with his myriad responsibilities.

This could partly be attributed to the sheer size of the school, now nearing 400 students. There were several schools in the country of this size, but Swaneng Hill claimed to be different and was increasingly recognised as such. A school like this, with all its innovation, imaginative teaching, and practical community and voluntary work – the very essence of 'the spirit of Swaneng' – required Patrick's constant energy and attention.

It called on every ounce of his charisma to inspire new young volunteer teachers and the whole student body. This dependence on Patrick was highlighted by Carl Gunnar Marstrand, the Danida volunteer at the Farmers' Brigade, who observed that the expatriates at the school and the brigades '[were all] alight with idealism … Yet, without a stout and dynamic personality as PvR to co-ordinate and find direction for our efforts, rather little would have come of our idealism in terms of creating any durable effects.'[1]

By 1969, however, Patrick was seldom in direct touch with the students, and many of them were becoming increasingly sceptical about doing their own catering and giving up their Saturday mornings for manual and community work when they had 'more important' revision for exams to do.

Figure 13.1: The Van Rensburg family at Swaneng c.1970: Patrick, Tom, Liz and Mothusi. (By kind permission of the Van Rensburg family collection)

That October Patrick sought the advice of several of his most trusted members of staff: Lawrence Notha, Oats Pitso and Daniel Jankie. Oats and Daniel, former students, had joined the staff, Oats as a teacher of Setswana and Daniel as coordinator between brigades and school. From these discussions it became clear that Patrick was losing touch with student thinking.

In the early years he had known every one of the students by name, had paid close attention to their concerns and aspirations, and had been able to encourage and inspire them to take responsibility for their own discipline and voluntary work. Now it seemed that the school had just got too big for one person to handle in that way.

Size, however, was not the only problem. There was also Patrick's preoccupation with a never-ending stream of new educational and developmental projects. He may have, in his own mind, already 'moved on' from Swaneng Hill. This, however, remained unspoken in the discussions, and it was decided that dividing the students into four 'houses' would make the school more manageable and personal. Leaving Lawrence Notha to take charge of this reorganisation, Patrick departed for a conference in Moshi, Tanzania.

At the end of October he returned in high spirits amid a welcome shower of rain. During the inevitable party that followed he expounded his latest idea – to build a co-operative hotel. In Moshi he had stayed in a hotel built and owned by a coffee growers' co-operative. Serowe, he declared, needed just such a hotel. The Serowe Hotel was too expensive and too dominated by the old white élite. He would approach the consumers' co-operative and get their support.

The co-op agreed to raise the capital and was allocated land on the side of Serowe Hill, overlooking the centre of town. The hotel was designed piecemeal by Patrick. The central building would contain a bar and restaurant, with an open balcony overlooking the town, while accommodation rondavels with covered walkways would stretch out on either side.

The buildings would be constructed of local stone, with thatched roofs, in what had become Patrick's version of modernised traditional Botswana architecture. The building was undertaken through the early 1970s by the

Figure 13.2: The Tshwaragano Hotel, Serowe. (By kind permission of Benny Wielandt)

Builders' Brigade and their trainee graduates, one of whom, Nthaga Keoraletse, recalls doing the thatching.[2] The hotel was largely responsible for spawning the Thatchers' Brigade, an offshoot of the Builders' Brigade. Although still far from complete, the hotel opened in 1971 as the Tshwaragano ('working together') Hotel and became the favoured haunt of the staff of Swaneng and the brigades.

Meanwhile, problems for Patrick had continued to mount through 1969. On 16 December the trainees of the Farmers' Brigade came out on strike, although the word 'strike' was never used. With 60 cows to be milked and 2 000 chickens to be fed, a speedy resolution was imperative. Carl Marstrand and Charles Gott 'heroically took care of the animals',[3] while Vernon Gibberd took the problem to Patrick.

It was indicative of Patrick's loss of influence with the students and trainees that he did not, as he would have done in earlier years, speak directly to the trainees himself. Perhaps he saw this as a wider cultural problem, for he sought the help and advice of the chief, *Kgosi* Sekgoma Khama, who had taken over as acting *kgosi* from his older brother, Leapeetswe, who was on study leave in the UK.

Sekgoma offered to listen to the trainees' grievances and that evening he, Patrick, Vernon Gibberd, Carl Marstrand, Tom Holzinger and the striking trainees crowded into the Marstrand house on the farm site. The trainees seemed comfortable with *Kgosi* Sekgoma in the room, which made it more like a *kgotla* meeting, with every person free to speak his mind. Most of them spoke very well, partly in English, partly in Setswana.[4]

Basically, they felt their concerns were not being listened to. Their complaints were essentially threefold. First, there was too much manual labour with not enough financial reward. They felt they were being used as free labour on the farm. They shared facilities with the school students and contrasted their half-day's labour seven days a week with the small amount of voluntary practical work performed by the others.

This led to the second complaint: dissatisfaction with the quantity and quality of their classroom learning. As far as they were concerned, 'education' entailed classroom work. Finally, the first cohort would soon complete their training and they complained that there was nothing for them at the end – no certificates and no jobs.

From Patrick's viewpoint, they clearly failed to realise the level and value of knowledge, skills and experience that they acquired and developed through practical farm work. And they failed to appreciate that it was production from the farm that largely paid for their training. As far as employment was concerned, Patrick, and Robert Oakeshott for that matter, had assumed that the trainees would see the entrepreneurial potential in the modern farming techniques they had been taught and would become self-employed farmers. This entrepreneurial spirit would somehow emerge from their enhanced skills and academic learning, with its special emphasis on Development Studies. Fortunately, Patrick realised this was not the time to give the striking trainees a lecture on the subject and after they had expressed their grievances, they withdrew.

After further discussion with the staff it was agreed that, rather than expel the lot, as the *kgosi* had suggested, the final-year trainees would be sent home for a two-week holiday. On their return their allowances would be slightly increased and efforts would be made to set up some sort of co-operative venture when they graduated the following year.[5]

In the Swaneng Hill School Newsletter, written just after the event, Patrick showed no recognition of the depth of the crisis. Indeed, neither here nor in his later memoir was a 'strike' as such even acknowledged. He referred in the newsletter to a single disgruntled trainee who had been 'deliberately and systematically spreading mistrust and ... refusing to obey instructions'.[6]

This was a very different attitude from the earlier insistence that students and trainees be involved in decision-making. It illustrated that in stressful times, when he was not getting his own way, Patrick could develop 'tunnel vision' and become quite autocratic. In his book *The Serowe Brigades*, written seven years later and published in 1978, he refers only to some resentment among the trainees 'in the early days' about the amount of work they had to do.[7]

The strike had, in fact, revealed a weakness at the heart of the brigade system: namely, the lack of employment opportunities for many of the trainee graduates, who were not culturally attuned to becoming self-employed entrepreneurs. This applied particularly to the trainees of the Farmers' Brigade, for whom setting up a farming project required far too large a capital outlay.

Figure 13.3: The Farmers' Brigade delivering fresh milk in Serowe. (By kind permission of the Khama Memorial Museum, Serowe)

The following year, in response to Patrick's promise to set up a co-operative project for the qualifying trainees, a group of them formed 'The 1970 Settlers' Association'. They were led by Tom Holzinger and Phenyo Nthobatsang, an agronomist with experience in irrigated horticulture in South Africa. They established an irrigated enterprise near the new mining town of Selebi-Phikwe, selling fresh vegetables to the mining community. After only six months, however, the project had to be abandoned because of problems with the water supply.[8]

* * *

Ever since settling in Botswana Patrick had kept in close touch with friends and contacts in and from South Africa. Besides his commitment to his Scandinavian donors to take up to 10 per cent of South African students, there were always a number of South Africans on the staff of Swaneng and the brigades. Some of these were refugees, like Lawrence Notha and Alie Fataar, while others, usually white, were volunteers.

It was well known among the anti-apartheid community in South Africa that Patrick van Rensburg was a safe pair of hands in Botswana.

South African refugees could always be confident that he would do what he could to help them, Indeed, Patrick was well aware that Lawrence was secretly involved in the underground network that conveyed ANC refugees to Zambia and other points north.

In June 1969 Patrick took on an experienced teacher and refugee friend of Notha, David Ngqaleni, to teach Science. Unfortunately, David had not yet been granted refugee status, which left him under constant threat of being returned to South Africa. The Botswana government was under pressure from its powerful and hostile neighbour, which, at any moment, could isolate and cripple the country economically. Nevertheless, it stood by its international obligation to accept and respect political refugees, although in doing so it faced South African assertions that it was 'harbouring terrorists'.[9]

David's position was, therefore, very precarious and his situation reached a crisis point in December 1969, when he was issued with an expulsion order, to take effect on Monday 5 January 1970. He had appealed against it but had heard nothing. With time running out Patrick urged him to try to get a personal interview with President Khama, who was visiting Serowe for a few days before Christmas. But his request for an interview was turned down.

Patrick was furious. Throughout his time in Botswana a powerful underlying motivation for his innovative educational and developmental work was to create a proven model of successful, self-reliant and sustainable development that could, one day, be replicated in his beloved South Africa, if and when he was ever allowed to return.

In the meantime, he felt he must do what he could for the liberation struggle – which, in his case, was to take on refugees as students and as teachers. This was now being thrown back in his face. To Patrick it was simply obvious that David Ngqaleni was a genuine and vulnerable refugee who needed a safe haven, yet Botswana, the country to which Patrick had given so much of his restless heart and his physical and mental energy, was on the verge of sending this vulnerable man back to almost certain imprisonment and probable torture and early death in South Africa. Surely this was just a piece of bureaucratic heavy-handedness?

If it was not and David Ngqaleni really was to be returned to South Africa, Botswana was not a country to which he wanted to give any more of his time. He mulled over his options that night, discussing the matter with Liz, and she agreed. The following day, Tuesday 23 December, he phoned the Khama home in Serowe and left a message with Lady Ruth Khama to the effect that if David was driven out Patrick would resign all his commitments and leave the country. The next morning he heard from Seretse Khama's personal adviser in Gaborone that the president had already turned down David's appeal.[10]

Patrick told Sheila of his threat to resign and leave the country and they discussed where he might go. Presuming he would set up another Swaneng-type school, Sheila assured him she would do her best to follow him, as would many of the Swaneng staff. 'I am so thankful,' she wrote, 'that Pat has reverted to thinking about individuals and his loyalties to them that I am prepared to do whatever he thinks best.'[11]

Patrick was scheduled to leave the country for a fundraising trip to Europe on 2 January, just three days before David's time ran out, and he resolved to make one last attempt to get the expulsion order rescinded. While passing through Gaborone on his way to catch a flight to Lusaka and London he visited the president's office in person and got the expulsion order delayed, at least until after his return from Europe. David was finally told he must leave by the end of February, at which point he moved to the safety of Zambia and Swaneng lost a good Science teacher.[12]

By then three more South Africans had joined the Swaneng staff. They were Cliff Meyer, Jackie Cock and Jackie's friend Dottie Ewan. They came as volunteers rather than refugees and were prepared to stay for the long haul. Patrick noted that Cliff Meyer, who had abandoned training as a Catholic priest and had worked as a journalist in Rhodesia and taught in Lesotho, 'quickly took to our policies – as did Jackie Cock and Dottie Ewan. All three … understood what we were attempting at Swaneng and all were to make significant contributions to its development.'[13]

As fellow South Africans they felt a particular loyalty to Patrick and proved valuable friends in the time of crisis that lay ahead. Jackie went on to become a professor of Sociology at the University of the Witwatersrand in Johannesburg and wrote *Maids and Madams*, about domestic workers in South Africa.[14]

* * *

Patrick's brief fundraising trip included the UK, the Netherlands, Germany and Sweden. In Uppsala Sida agreed to pay him a regular salary, which more or less doubled what he had been receiving, although it was no more than a local Botswana salary at that level. Patrick, however, paid it straight into the general Swaneng account and only drew out what he needed for his and his family's very modest lifestyle. Liz did not receive a salary for her work.

Beyond that, it was becoming increasingly difficult to raise money for Swaneng Hill. The school had been going for seven years and donors felt it was time for the Botswana government to take over funding responsibility. The latter, however, while increasingly drawing Swaneng's running costs into the general Department of Education budget, was not yet covering the school's capital costs.

Scandinavian donors were now concentrating their funding on the brigades, Shashe River School, and the new Swaneng-type school at Mahalapye, due to open in 1971 and to become known as Madiba Secondary School. Patrick did, however, manage to interest a German aid agency, the Evangelische für Entwicklungshilfe, in his self-help education ideas. The agency promised a significant contribution of DM510 000 for new buildings at Swaneng Hill.[15]

By this time it was clear that responsibility for the expanding school network was too much for the original Swaneng board, which ultimately meant Patrick himself. And, with the government becoming more financially involved, a new governing structure was required. Patrick drew up a proposal for a board that contained representatives from the Department of Education and the Central District civil authority, together with a number of elected representatives from the local community.

In early May the government presented its preferred format, which, to Patrick's dismay, contained no elected element and, apart from the school principal, was made up entirely of appointed civil servants.[16]

Patrick had organised a national seminar to be held at Swaneng at the end of May 1970 and had invited delegates from interested government departments and from schools across the country. The aim was to discuss the integration of practical and academic learning within the ethos of voluntary community work, as practised at Swaneng Hill and Shashe River.

He hoped the seminar would spread the word to other schools in the country and get his ideas accepted as national education policy. Vice-President Masire, a known supporter of Patrick's ideas, was expected to attend. This made it all the more frustrating for Patrick when school reassembled on Wednesday 13 May and the final-year students – the Fifth Formers – refused to take part in community voluntary work. As before, they pleaded pressure of work: the fact that they were revising for their end-of-year School Certificate examinations, the results of which would determine their future educational and employment opportunities.

According to Sheila, 'Community work on a House basis is not going well. Roughly a third of those who should attend turn up and Pat is feeling explosive.' The following morning at school assembly

> Pat really went to town … He said he would be guided by the students. If they didn't want to do community work, then he would return the money recently sent by Germany and explain that he had obtained it on false pretences. And he himself would work shorter hours and would make no effort to recruit more members of staff on a voluntary basis. The choice was the students[']. His voice rose and it was most dramatic, staff shaking in their shoes.[17]

It was 'a gambler's speech', and badly timed, as the school had three days off, with a public holiday on the Monday. According to Sheila, 'The Fifth are all too much inclined, at this stage, to think that they have got almost all they need from the school and are about to emerge as the elite of the country.' As for Patrick, she succinctly observed, 'he does in some ways regard [the school] as a millstone round his neck and would much prefer to concentrate on the brigades'.[18] When she met Patrick that afternoon, however, she found him 'in a fairly elated frame of mind'. He was clearly enjoying the battle; but she feared he was on a 'self-destroying route'.[19]

Robert Oakeshott, a man of constant analytical frame of mind, probably got it right when he wrote of Patrick a few weeks later:

> he is a person whose equilibrium significantly depends on being in an 'embattled' situation. Perhaps *because* he has kicked over all his family

background he needs to be faced all the time with a 'back-to-the-wall' type of challenge ... [and] what really disturbs him is the relatively high privilege of students here [at Shashe] and at Swaneng.[20]

The acting director of education, Dr N. O. H. Setidisho,[21] arrived on Tuesday 26 May 1970 and, with the delegates for the national seminar due at the weekend, Patrick's task was twofold: win over 'Dr No', as the Swaneng staff nicknamed Setidisho,[22] and get the Fifth Formers into line.

That evening he and Liz invited Setidisho to dinner. Also present was Robert Kgasa, a Tiger Kloof–trained skilled tanner who had recently joined the staff as manager of the Tanners' Brigade and was living with the Van Rensburgs until a house had been built for him. One can imagine that the conversation revolved around Swaneng and the brigades, with Patrick arguing that what made Swaneng special was what went on *in addition* to normal academic learning. Setidisho was a quiet man, and the conversation was probably mostly a Patrick monologue.

Figure 13.4: Robert Kgasa supervising the Tanners' Brigade. (Van Rensburg family collection; photographer unknown)

The next morning Patrick took Setidisho on the customary tour of the school and the brigades. This, as he later recalled, had impressed and inspired hundreds of visitors over the years,[23] and, as usual, he stressed that most of it had been built through the voluntary labour of the students. The tour, combined with Patrick's charisma and enthusiastic patter, had got many visitors to loosen their purse strings, but it seemed to leave Dr Setidisho cold. He was unresponsive and expressionless throughout, just as district education officer Stanley Hann had been on an earlier visit. Hann, whom Patrick described as a 'British colonial re-tread from Zanzibar',[24] was due later that day.

Patrick returned home exasperated and in despair. He poured out his frustrations to Liz. The acting director of education clearly had no understanding of what the two of them, and scores of volunteer teachers, had worked so hard to achieve over the previous eight years. It made him angry to think that Setidisho would probably be chairman of the new Swaneng board of governors, with Hann likely to be secretary. Patrick had 'a sad foreboding' that the new board would put paid to the combination of work and study at Swaneng. And if that were to happen, 'the Fifth would have won, by default'.[25] He turned his anger on the Fifth.

That afternoon a very distraught Patrick went to see Tom Holzinger with a request that he go and rouse the Farmers' Brigade trainees and bring them to the school to confront the students. Tom believed that Patrick had been 'overdosing on Mao' and saw the present conflict with the Fifth in terms of class struggle. Choosing his words carefully, Tom slowed the conversation down and tried to explain that although it seemed a good idea, the trainees would not understand the request. People were simply not ready for a class struggle from below. So it became, in Tom's words, 'a one-man class struggle'.[26]

That evening Patrick, Liz, Jackie Cock and Dottie Ewan were invited to Sheila Bagnall's house for dinner.[27] Setidisho had been invited, but declined, probably perceiving that he would face another assault on his conservative perception of education. That evening Patrick had clearly already been drinking and, according to Sheila, was 'ranting on' about the élitism of the Fifth.

After dinner Patrick and Liz went up to their house, but at about 2 am, Dottie and Jackie heard raised voices and Patrick turned up at their house in a highly excitable state. He was determined to make some sort of demonstration against the Fifth and threatened to hide their books.

They talked with him for a long time and felt they had calmed him down, but when he left he did not go home to bed.[28] Instead, he went to the Fifth Form classroom and chalked anti-élitist slogans on the board and on their raised desktops. On the wall outside he wrote: 'Elitist Fifth. Up the Brigades'. Then he cooked himself some breakfast in the staff canteen and was ready at dawn to show Setidisho and Hann the early morning milking at the Farmers' Brigade.

He addressed the morning assembly, making a speech highly critical of the Fifth Form students. After assembly, when the Fifth saw what had been done overnight to their classroom, they refused to enter. Some said they should send for a witch doctor to cleanse it ... so much for their scientific education.

By then Patrick had begun to realise that he might have gone too far. He went home and sent for the Fifth. He told them he had written the slogans and was going to resign. As they left, Dr Setidisho came to the house. Patrick explained the anti-élitist motivation for what he had done and offered his resignation.

Setidisho was remarkably conciliatory. He refused to accept the resignation and said Patrick should take a holiday.[29] Then, just as Setidisho was leaving, a long line of students traipsed up the hill, some in tears and carrying posters reading 'DON'T RESIGN' and 'WE LOVE YOU'. By this time Patrick, too, was weeping.

Sheila called a staff meeting. It was agreed the weekend's seminar would have to be postponed. Among those expected for the seminar was Vice-President Masire. The police were very supportive and used their radio to send messages around the country cancelling the event.

Meanwhile, Patrick and Liz, both of whom had been up all night and were in a highly emotional state, retired to bed and slept for much of the day. That evening Dottie and Jackie went up to the Van Rensburg house to cook supper and invited Sheila to join them. Liz was still asleep, but Patrick was awake – weepy but cheerful. During the evening staff came in and out, assuring Patrick of their support. By way of immediate support, they contributed to a fund to pay for Patrick and the family to go to Chobe Lodge in the far north of the country for a couple of weeks' holiday.

One of the South African volunteers, Mark Gandar, son of the campaigning liberal editor of the *Rand Daily Mail* whom Patrick had known and written for in Johannesburg, had a Land Rover and generously offered to drive them there.

The next morning, Friday 29 May, Patrick insisted on speaking to the assembly. According to Sheila, writing the following day, he apologised for his behaviour and recanted his comments on the Fifth.[30] Writing his memoir many years later, however, and having read Sheila's published letters, Patrick insisted he had not apologised or recanted his remarks. Rather, he had 'expressed sadness and regret that the negativity of some students had forced [him] to take an action that [he] would have preferred not to'.[31]

Given his still exhausted and stressed state that Friday morning, it is likely that Sheila's more immediate memory is correct and that Patrick's own memory, expressed some thirty years later, is the truth that he felt he *should* have spoken. Straight after the assembly Patrick, Liz and the two boys departed with Mark Gandar.

They travelled up the unmade 'road' alongside the Rhodesian border to Kasane, 500 kilometres north of Francistown, and arrived at Chobe Lodge the next day. Gandar returned immediately, via the better roads of Rhodesia, from which Patrick and Liz had been banned since 1966. Sheila hoped that Patrick would stay away for a good long rest, but knew that was unlikely: there were two planes a week between Livingstone (across the border in Zambia) and Francistown.

Sure enough, in a little under two weeks Patrick was back in Swaneng, apparently completely recovered. There can be no doubt that he had had what can only be called 'a breakdown', brought on by months, indeed years, of overwork, stress and untenable layers of responsibility. Robert Oakeshott agreed, observing: 'Heaven knows, after the eight years of strain and striving that he has gone through, it is not surprising.' He then added, as he had before, 'I also think that completely kicking over the cultural and family background traces in the way he did is almost bound to leave a person chronically un-relaxed.'[32]

Patrick himself, then and later, always denied any mental instability, however temporary, insisting that he had been absolutely clear-minded, despite the alcohol. To have admitted otherwise would have weakened the validity of his protest against the Fifth. He had merely 'done what needed to be done'.[33]

He asked Sheila to remain in charge of the school. It was not initially a formal appointment as acting principal – that would be in the gift of the new Swaneng board – but he would not be returning as principal and would be trying to get a Motswana principal appointed as soon as possible.

The original voluntarism that had defined Swaneng Hill School was a product of its time – seen by all in Serowe in the early 1960s as the only way to get a secondary school built in their community. For Patrick it was far more than that. Voluntarism was a key element in his struggle to prevent his school from becoming a source of élitism. Eight years later the school was basically built. The impetus for voluntarism was wavering and it was clear that the new government-controlled board would want to reshape the school in the standard academic mould.

Although he had come to the realisation through the May crisis, Patrick saw the way the wind was blowing and that it was time from him to withdraw from the school. As he had earlier remarked to Sheila, he was an innovator, not a consolidator, and he had plenty of ideas brewing for pursuing his vision of practical, productive education for rural development.

* * *

Within a month of the crisis at Swaneng Hill the government began the process of taking over responsibility for the running of the school. Dr Setidisho and Mr Hann arrived and demanded to see a list of the current students and papers relating to the accounts and other matters. It was to be another five months before the new Swaneng school board and executive were up and running, but it was the beginning of the end for Patrick's independent, private, self-help school.

In his final negotiations with the Ministry of Education over the future of the school, and in a spirit of compromise on their part, Patrick 'secured their support for some elements of policy, namely, the diversified curriculum, including practical subjects and Development Studies'.[34] Until he had another house built he continued to live in the principal's house at the top of the hill and was still very much around the school and brigade complex, making ad hoc decisions, to the immense frustration of 'acting principal' Sheila Bagnall.[35]

By July, literally only weeks after his enforced holiday, Patrick was back in full developmental form. Attending a conference in Gaborone on rural development, he promoted his alternative, practical education, through brigades, as a means of increasing local productivity and raising rural standards of living.[36]

At the end of that month he went to the Caribbean – Jamaica, Trinidad and Guyana – for a month's worth of conferences, probably funded by one of the Scandinavian agencies. He returned at the end of August recharged with enthusiasm. He had met a headmaster from Guyana who extracted fifteen hours of manual work a week from his students. Sheila warned him not to dream of trying to implement that at Swaneng.[37]

Things seemed to be going Patrick's way through September. The local district officer, Simon Gillett, remarked that he regularly came across ex-Swaneng students and found them 'much readier to think for themselves than students from other schools',[38] while President Sir Seretse Khama made a speech in Mahalapye in which he said, 'I am convinced that the country needs more schools of the Swaneng type'.[39]

With the new 'Swaneng-type' school due to be opened in Mahalapye, Patrick allowed this compliment to convince him that Seretse was throwing his support behind all his educational ideas. A week later Mike Hawkes and his wife Jan returned to Swaneng with their little son David and their six-week-old daughter Rachel, after nine months in the UK.

Mike had returned on Patrick's assurance the previous year that he would take on the headship of the proposed new school in Mahalapye. In early 1971 Mike and his family moved to Mahalapye, where he started the school in some unused primary school buildings. He set up a Builders' Brigade and got the construction of Madiba Secondary School under way. Patrick, who had initiated the idea of the Mahalapye school and been heavily involved throughout the planning stages, rarely visited the site, apart from attending some of the early work camps.[40] He had moved on from secondary schooling.

* * *

Figure 13.5: Volunteer students completing a wall of the Swaneng Hill school hall. (By kind permission of Karl-Hermann Handwerk)

In October 1970 Swaneng Hill's school hall was officially opened by President Khama. Patrick was in his element, showing off the fruits of his ideas. In his speech of welcome to President Sir Seretse and Lady Khama he spoke of the history of self-help that prevailed at Swaneng, pointing out that the hall itself had been built entirely by the students and staff of the school, working mostly at weekends for three years. He described it as 'a symbol of great determination and a noble achievement'. Even the chairs they were sitting on had been made by students; they were the product of the Engineering Brigade.[41]

In his reply President Khama spoke of how impressed he had been by the work of the brigades. He praised the construction of the hall, the largest of its kind in the country, as symbolic of Botswana's independence. And he was so proud of the steel-tubed chair that had been presented to him by the Engineering Brigade that he waved it in the air in triumph. The moment was captured by a photographer and later printed in Serowe's *Mmegi wa Dikgang* newspaper, which, after a gap of two years, restarted in February 1971.[42]

The triumphal opening of the school hall was really Patrick's swansong as far as Swaneng Hill School was concerned. He was still attending staff meetings, but he no longer had a close rapport with many of the staff, some of whom wanted more democracy in staff meetings. Patrick, who in this period of losing control of what was still widely regarded as *his* school, could be inclined to show elements of autocracy.

He had lost some of the subtlety of persuasive interaction with expatriate staff as he became ever more convinced that he knew best when it came to education for development. He insisted there must be a limit to staff democracy, especially as most were on short contracts. On this matter he had the support of Sheila Bagnall, who confided to a friend, 'The staff are still a band of stroppy young things, though mercifully and usually split over every issue'.[43]

The executive of the new Swaneng school board was made up of government appointees, with no official representation from any of the three schools involved – Swaneng Hill, Shashe River or Madiba – although Sheila was invited to sit in on the meetings to answer any questions that arose.

One of the most hurtful recommendations that emerged from the executive's first meeting, on 23 November 1960, was that Patrick should live off-site and should only be on the school campus when accompanied by a member of the executive.[44] It was clearly an attempt to turn the loyalty of the school – staff and students – away from the founder of Swaneng Hill and towards the new executive.

Clearly they did not know how to handle the charismatic figure of Patrick van Rensburg. While he was still living on-site Patrick cheerfully ignored the recommendation. Sheila, who appears to have been embarrassed by the executive's decision, was unwilling to enforce it, despite finding Patrick's ever-present and spontaneous decision-making undermining and intolerable.[45]

14 | Education with Production, the 1970s

With Patrick no longer responsible for Swaneng Hill School, he and Liz were now free to move down into the village and give their two Botswana-born boys, then aged seven and four, a chance to integrate with local village children.[1] They identified and gained approval for a plot just across the main road from the Swaneng Hill's gates, and construction of the new home, to Patrick's own idiosyncratic design, began in January 1971. It was built by the Builders' Brigade, regularly assisted by Patrick himself, in local stone with a thatched roof.

By April 1972 it was sufficiently completed for the family to move in. This was their first permanent, personal home and it prompted the couple to reassess their lives and think of their long-term future. Patrick applied for Botswana citizenship, which was granted by directive from President Khama in 1973. Liz retained her British passport, on which their two young sons were included, so they would have the freedom when they were adults to choose between British and Botswana citizenship.[2]

* * *

By this time Bessie Head and her son, Howard, were back in Serowe. She was now an established novelist. When she returned in 1969 she had completed the typescript of her second novel, *Maru*, and had just sold the paperback rights to *When Rain Clouds Gather*. The contract had earned her the princely sum of £1 000 and for the first time in her life she had enough capital to build herself a proper home.

Patrick helped get her a plot bordering the eastern edge of the Swaneng Hill complex, and the Builders' Brigade built her a small two-bedroom house at a cost of £700. She called it 'Rain Clouds' and moved in that November.[3]

Figure 14.1: Bessie Head arrives by bicycle at the home of Danish volunteer Benny Wielandt. (By kind permission of Benny Wielandt)

Although her relationship with Patrick was often fractious, he had always been a rock of stability on whom she could call in times of need. She was thus very distressed by Patrick's breakdown during the school crisis of May 1970. Indeed, she may have been influenced by the manner of his demonstration against the Fifth when she reached a crisis of her own.

Over Christmas 1970 Bessie became seriously ill. She began hearing voices in her head and became fixated on the delusion that Vice-President Masire had been assassinated and that President Seretse Khama was covering up the crime. One morning in January 1971 she cycled into the centre of Serowe and calmly put up a poster on a wall in front of the post office on which she claimed that President Khama had covered up the assassination of the vice-president.

To make matters worse, she wrote that the president had committed incest with his daughter. She signed this gross slander 'Bessie Head'. Soon after she got back home the police arrived and arrested her. By the time she got to court she was raving, and the magistrate ordered her to be admitted to the Serowe hospital. Stan and Margaret Moore, bursar and teacher respectively at Swaneng Hill, had become close to Bessie and they took in Howard, while Patrick undertook the awkward task of going to Gaborone to placate President Khama. In fact, he found the president to be 'understanding and generous', and his handling of the situation made 'people generally more tolerant of Bessie's behaviour'.[4] Patrick and the Moores also wrote to Bessie's large circle of literary friends explaining what had happened.

In March Bessie was moved to the psychiatric hospital in Lobatse. Friends rallied round in her support and Naomi Mitchison wrote to assure her that she had just spoken to Quett Masire on the phone and he was still very much alive. Somewhere from deep within herself Bessie summoned up the strength in the next couple of months to retake control of her life and by June she was back in Serowe, though still far from fully recovered.[5] She spent most days working peacefully in her vegetable garden, where she communed with her friend Bosele Sianana. This seemed to help bring her back to stability.

Bessie's income from writing was small and irregular and by August 1972 she was broke again. Once more she appealed to Patrick for help. He agreed to pay her R20 a month, just enough to cover food for herself and Howard; but she clearly needed more regular support to enable her to concentrate on her real talent, writing.

Patrick wrote to Randolph Vigne and together they approached Canon Collins, who Patrick knew had a wide circle of potential donors. Sure enough, Collins was able to raise enough money to provide Bessie with a small regular income to pay for her minimal needs.[6] This left her free to begin work on what she referred to as her 'Serowe book'.

The idea of a collection of stories about the people of Serowe, past and present, had been suggested to Bessie by the British publisher Penguin. The book was to be based mostly on an extensive array of interviews with people from every social stratum of Serowe society. She told Neil Parsons in 1974 that at first she did not know where to start (not being well connected with Serowe, as opposed to Swaneng, people) until she read a copy of his PhD thesis on the history of the Bamangwato, which he had deposited with the Bamangwato Tribal Administration in 1973.[7]

She started by interviewing the interviewees listed in the thesis, and from there she was able to develop her own cast of contacts. By the time she had finished, however, Penguin had lost interest and the book, which would become her most famous work, *Serowe: Village of the Rain Wind*, was not published until 1981, when it was accepted for the Heinemann African Writers Series.

She had divided the book into sections. The history of the Bamangwato and their settlement in Serowe was treated as the era of that historic figure 'Khama the Great', Seretse's grandfather. The colonial period was that of Seretse's uncle and regent, Tshekedi Khama, while the third section was portrayed as the era of Patrick van Rensburg – quite an accolade for someone who only became a citizen of Botswana in 1973. Within this section Patrick and his work at Swaneng and with the brigades featured prominently.[8]

* * *

Patrick's ideas about an alternative model of education had originally been inspired by the initiative of the first cohort of Swaneng students. From their example he had evolved the school's communal, self-help principles and the concept of brigades, through a process of trial and error, during which he became increasingly critical of the established, competitive system of academic secondary education that did little more than add a new layer of élitism to society.

What was needed, he had argued at Moshi in October 1969 and again at a conference in Gaborone in July 1970, was a model of education that involved the total rural population.[9] Lasting rural development should be based on far more than the export of cattle, which, in any case, mainly benefited the traditional élite.

It must include the internal exchange of goods, manufactured within the rural areas, using appropriate technology and skills that local people

Figure 14.2: The wedding of Sekgoma Khama in April 1974 was an occasion for great celebration in Serowe. (By kind permission of Benny Wielandt)

could readily acquire, and drawing on local resources, be these animal, vegetable or mineral. He cited Chinese and Indian examples of 'small-scale, labour-intensive, inexpensive technology production of village needs in consumer goods'.[10]

It was vital, he had argued at Moshi, that the modern sector 'should not drain the best brains away from rural development. Disequilibrium must be minimised. Modern sector development and rural development must be harmonised.' His solution to the challenge of harmonised development was the brigades, for brigade training had the potential to 'spearhead' development. Brigades need not simply be 'the last resort for the frustrated ambition of school leavers'.[11]

Relinquishing control of the school left Patrick free to pursue the further development of Education with Production (EwP) through the expansion of the brigades. Sheila Bagnall, confirmed in the post of principal of Swaneng Hill in March 1971, was happy to offload responsibility for the brigades to Patrick.

At her urging, the Swaneng Hill board approved the conversion of the Serowe Youth Development Association (Syda) into an entirely separate Serowe Brigades Development Trust (SBDT). The new trust, with Patrick as executive secretary, was formally inaugurated in August 1972. Patrick was now free to pursue his dream of placing the brigades centre stage in the economic development of Serowe.

Realising that he needed an administration centre from which to bring his dream to fruition, one of the first things he did was oversee the construction of an office building. As the building neared completion in 1973, he appealed to War on Want to finance a full-time secretary. The British charity found him Jenny Peel and, as Patrick was on one of his fundraising trips to the UK, they arranged to meet in the lounge of the Paddington Station Hotel. Jenny was to recall: 'My first view of Pat was of a large bearded figure scrabbling about on the floor among heaps of papers which he'd just knocked off a table. He definitely looked as though he and his papers need organising.'[12]

From the early 1970s Patrick oversaw a rapid expansion in the range of brigades in Serowe, to such an extent that by the mid-1970s they constituted the dominant productive activity in the town. Mechanics', Tanners' and Printers' brigades had been added to the original Builders', Farmers' and Textile brigades. Work on Patrick's latest initiative, the Tshwaragano Hotel, spawned a number of further brigades, including one for carpenters, as a breakaway from the builders, and others for electricians, plumbers, stonemasons and thatchers.

If Patrick saw a need, such as bookkeeper training, he created a brigade to cater for it. A Food-Processing Brigade turned sunflower seeds into cooking oil, groundnuts into peanut butter, and tomatoes and chillies into a range of sauces.[13] From 1976 a Dam-Building Brigade, under the instruction of Dutch volunteer Wouter van der Wall Bake, began constructing dams for the rural communities within a couple of hours' tractor drive from Serowe.[14]

Patrick's dream was to create for Serowe and the surrounding district a self-sufficient community that would become a model for rural development, not only in Botswana, but throughout the developing world. And by the mid-1970s it seemed he was achieving that goal.

District commissioner and chairman of the SBDT, Mr N. E. K. Sebele, reported in 1976: 'I have seen Mr van Rensburg work with indefatigable zeal, sometimes against odds, to promote Brigades. His efforts were soon crowned with success as the idea was accepted by Government, who consequently encouraged the formation of Brigades all over the country.'[15]

Government encouragement came in the form of regular subsidies paid to the individual brigade trusts that had been formed in all the main rural centres of population. Rather than see the brigades as engines of growth within their rural communities, however, the Ministry of Education regarded them as low-cost vocational training centres, designed to help primary school 'drop-outs' into employment in the formal economy, most of which was centred on Gaborone and other towns close to the 'line of rail'.

Patrick saw this as distorting his concept of the brigades as a spearhead for self-sufficient rural development and he was determined to keep the Serowe brigades free from government financial support for as long as possible. He recognised that they suffered from low productivity and, at best, covered only about two-thirds of the cost of the education and training they offered, but they more than made up for this by their service to the community in providing skills and opportunities to the neglected rural majority. As far as he was concerned, low productivity was little more than a frustration, illustrated by his rhetorical question: 'Why can't the Batswana be more like the Chinese?'[16]

Frank Taylor, whom Patrick had brought to Serowe to market the textiles and other products of the brigades, was not so sanguine. He had previously worked in marketing for the game industry in Francistown and came to see low productivity as a fundamental flaw at the heart of the brigade system. In his view, a higher priority should be placed on greater productivity combined with quality control.

As it was, cost covering was an illusion; the project was subsidised by foreign aid and expatriate volunteers. Patrick, on the other hand, eschewed profit and focused on the socialist, co-operative element of the brigade

Figure 14.3a: Electricians' Brigade installing electricity at the Tshwaragano Hotel. (Van Rensburg family collection; photographer unknown)

Figure 14.3b: Mechanical Brigade installing a new generator. (By kind permission of the late Aaron Kibel's family)

Figure 14.3c: Mobile Plumbers' Brigade drilling a borehole under the supervision of a Danish volunteer. (By kind permission of Benny Wielandt)

Figure 14.3d: Trainee weaving a tapestry design for a carpet. (Van Rensburg family collection; photographer unknown)

Figure 14.3e: The first weaving and dressmaking workroom, with (*extreme right*) Lily Mapula, instructor. (Van Rensburg family collection; photographer unknown)

concept. The difference in outlook between the two men came to a head in 1973 and Frank resigned. He left Serowe and the two men rarely spoke again.[17]

* * *

Working separately but parallel to the brigades was Patrick's co-operative and self-help project for unemployed adults with little or no education. It was called Boiteko ('self-help') and was based on similar principles to the brigades: training in productive skills with a view to enabling the people to become more self-sufficient, but in a co-operative manner.

It originated in 1969, with the assistance of Joel Pelotona, the sub-chief of the local Mere ward and an artist who taught design in the textile workshop.[18] Starting with about ten poor, local, unemployed people with little or no education, mainly but not exclusively women, Boiteko provided them with a focus, and some hope. They would come together to learn new craft skills from each other and from the staff and trainees of the brigades, together with a few volunteer students from Swaneng.

The range of skills in building, spinning and weaving, dressmaking, gardening, tanning and leatherwork gradually built up. Later, pottery and simple food-processing were added to the range, and membership rose in the mid-1970s to a peak of about forty. Liz was heavily involved in the spinning and weaving side of Boiteko, as well as continuing her commitment to the brigades' textile workshop. Although a bakery and cooking unit failed to compete with the commercial sector, a knitting unit did quite well, selling to tourist outlets in Serowe and Gaborone.[19]

Patrick's aim was to create a self-sufficient community. Members exchanged their products in what he called a 'swap-shop', for many of them had no access to cash. Payment was initially in vouchers, but that scheme excluded members from the wider Serowe cash economy and it was soon abandoned. A cash system was gradually introduced and a community market was established. Earnings from sales were pooled and shared among the members. This created some resentment as there was too great a variation in the hours worked.

Boiteko was supposed to be a self-sustaining project, though it never really was; it was always subsidised, either directly by Patrick, with cash and product donations from various outside sources, or by training input and secretarial and accountancy services from the staff, trainees and students of the brigades and Swaneng Hill.[20] Nevertheless, both Patrick and Liz regarded it as an important factor in the promotion and maintenance of the co-operative spirit and idealistic voluntarism that they had known in Serowe in the early 1960s.

The spirit of Boiteko was most evident in the building of a durable stone community centre and houses for the members. All the materials were locally available, and the new techniques were readily learned. But it needed a lot of hard co-operative labour. A small group of young men burnt the lime, which they sold to Boiteko, while another group used donkey transport to carry the slaked lime, river sand, manure and water for the mortar, and stones for the building.[21]

Patrick hoped that each of the Boiteko women would have a stone rondavel to live in and a number were built, although only one remains, still occupied in 2018 by Bosele Sianana, one of the original Boiteko women.[22] The community centre was used for childcare, communal meals and some primary health and literacy education. Communal cooperation within Boiteko, however, was constantly being challenged by pressure from the cash earnings of those engaged in the burgeoning modern sector.

Bessie Head was a prominent critic of Patrick's concept of communalism within Boiteko. She grew fruit, vegetables and seedlings for sale or exchange in the Boiteko store and had been working with the gardeners for some time, successfully teaching thirteen young women the principles of managing their vegetable plots. What they grew was for their own consumption, or for sale, to provide a small cash income.

In January 1976 Patrick proposed having an additional, communal garden, the products of which would be for the Boiteko community as a whole, and asked Bessie to manage it. He specifically stipulated that in order to instil a greater sense of community commitment within Boiteko the communal plot was to be worked separately from the individual plots, on a voluntary basis on Saturday mornings. On this point he clashed with Bessie.

Bessie understood the pressures the women were under. They worked long hours for Boiteko during the week, and on Saturdays they had other social pressures and family obligations to attend to. As their manager,

Bessie told the women there was no need to work at weekends. According to Bessie's account, Patrick was furious. He came to her house with the Boiteko manager, Kopano Lekoma, and harangued her for undermining the whole communal spirit of Boiteko.

She explained her reasons, including her belief that it was fundamentally wrong for people not to be paid for work done. It was one thing for them to work for themselves on their own plots and earn what they could from selling their produce, but if they were to work for the wider community they should be paid a salary. Patrick would not hear of it, and Bessie resigned.[23]

The natural neighbourliness of village life had, perhaps, deceived an idealistic incomer like Patrick. Batswana were individualists at heart and only engaged in voluntarism and communalism out of necessity, or, in former years, at the specific direction of the chief. As Bessie saw it, Patrick was now acting like a dictatorial chief.

In a fury she typed a two-page 'List of Complaints Against Pat Van Rensburg, Kopano, and Boiteko Management', in which she accused Patrick of degrading and exploiting the poor by expecting them to work for no money: 'I am sick of the farce and I will not delude 13 bright girls into believing that Boiteko offers them anything in its present form. It offers them NOTHING but poverty, hard work and starvation and I am not going to be a part of this evil game any more.'[24]

According to Kopano Lekoma and Liz van Rensburg, who reported on Boiteko to the SBDT in 1976, the decline in the communal spirit of Boiteko came about 'because members thought more in terms of earning money rather than providing service to each other'.[25] Patrick was forced to abandon his attempt to establish weekend voluntary work as part of the ethos of Boiteko.[26] He recognised that the co-operative spirit could not survive the commercial pressures of modern sector development that was becoming increasingly evident through the 1970s.

With copper-nickel from Selebi-Phikwe, diamonds from Orapa, and the Morupule coal-mining and power station complex near Palapye coming on stream from the early 1970s, government was able to make huge investments in the country's infrastructure. Schools, clinics, electrification and tarred roads began to penetrate the rural areas.

The country experienced the beginning of two decades of phenomenal economic growth. Employment opportunities in the modern sector, however, sucked labour out of the rural areas. Liz managed to keep the spinning section of Boiteko alive – at one time she had fourteen spinners, but Patrick's vision for rural development became ever more difficult to sustain.

Boiteko suffered economic and management problems in the late 1970s and more or less collapsed, though it was revived for some years in 1984, when Ditshwanelo Makwati assisted the remaining ten Boiteko women to regroup as the Boiteko Agricultural Management Association. This gave them greater structure as a group and access to government extension programmes. They grew vegetables on a one-hectare plot and ran a poultry unit of 480 hens for egg production. In this way they provided the local community with their daily needs in vegetables and eggs and made a small communally-shared income for themselves.[27]

* * *

In reaction to the individualist, capitalist mode of the modern sector that was gaining traction throughout Botswana society, Patrick became ever more heavily involved in Marxist philosophy, especially its Maoist interpretation. In the early 1970s Liz's brother-in-law, Aaron Kibel, had lent Patrick a copy of Karl Marx's *Capital*, and he found it a revelation.[28]

Through Marx's masterly analysis of the capitalist system, from its origins in medieval Europe to the fully industrialised capitalism of the late nineteenth century, Patrick felt he now had a theoretical understanding of what he had been grappling with for the past decade. The 'modern sector' that he often referred to, together with the élitism that he had struggled so hard to eliminate, were each the product of class struggle within a capitalist system.

Marx did not write a great deal about education, but what he did write must have gone a long way to strengthening in Patrick's mind what he believed to be the way in which the education of the masses should be structured. Marx believed that the education of the working class should be a combination of general mental education, gymnastics or organised physical education, and technical training. The latter should be combined with productive activity, so that children would understand the whole process and organisation of production.[29] In due course Patrick was to develop this into a curriculum that he called 'Fundamentals of Production'.[30]

The practical interpretation of Marxism that Patrick considered most appropriate for Botswana was that practised in China and Cuba. He favoured their focus on rural development rather than the centralised industrialisation of the Soviet Union's command economy. Besides, he probably still distrusted Soviet communism, not only because of the invasion of Hungary in 1956, but also because of the more recent invasion of Czechoslovakia in 1968. His analysis of contemporary Botswana was also influenced by the new conceptual framework of neo-Marxist dependency theory, typified by Andre Gunder Frank's book *Capitalism and Underdevelopment in Latin America: Historical Studies of Chile and Brazil.*[31]

A deeper understanding of Marxist theory helped Patrick in his lively discussions with his avowedly socialist friend Dr Kenneth Koma, Botswana's leading opposition politician and co-founder of the left-wing Botswana National Front (BNF). Koma had the distinction of being the most widely read and highly educated politician in the country, with a doctorate in Political Science from the Soviet Union's Academy of Sciences in Moscow.[32]

Koma's home was in Mahalapye and he was a regular visitor to Serowe, where he and Patrick enjoyed intense conversations about education, development, politics and 'the emancipation of the masses'. When interviewed in old age Patrick said about his relationship with Kenneth Koma, 'I liked Ken more than any other person I have met here'.[33] It was this close friendship, combined with the number of BNF members employed in the brigades, that led key members of the governing Botswana Democratic Party (BDP) to take up the old refrain of colonial civil servants that Patrick was a communist sympathiser, not to be trusted.

As if to confirm their suspicions, Patrick ran study groups for a small and select group of brigade staff and a few others, expatriate and local, on socialist theory and practice. Ted Comick, a young American volunteer who had worked briefly in the trade union movement after graduating from university, was instrumental in establishing the study groups after his arrival in 1974. He was well versed in Marxist theory and played a critical role in the establishment of the study groups.[34]

Attendance was by Patrick's invitation. He divided the members into groups, apparently according to what he believed was their degree of socialist commitment. He would set them papers and chapters of books to read and they would gather at the Van Rensburg home on Saturday after-noons, under a tree in the yard, and discuss their findings.

Patrick was such a charismatic figure that the members of the groups, mostly idealistic expatriate volunteers, were prepared to give up part of their Saturday afternoons to discuss socialist theory and practice. In this way, he believed, through the brigades' teachers and trainers, he was pro-moting the socialist cause of anti-élitism and the establishment of a more egalitarian society. It was also a way for him to gain personal and intellec-tual support for his ever-evolving theory of EwP.

* * *

Figure 14.4: Former president Quett Masire in conversation with the author at his home in Gaborone in 2017. (Photograph: Kevin Shillington)

Despite the tendency of some within government to distrust Patrick and his educational ideas, for much of the 1970s he served on the government's Rural Development Council, chaired by Quett Masire. Many years later, in an interview for this book, Masire spoke fondly of Patrick and his stimulating contributions to discussions on rural development policy.

'He was a ball of fire,' he recalled with a laugh. 'I was head over heels in love with him.' However, he admitted, 'we clashed now and again'.[35] And he was right in this latter recollection, for relations between Patrick and the Botswana government, even Masire, were not always cordial. While Patrick's citizenship granted his family stability in the country, it also left him free to criticise government policy. And through the 1970s he found much to criticise.

He was to observe of this period that 'the sudden, new accretion of wealth [from mining] had dramatically, in a short space of time, unleashed a new optimism and faith in Botswana's formal sector development', to the detriment of the rural majority.[36] Although Patrick avoided joining the official opposition, the BNF, these developments drew him ever closer to the socialist wing of that party.[37]

The BNF's rhetoric at this time condemned the growing inequality and the government's neglect of the 80 per cent who had little share in the benefits of the burgeoning modern sector. Patrick's close association with members of the BNF did not go unnoticed by the governing BDP, whose heartland lay in Serowe.

In April 1977 the National Commission on Education published its report, *Education for Kagisano* ('living together in harmony and friendship'). Beyond acceptance of the brigades as a useful form of cheap vocational training for 'primary school drop-outs', there was no indication that any of Patrick's ideas about self-sufficient rural development were being taken on board. Indeed, quite the opposite.

In an appendix to the *Kagisano* report Patrick's Development Studies course was described by a senior official of the secondary curriculum task force as 'emphasising those aspects which can produce a disgruntled and discontented citizen rather than one who is patriotic and dedicated'.[38] He might as well have added, 'and votes for the BDP'. In a direct jibe at Patrick's volunteers, the official claimed that the dangers posed by Development Studies were aggravated when taught by 'inexperienced [expatriates] with little understanding of or commitment to Botswana'.[39] Patrick got his chance to respond a few months later, when he was invited to open the annual Kanye Agricultural Show.

Despite being Masire's hometown, Kanye was a hotbed of political opposition. The show's chairman, Bathoen Gaseitsiwe, was MP for Kanye South and leader of the BNF in Parliament. The invitation extended to Patrick was a bold move by the show's organising committee, for an agricultural show in independent Botswana had never previously been opened by someone who was neither a minister nor even an MP.

But Patrick was still on the government's Rural Development Council and, in a speech of welcome, Gaseitsiwe's son, *Kgosi* Seepapitso IV, declared, in the presence of both the vice-president and the minister of external affairs, 'Pat van Rensburg is the right person ... for introducing something different from the traditional show-opening ministerial speeches'.[40] And Patrick did not disappoint. He started by declaring that he was not a government critic, yet he criticised everything about government policy except its support for the Southern African liberation struggle:

> We have overthrown foreign political rule but have kept the colonial game and its rules – taxation and aid budgets, recruitment of expatriates and bringing in foreign companies – to build for us things like roads and schools which we can simply build by mobilising the men and women to do it for themselves through meaningful self-reliance.

He cited China and Cuba as examples of countries that rejected foreign companies and their accompanying professional experts.[41]

He returned to this theme when he addressed an audience at the University College of Botswana in November 1977,[42] although this time he combined it with setting out his vision for the transformation of society through EwP. He acknowledged that the government had achieved a lot in terms of infrastructure development in the previous ten years, but he was highly critical of the slavish copying of methods of development practised in developed capitalist countries, which increased inequality and led to rural stagnation and deprivation.

Such models of development relied heavily on sophisticated technology, which increased dependence on an academic education that was both expensive and selective. And you could not have selection without rejection. To avoid this, he argued, education should be redesigned as 'a new dynamic complex'. It must be continuous and lifelong, integrated with production and involving the whole society in skills transformation. The nation should be one big classroom, with 'everyone a worker, learner and teacher'. The people needed to be productively mobilised to meet the basic needs of life for everyone. The country had the resources; it just needed the political will and the organisation.[43]

Government ministers responded in Parliament the following week. Minister of Commerce and Industry M. P. K. Nwako said that Van Rensburg's criticism of government development policy was 'aimed at perverting our youth and retarding the progress of this country'. His attack was headlined on the front page of the government's *Daily News*: 'VAN RENSBURG "PERVERTER OF OUR YOUTH"'.[44] Minister of Education K. P. Morake followed up the attack, repeating Nwako's 'perverting' allegation, and pointing out that Van Rensburg's own brigades had been financed by money from outside.[45]

Nwako was from the Serowe/Palapye area, while Morake was from Tonota, so both ministers were well aware of what Patrick was up to in Serowe. What lay behind the specific perversion accusation was ministerial awareness of Patrick's Marxist study groups for teachers and trainers at his home in Serowe. In winding up the debate Vice-President Masire, usually a supporter, accused Patrick of decrying Botswana's democratic principles: '[He] admires other countries' political strategies [referring to China and Cuba] and would like to see them implemented. The democratic system of the country allows him to do so, but he has now moved "heaven and earth" to prove his political involvement.'[46]

He went on to link Van Rensburg with opposition leader Kenneth Koma, who had circulated a manifesto calling for demonstrations. Masire used Koma's manifesto to declare that the Botswana National Front was a revolutionary party and that Patrick, by association, was a revolutionary.[47] It was all political posturing, but clearly Patrick's criticism had hit a nerve in government circles.

***

Government hostility towards Patrick continued through 1978 as the Serowe brigades experienced a managerial and financial crisis. Under pressure of wage inflation from the modern sector, the brigades were forced to apply to government for financial support. As Patrick had feared, government saw this as an opportunity to bring the brigades into line with its vision of a low-cost form of vocational training for the modern sector rather than Patrick's vision of a dynamic catalyst for achieving rural self-sufficiency.

Selective government grants, however, were never enough to make the Serowe brigades financially viable, and it was clear by 1978 that many were heading for bankruptcy. At the same time, Patrick sensed the hostility of the local BDP élite, both to himself and to those in the BNF who provided much of the management of the brigades. In 1978 he resigned as secretary of the SBDT, with effect from the end of 1979.

The government regarded the management and training staff as employees of the Ministry of Education and for that reason the staff demanded pay parity with the teaching sector. This hastened the brigades' bankruptcy. By 1980 many of them had folded and the attempt to give effect to Patrick's vision of rural self-sufficiency had largely collapsed. A few of the brigades carried on through the 1980s and, ironically, when the technical college in Palapye was looking for practical experience for its trainees, it sent some of them to the surviving Mechanical Brigade workshop in Serowe.

* * *

By contrast, in developmental circles beyond Botswana Patrick's ideas were being received very positively. His most important allies in this respect were based in Sweden, in particular at the Dag Hammarskjöld Foundation (DHF).

The intention of the foundation was to organise seminars and courses on a wide range of themes relating to social, economic and cultural development in developing countries. Patrick's educational ideas, combined as they were with the economic and cultural development of the neglected majority, fitted perfectly into its primary aims.

Like Hammarskjöld himself, Patrick was a man of dogged determination who stood up for his beliefs, no matter who tried to deflect him.

This must have appealed to the Swedes, who were to become his close allies in the developmental challenges that lay ahead. Their relationship had begun with Patrick's Scandinavian lecture tours of 1965 and 1967 and been consolidated by the visit to Serowe of Sven Hamrell and Thord Palmlund in 1966 and another by Hamrell and Olle Nordberg in 1969, by which time Hamrell was executive director of the DHF, with Nordberg as administrative secretary.

It was clear to Sven and Olle that Patrick had a replicable model of development that could and should be spread widely in the developing world. They became close friends with Patrick and were key to the international dissemination of his ideas. Indeed, their unfailing support for so many years was crucial in strengthening Patrick's confidence in his projects and ideas. He always stressed how much he valued their friendship and solidarity.[48]

In 1971 they visited Botswana with a proposal for an international seminar based on Patrick's vision of alternative education. The Botswana government failed to take up the idea, but the Tanzanians were prepared to support it. Sven invited Patrick to take a sabbatical of several months in Uppsala in 1972 and 1973, during which time he wrote the story of the Swaneng years, combined with his vision of 'Education for Employment in Africa'. This provided the theme on which the seminar, or series of seminars, would be based.

Sven circulated the unpublished manuscript to an international audience of education and development specialists as preliminary reading for the seminar.[49] Technical issues delayed the seminar and, in the meantime, the foundation published Patrick's manuscript as *Report from Swaneng Hill: Education and Employment in an African Country.*[50] It was his first major publication since *Guilty Land* in 1962 and it was widely circulated in development circles.

The much delayed seminar, centred on the theme of the book, finally took place in Dar es Salaam in late May 1974.[51] Co-sponsored by the DHF and the Institute of Development Studies (IDS) of the University of Dar es Salaam, the seminar was opened with an inspirational keynote speech by Tanzanian president Julius Nyerere.[52] Patrick was co-director of the meeting, alongside Ibrahim Kaduna, the director of the IDS, and Professor Joseph Ki-Zerbo, the renowned historian and educationist from Upper Volta.[53]

Although Patrick was hoping to learn from the delegates, his own alternative vision dominated the seminar, especially because it meshed so closely with Nyerere's self-reliance philosophy. Rather than looking at 'education' and its curriculum as a universal norm that would lead to employment as though by osmosis, Patrick placed production co-operatives at the heart of education, with academic elements attached to service the whole.[54]

His experiments hitherto had been small and particular to Botswana, but they had shown that his model could raise the incomes of ordinary people, which was surely the primary sign of success. He appealed to the educationists, ministers and others at the seminar to have faith in those 'ordinary people'. With that faith, and some local adaptation, he assured them, the model could be widely replicated and develop into a mass movement.

Aside from a range of representatives from the Southern African liberation movements that were based in Dar es Salaam, the seminar attracted 19 official delegates, mostly from African countries, and 17 lecturers and support personnel. Among the latter was Liz van Rensburg, who, with their two children, had accompanied her husband. Liz had prepared an exhibition of photographs and artefacts illustrating the achievements of Swaneng and the brigades. The exhibition, together with some exhibits from other African countries, was on display throughout the seminar.

Patrick's exposure through the Dar es Salaam seminar greatly enhanced his international reputation and emboldened him to summarise his vision in an article entitled 'The Need for a Revolution in Education', which was published in the international journal *Africa*.[55] Through the next decade and beyond Patrick was to play a leading role in a series of Dag Hammarskjöld seminars dedicated to issues of education and development in 'Third World' countries, with the range of invited delegates considerably widened beyond Africa. Olle Nordberg has revealed that Patrick was not always at ease at these big international conferences, preferring the immediate and the practical solution to specific problems:

Pat was a very hard-working person with practical aims and [dirt] under his nails and expecting tangible results. He was not a speaker to a world audience with sweeping formulations; he wanted to get things done. [But] he wished to show solidarity with Sven, who had helped him a lot.[56]

More to his liking was a follow-up to the Dar es Salaam seminar, which took place in Maputo, Mozambique, in April 1978, with Patrick again chief rapporteur and co-director. Mozambique had a strong tradition of Marxist-based self-help education, developed during the long liberation war that had only ended in 1975, and the minister for education, Graça Machel, the wife of President Samora Machel (and later of President Nelson Mandela), chaired and opened the seminar.[57]

By this time Patrick was convinced of the transformative potential of education for development and the following year he reported on an Uppsala seminar in which he stressed that 'development' was not an abstract concept. It must always be predicated upon the questions: 'What? For Whom? and How?'[58] Education, he argued, had the potential to go beyond mere skills training. It must be linked to restructuring society from the ground up and, in doing so, must expect class struggle and conflict.

***

The DHF's financial underpinning of Patrick's vision from the 1970s and funding support for the brigades from Sida (Sweden), Danida (Denmark) and the Bernard van Leer Foundation (the Netherlands) ensured that the name Van Rensburg became recognised by those in international circles working in the fields of alternative education and development. He had certainly gained the fame that he had craved as an awkward and sexually shy young man in his late teens and early twenties.

Much of the idealistic young expatriate community of Serowe had been attracted there by Patrick's exciting and innovative work. Many had read *Guilty Land*, by way of introduction to the man. It was a heady atmosphere. Patrick was a powerful and charismatic figure with an ability and willingness to listen that made him very attractive to many of the impressionable young expatriate women in Serowe, and there is no doubt that he took advantage of the sexual temptations that he saw all around him.

He was often away from home, within Botswana as well as travelling abroad for fundraising and conferences. Even when he was in Serowe, demands on his time were constant, and family relationships were bound to suffer. His elder son Tom's[59] earliest memories, in the late 1960s, were of a very attentive father, always keen to read to him and to explain how things worked, emphasising the need to develop skills of both hands and mind.[60] By contrast, his younger son Mothusi's early memories of his father in the 1970s were of a man who was always working.

It was Liz who would push for a holiday 'for the boys', and hopefully to give Patrick a rest. But whether they went to Chobe to visit the game park or to a safari lodge near Maun, Patrick was always absorbed in his papers: proposals for new projects, reports on old ones, appeals for funding and drafts of seminar papers. Indeed, if they travelled by car, for instance on the long and dusty journey to Maun, he would bring a whole suitcase of papers with him.[61] He always wrote in longhand, relying on someone else – his secretary or Liz – to do the typing.

By 1978 Liz had decided it was time for her and the two boys to leave Botswana and settle in the UK. Apart from the fact that Patrick must have been a very difficult man to live with, Liz was concerned about the health of her elder son. Tom suffered from a curable childhood illness, which required particular drugs, available locally only from South Africa,[62] which was out of bounds for the whole Van Rensburg family, and receiving drugs via friends or by post was proving unreliable.

At one stage Liz had written to the South African authorities asking for special permission for a one-off visit for herself and Tom to see a specialist in Johannesburg, but the request was turned down. It appears it was this that tipped the balance in her decision to leave with the two boys.[63] They settled in Leicester in September 1978, in time for Liz to get the boys into school for the beginning of the new school year.

It was not a formal separation for the couple. Liz continued to provide Patrick with all the moral support she could. He always visited the family when he was in England, and they went on holidays together; but the original joint commitment that had carried them overland through Africa and through all the triumphs and vicissitudes of Swaneng and Serowe in the 1960s was no more. With Liz no longer at his side, Patrick felt a renewed urge to prove himself and his ideas, for which he looked beyond the confines of Botswana.

15 | Foundation for Education with Production and Spreading the Word, the 1980s

Revolution was in the air in 1979 – not just in Iran, Grenada and Nicaragua, but in Africa too, with the overthrow of several brutal dictatorships. Patrick sensed it in Southern Africa. It was clear that in neighbouring Zimbabwe the Smith regime's 'internal settlement' could not hold out much longer. And, viewed from Botswana, it was even possible to believe that South Africa itself was about to enter the final decade of its road to liberation.

The time was right for Patrick to throw his full weight into the struggle. He believed that his model of EwP was the way to ensure that when both Zimbabwe and South Africa were liberated the old colonial and contemporary capitalist models of education for exploitation could be swept aside. With his help they would be replaced by a socialist vision of education that would transform society to the benefit of the masses.

Influenced by the Marxist analysis of his Serowe study groups, Patrick now saw the challenge ahead in terms of class struggle and the beneficiaries of the capitalist model of education as the 'black petty bourgeoisie' rather than the vaguer term 'élite'.[1] It was they, in Botswana and Zimbabwe (and ultimately in South Africa), who were putting barriers in the way of his alternative model of education.

He saw the opportunity to start the fight back against those forces with the dramatic outflow from South Africa of child refugees following the Soweto uprising of 1976. Many passed through Botswana on their way to Zambia and ultimately Tanzania, where they became the responsibility of the ANC leadership. Most of these refugees had been politicised by the Black Consciousness movement and regarded the ANC as old-fashioned. Once they reached exile, however, they found the ANC was the only organisation able and prepared to take them on, offer them training and educate them politically.[2]

Patrick had worked with the ANC since his early Swaneng days and may even have secretly helped his friend and colleague Lawrence Notha to transfer refugees northwards.[3] He supported most of the ANC's policies and, over the years, employed a considerable number of South Africans, many of whom he knew were secretly members of the ANC.

He regularly met with the ANC hierarchy in Lusaka and Dar es Salaam, but there appears to be no evidence that he ever actually joined the party, which, from 1969, had been open to all races. The ANC in exile was a strictly controlled hierarchical organisation. To have formally become a member would have severely restricted Patrick's ability to pursue his own independent educational and developmental path, which, by this stage, went far beyond the liberation of South Africa.

The ANC's initial efforts to provide a school for the Soweto refugees were quickly overwhelmed by sheer numbers, and in 1977 the Tanzanian government made a farm available near the village of Mazimba in Morogoro district to the west of Dar es Salaam. The school was formally opened by ANC president Oliver Tambo in 1979. It was named the Solomon Mahlangu Freedom College (SOMAFCO), in honour of a young freedom fighter who had been captured in South Africa and executed on 6 April 1979. The ANC drafted in cadres to set up and run the school and when Patrick first visited, in 1978, they were making temporary use of empty farm buildings.

Patrick saw the Mazimba farm as an ideal context for Education with Production (EwP). The productive side of EwP would not only feed and clothe the students, it would help cover much of the teaching and other running costs of the school. Some from within the ANC had been observers at Patrick's Dar es Salaam seminar in 1974 and, grateful for any help, they welcomed the ideas of such an experienced educational practitioner.

Patrick knew that the ANC was going to have to manage the project for itself and the most he could do was advise and perhaps influence it. He invited fourteen ANC cadres to Serowe to undergo a one-year intensive course within the brigade system. They would be trained in specific technical skills and would absorb the principles of EwP. He hoped this would persuade the ANC to establish EwP at the core of its school curriculum, with an eye to its future adoption in South Africa.

The candidates who arrived for the course in Serowe in January 1979 were not the idealistic material Patrick could have done with. They were mostly older people who had been sitting it out in Tanzania and welcomed the chance to be nearer home and do something different. Two of them even naïvely slipped back into South Africa, and were promptly arrested.[4]

Nevertheless, Patrick's presentation of EwP as 'education for liberation' at a Lusaka seminar in 1980 (see below) had its influence on the ANC's Educational Council and EwP was perceived, at least in theory, 'as an ideological and material necessity'.[5] Besides, they were in Nyerere's country, where 'education for self-reliance' was taken as the natural order. There was the school farm to be run, and workshops for motor repair and carpentry were a necessary part of achieving any sort of self-sufficiency in rural Tanzania.

The students were divided into 'brigades', named after ANC leaders like Tambo and Luthuli, and these worked in rotation on various productive projects, especially on the farm. But this was only for a few hours a week. It was regarded, by students and ANC leaders alike, as time away from academic work, which they saw as the real purpose of education. They failed to appreciate the beneficial links between productive work and the classroom, especially in those difficult theoretical subjects, Science and Mathematics. The farm and the various workshops were run by local paid labour, who often regarded the students as getting in the way of their work.[6]

In those early years SOMAFCO may have appeared to practise EwP, but it was never fully integrated into educational policy, despite Patrick's best efforts and regular visits to the school. In January 1982 he co-directed a Dag Hammarskjöld Foundation–funded workshop at SOMAFCO with the purpose of devising a suitable curriculum for the college.[7] It became clear from discussions, however, that despite a nominal commitment to EwP, the school's primary purpose was formal academic work, aimed at obtaining certificates. The priority of ANC educationists was to upgrade general levels of black education, which had been deliberately kept at a low level under 'Bantu Education'.

Hendrik Verwoerd, in explaining the purpose of the Bantu Education Act of 1953, had declared: 'There is no place for [the African] in the European community above the level of certain forms of labour.'[8] Black people were to be educated for their restricted role as manual and low-skilled labourers. Education in Science and Mathematics and much of the humanities was thus severely restricted.

The primary role of the ANC in exile was thus to counteract this racist educational degradation and prepare those with ability to be ready to take control of the commanding heights of the professions and the economy following the liberation of South Africa.[9] Manual work was thus considered a low priority and that undertaken by the students on the farm and in the workshops became voluntary.

By the mid-1980s it had become little more than occasional days spent cleaning the school grounds in preparation for a special occasion.[10] Nevertheless, Patrick was still considered a valued educational adviser for the ANC and he was regularly invited to SOMAFCO to attend meetings of the party's National Education Council.

* * *

In December 1979 the Lancaster House Agreement, under which Zimbabwe would gain its independence the following year, was signed in London. War veterans and refugees began to pour back into the country; and elections, won overwhelmingly by Robert Mugabe's Zimbabwe African National Union (Zanu),[11] took place over three days, from 28 February to 1 March.[12] Zimbabwe formally gained its independence on 18 April, with Mugabe as prime minister and Canaan Banana as ceremonial president.

By this time Patrick had cut most of his direct ties with his various projects in Serowe, and from late 1979 or early 1980 he was based mostly in Gaborone, staying usually with Mike Tiller, a former Swaneng volunteer, and his partner, Amina. But he was always on the move.

There was a possibility that he would establish his centre of operations in Zimbabwe, which was already being seen by radical activists as a beacon of hope for the liberation of the whole of Southern Africa. By now he was thinking regional and even global rather than local and planned to set up a 'Foundation for Education with Production' (FEP). Zimbabwe seemed the ideal place to start.

The Zimbabweans had already, of necessity, been practising a form of EwP in their self-built bush schools in Mozambique and Zambia[13] and Patrick accepted at face value Mugabe's professed commitment to socialism. He thus had strong hopes that the new government would appreciate the transformative potential of Education with Production.

In the months following the Zimbabwe election Patrick contacted a number of key African educationists and intellectuals he had got to know through his series of seminars in the 1970s. They included the historian Professor Joseph Ki-Zerbo of Burkina Faso; the exiled Ugandan lawyer and leftist academic Dr Dan Nabudere, based in Dar es Salaam; Professor Nicholas Kuhanga, former Tanzanian minister of education and newly appointed vice-chancellor of the University of Dar es Salaam; and Mohammed Tikly, an exiled South African educationist who was to go on to become the director of SOMAFCO from 1982 to 1987.

He put to them his proposal to establish a foundation that would coordinate, promote and guide the spread of EwP. They agreed to put their names and reputations forward in support, at least in an honorary capacity. Meanwhile, Patrick visited Sweden, where he had a critically important meeting with Ernst Michanek, the legendary director-general of Sida. Michanek, who had attended the 1978 EwP seminar in Maputo, agreed to fund the FEP for ten years, which would cover the agreed expenses of the new foundation until 1990.

Figure 15.1: The DHF Conference in Maputo, April 1978: *Sitting at the head table, from left*: unidentified man, Pamela Roberto (Mozambique Ministry of Education and co-director of the conference), Ernst Michanek (director-general of Sida and chair of the board of trustees of the DHF), Graça Machel (Mozambique minister of education and president of the conference), Patrick van Rensburg (chief rapporteur and co-director of the conference), two unidentified men. (Van Rensburg family collection; photographer unknown)

With this level of intellectual and financial support Patrick was able to launch the FEP in Harare on 25 September 1980.[14] He had invited a wide range of people to the event and, at his proposal, Dr Nabudere was elected chairman of the board of trustees, with Vice-Chancellor Kuhanga as vice-chairman. Other international academics who became founding trustees were Ms Augusta Henriques of Guinea-Bissau, Professor Micere Mugo of Kenya and Mr Thomas Vaeth of Zimbabwe. Their nominal leadership of the FEP gave the birth of the new body international and intellectual weight.

Patrick, who had conceived the foundation, was duly elected executive director, placing him in firm control of the day-to-day running of the organisation.[15] In 1982 Nabudere moved to the UK and Kuhanga took over the chairmanship.

A few weeks after the founding of the FEP Patrick went to Lusaka, where he co-directed a seminar on 'Education and Culture for Liberation in Southern Africa'. The meeting was designed primarily for the region's liberation movements, which had been observers at but not participants in the Dar es Salaam and Maputo seminars in the 1970s. In his report on the seminar Patrick observed optimistically that 'concepts like education and production, which had to be introduced somewhat tentatively only a few years ago, are now readily accepted and steadily gaining ground in the debate on the future educational policies in southern Africa'.[16]

Neil Parsons, who had attended an early conference introducing EwP to Zimbabwe, has recalled that it was packed with school teachers whose experience dated from pre-liberation days and that they were initially hesitant about the value of EwP. They warmed to the concept, however, when they learned that Patrick van Rensburg was the author of *Guilty Land*, a book that had impressed them in their youth.[17]

Patrick had high hopes for the future of his new foundation, although in the course of 1981 it became clear that his concept of the purpose of the FEP was at odds with that of the Zimbabweans. He took it for granted that EwP would in due course be applied throughout the Zimbabwean educational system, as an engine of social and economic transformation. The Zimbabweans saw it differently.

They were tied by the terms of the Lancaster House Agreement to the current educational system and the retention of the colonial civil servants who ran it.[18] The majority of Zimbabweans went along with this: they wanted universal access to the privileged form of education hitherto reserved for whites. The FEP was thus viewed as a means of temporarily absorbing the school-age refugees and war veteran teachers who would shortly be returning from their bush schools and holding centres in Zambia and Mozambique.

In order to cater for them, Patrick used his first grant from Sida to purchase Blue Water Farm, near the village of Bromley, 48 kilometres south-east of Harare. This, he believed, would provide a base for both an EwP school and the international headquarters of the FEP.

Over several months in late 1980 and early 1981 'tens of thousands of starving children … [and] their unpaid and equally starving teachers'[19] poured back into Zimbabwe, to be settled on Blue Water and other farms recently vacated by emigrating white settlers.

Although the minister of education, returned refugee Dzingai Mutumbuka, was initially supportive of EwP, his ministry officials were not. They saw the farms and their schools as hotbeds of communism, and in this critical period they made a point of depriving them of food and other basic resources, hoping to starve them into dispersal. That the schools and their students survived at all was due both to the generosity of international donors and to the dedication of the war veterans and party cadres, who worked long hours, often for no pay, to keep the students alive and to give them a practical and useful education.[20]

Even within EwP circles Patrick was out of line with Zimbabwean thinking.[21] At a meeting of the FEP's board of trustees in June 1981, he proposed setting up national committees in each country that practised some form of EwP. These would advise the FEP, but it would be the FEP as directed by Patrick that would initiate new projects.

The Zimbabweans totally disagreed. They wanted to reverse the relationship. In this post-colonial era they needed control of their own EwP programme, with power to initiate their own projects. They had already decided to form their own version, which they called 'ZIMFEP' and which Patrick viewed as little more than a 'National Committee' under the control of the FEP. The Zimbabweans, however, insisted that while they recognised their indebtedness to Patrick for his inspiration, his work and his experience, the role of his international FEP should be that of adviser, not the other way around.[22]

There was a further point of disagreement. Patrick planned to hire expatriate trainees and other experts who would be the guarantors of the high-quality training that he knew from his Botswana experience attracted international donor support. The Zimbabwean experience in Zambia, however, had been that expatriate-dominated projects did not long outlive the departure of the expatriates. The Zimbabweans wanted home-grown projects that really lasted, even if that meant some early compromises on the quality of the training.[23]

Faced with such a challenge Patrick reluctantly bowed to the democratic will and agreed to withdraw the headquarters of the FEP to Botswana. The FEP's trustees approved the use of a Sida grant to acquire land for the FEP in Gaborone. ZIMFEP was formally inaugurated in Harare on 6 August 1981, with Education Minister Mutumbuka as founder and President Canaan Banana as patron.[24]

Patrick found his defeat in Zimbabwe particularly bruising and in due course, as he observed that EwP in Zimbabwe was confined to the farm schools for returned refugees and not allowed to spread to the rest of the education establishment, he felt that his former ally Dzingai Mutumbuka had betrayed the cause. He was to regard him as the devil incarnate, a view confirmed in his mind when Mutumbuka joined the World Bank in Washington in 1990.[25]

Meanwhile, Fay Chung, who had run Zanu's EwP-type bush schools for refugees in Mozambique, joined the Ministry of Education in Harare in 1980. She remained loyal to the cause and became chair of ZIMFEP. After several months of negotiation between the FEP, Sida and the Zimbabweans, it was agreed that Blue Water Farm and other FEP assets in Zimbabwe would be transferred to ZIMFEP.

* * *

Patrick was never celibate for long and soon after settling in Gaborone in 1980 he had met Rosemary Forbes, the head of a Canadian volunteer agency. She lived in the same block of flats as her close friend from Somalia, Amina Dirie, and her partner Mike Tiller. Mike, a former Swaneng volunteer, had been one of Patrick's best friends in Serowe in the 1960s and Patrick always stayed with the couple when he was in Gaborone.

One day Patrick turned up at the flat to find that Amina was away. He went next door to Rosemary's flat to ask where she was and when she would be back, and they got talking. It was 1 May, Rosemary's thirtieth birthday. She was on her own and feeling depressed at the idea that life was slipping by. Patrick was a good listener and she unburdened her negative thoughts about lost youth. Patrick, at forty-eight, assured her that, on the contrary, thirty was a great age. One month after his own thirtieth birthday he had published his first book and then set off on that most exciting and transformative journey, up the Nile and down the length of Africa. The age of thirty had marked the start of the most important work of his life.[26]

Hitherto Rosemary had never considered herself interested in older men, but Patrick was different; he was dedicated to his vision and at the same time full of empathy, humour and enthusiasm for life. She learned from him that it was not age that mattered but the way one lived one's life. They became friends and when she attended a conference in Harare in November 1980 he went with her. They stayed together in a friend's house for the duration of the conference. Thereafter they became more than just good friends and he moved into her flat in Gaborone.

The arrangement suited Patrick very well. Rosemary's flat was on the ground floor, making it easily accessible to visitors, and her living room became his office. FEP people were always there and Rosemary lost the use of her dining table to Patrick's mass of documents. She recalls that in frustration she protested, 'You are one thing. You and your stuff are too much.' She spilt red wine over his documents. He went out and got himself an office. Ten years later he still referred to his 'red documents' with the quip, 'there was a red line and you crossed it'.

After two years of living on his own Patrick was looking pretty bedraggled when he moved in with Rosemary. She got him into some decent clothes. He trimmed his beard, took up running to keep himself fit, and started taking some pride in how he looked.[27]

In mid-1984 Rosemary returned to Canada, but almost immediately was asked to go back to Gaborone to manage the work of the

World University Service of Canada (WUSC) in Botswana. She stayed until 1987, during which time she gave birth to her and Patrick's daughter, Joanna. On 13 May 1986, one week before her due date, Rosemary drove herself to a Johannesburg hospital as it was to be her first delivery, at the age of thirty-six. She arranged to be induced the following day, 14 May.

She would have liked to register her daughter as a Van Rensburg, but as Patrick was barred from entering South Africa he was not there to confirm his paternity, so Joanna was registered under Rosemary's surname, Forbes. After the birth Rosemary stayed with a friend in Johannesburg while she arranged for Joanna to get both British and Canadian passports, before driving back to Gaborone with her newborn infant a week later.

***

Although Patrick had been forced out of the Zimbabwe project much against his will he kept in touch with loyal Zimbabwean colleagues from his base in Gaborone and managed to establish an amicable FEP–ZIMFEP link in an advisory capacity. He set up Tshwaragano Enterprises, an organisation that started as a Builders' Brigade and in due course was converted into a co-operative. Within weeks of the formal setting up of ZIMFEP in August 1981, Patrick took twenty-two Tshwaragano trainees to a work camp at Blue Water Farm, where they assisted in digging the foundations of the classrooms for ZIMFEP's Rusununguko School.

The first principal of Rusununguko was Swaneng's George Matiza, who, in the 1960s, had been a pupil under Patrick's leadership. He had been one of the successful graduates of the Village Development course and had gone on to teach at Swaneng Hill School. Thus, through him, the influence of Patrick van Rensburg was very much alive at Rusununguko School.

Back in Gaborone, the Tshwaragano trainees began constructing houses and workshops for Tshwaragano Enterprises and then an office block for the FEP in the Maruapula district on the northern edge of central Gaborone that became the organisation's new headquarters.

In 1980 and 1981 Patrick gathered round him in Gaborone Stephen Castles, who, in 1979, had been co-author of a book on socialist education;[28] Irene Staunton, a Zimbabwean who had worked as a publisher's editor while in exile in London; and John Conradie, a South African who had settled in Zimbabwe in the early 1960s to teach History at the University College of Rhodesia.

Jailed for terrorism in 1967 by the Smith regime, Conradie was released in November 1974 and exiled to Zambia, where he taught at the University of Zambia. He returned to Zimbabwe in 1980 but became disillusioned by the level of compromises the Zanu government was making with the old white regime and he went into voluntary exile in Botswana.[29] He became Patrick's right-hand man at the FEP and deputised for him when he was away, which was increasingly often in the 1980s and early 1990s.

Patrick had decided that the FEP would spread its ideas and influence in the region and beyond through seminars and publications. The lead publication would be an international journal entitled *Education with Production*. The first edition, edited by Stephen Castles, was published in December 1981. Loyal to his Serowe roots, Patrick had it printed by the Serowe Printers' Co-operative, which had emerged out of the former Serowe Printers' Brigade.

The journal was published approximately twice yearly, receiving articles on EwP from around the world as well as becoming a vehicle for publishing reports on seminars and conferences relating to the concept and practice of EwP. Irene Staunton took over the editorship in 1982 and continued with this and other work relating to FEP publications until 1984, when she and her partner, Murray McCartney, moved to Zimbabwe and Frank Youngman, professor of Adult Education at the University of Botswana, became editor of the journal.[30]

A major project in the 1980s for Patrick, the FEP and those associated with the foundation was to develop a complete curriculum for schools and education departments that were prepared to take on EwP, in part or in its entirety. By 1989 they had eight subjects lined up. Development Studies was already widely known, and Patrick added 'Cultural Studies' and 'Environment and Social Studies'.

While these three subjects provided the social and intellectual context for adult life, the rest were aimed at preparing students for the world of work. 'Fundamentals of Production' introduced students to the theoretical and practical workings of productive enterprises. English was taught as 'Language for Use', while Science and Mathematics followed a practical curriculum developed by ZIMFEP. Finally, 'Technical Studies' provided the training for the specific productive projects in which the school was involved.[31]

* * *

By this time Patrick had gained considerably in international status, thanks, in part, to Sven Hamrell. In February 1981 Sven had written to Jakob von Uexkull, a fellow Swede living in the UK's Isle of Man, who, the previous year, had founded the Right Livelihood Award (RLA) to 'honour and support courageous people and organisations that have found practical solutions to the root causes of global problems'.[32]

Whereas the Nobel Foundation rewarded the pinnacle of intellectual achievement in science and the arts, the Right Livelihood Award, dubbed by the media 'the Alternative Nobel Prize', recognised those individuals whose struggle for justice in the world was an inspiration to others, and those who devised and practised models of development for the social and economic benefit of humanity.

In line with these principles, Sven Hamrell recommended Patrick as a worthy candidate for the award, citing his work in devising a model of alternative education in Southern Africa that was also appropriate for many other parts of the developing world.

He referred Von Uexkull to Patrick's principal publications, *Report from Swaneng Hill* and *The Serowe Brigades*,[33] as well as to several of his published articles. After careful study and consideration, Von Uexkull and the Right Livelihood panel agreed with Hamrell, and in the latter half of 1981 Patrick received an invitation to come to Stockholm to receive one of that year's three awards. His fellow laureates were the British trade unionist Mike Cooley, 'for designing and promoting the theory and practice of human-centred, socially useful production', and the Australian Bill Mollison, 'for developing and promoting the theory and practice of permaculture'. Patrick van Rensburg's award was 'for designing school curricula to enable children in poor countries to acquire practical knowledge and skills for life'.[34]

In his acceptance speech Patrick was careful to acknowledge his indebtedness to the people of Sweden and, in particular, to the Dag Hammarskjöld Foundation, for their support of his work over the past fifteen years. He then went on to relate something of his personal background in South Africa by way of explaining what had led to his exile and the evolution of his alternative model of education in Botswana.

He explained his pioneering of Development Studies as an attempt to enable his students to analyse social development historically so that they would understand the development choices open to them. His aim was that in doing so they would become critics of the ubiquitous formal system of academic schooling that used a disproportionate amount of a poor country's meagre resources to educate a small minority to a high level. This not only neglected the well-being of the majority; it also rendered the country subservient to the interests of international industrial capitalism.

> I began to feel that education combined with production was important as a lever for change, because by involving people in production, by involving them in creating resources which helped to sustain their own education programmes, one was linking the school with society. One wanted them to be involved not only in production, in selling the things they made, in building within the community, but also in the social and cultural activities of society.[35]

As explained on the RLA website, the prize money that accompanies the award 'is only the start of a long relationship between the Laureate and the Foundation ... [The latter] sees its role as being the megaphone and shield for the Laureates, and provides them with long-term support.'[36] The money is not for private use; it is intended to further the laureates' ongoing work, although there are no formal restrictions placed upon it, and this trust seems never to have been abused.[37]

Patrick's share of the award money came to 17 000 Botswana pula (about the equivalent amount in US dollars at that time), which he banked as a special fund in the FEP's account. His first inclination was to use it towards setting up some kind of co-operative bank that would be owned by and extend credit to some of the poorest people in Botswana, but he soon realised that, at least for the time being, he would have to settle for something considerably less ambitious.[38]

* * *

The Right Livelihood Award recognised Patrick's work and provided funds to assist the furtherance of his projects, and it also established him as an international consultant in the field of education and development. This wider recognition began with a seminar on 'Education and Culture for Liberation in the Caribbean' that took place in Grenada on 22–26 November 1982.[39] The seminar was co-directed by Patrick, who had high hopes that the island nation would become a base for the spread of EwP throughout the West Indies.

His optimism was based on the transformation of the country being undertaken by the country's president, Maurice Bishop, a socialist vision-ary whose New Jewel Movement had seized power in 1979. Drawing inspiration from Julius Nyerere and from Castro's Cuba, Bishop based his policies on education for self-reliance and he was very attracted to Patrick's model of Education with Production.

The seminar was regarded as a great success and Patrick found in Maurice Bishop a kindred spirit. He was therefore deeply shocked when, less than a year later, and having just completed another trip to Grenada, he heard that Bishop had been overthrown and summarily executed.[40] A week later a US force invaded the island 'to restore order', and that spelt the end of EwP and the FEP in Grenada.

The killing of Maurice Bishop and the loss of the Grenada project was yet another major setback for Patrick, but he never stayed down for long. Indeed, setbacks seemed, if anything, to spur him on to ever greater efforts to promote his vision as widely as possible and 1983 became a particularly busy year for him.

In February he ran a Development Studies workshop for teachers in Molepolole, with attendees from Lesotho and Zimbabwe as well as Botswana. Development Studies had been taught at the Swaneng Hill, Shashe River and Madiba schools for many years and examined at junior secondary level since 1965. His aim now was to have it taught and examined at senior secondary level. It was another year before the various ministries of education and the Cambridge Examinations Syndicate were all on board, and the subject was finally examined at School Certificate level in Botswana in 1986.

In early April 1983 Patrick attended a conference in the Welsh capital, Cardiff, for the setting up of BritFEP, the initiative of some of his former Swaneng teaching colleagues. It was part of an attempt by socialist-minded people in Britain to provide an antidote to the right-wing policies of Margaret Thatcher's government. Patrick's paper was entitled 'Education for a New Society'. In the event, it was wishful thinking, for the Thatcher government was re-elected by a landslide two months later.

Immediately after the meeting in Cardiff Patrick flew to Alaska, where he had been invited to consult with Patrick Dubbs of the University of Alaska in Fairbanks. Dubbs, who was running a training programme for indigenous people in Alaska, had heard of Patrick's work through the Right Livelihood Award and was seeking his advice.

Patrick spent four days in discussion with Dubbs and his colleagues before being flown to the remote settlement of Huslia, 250 air miles north-west of Fairbanks. In the next five days he was shown around the villages of Huslia district and met with the staff and students of Huslia School. He discussed their problems and hopes for the future and showed them a film of Serowe and the brigades.

Dubbs feared the loss of the Alaskan people's traditional hunting-based economy and culture, which was being undermined by the penetration of the US capitalist economy and its imports. Traditional skills and self-sufficiency were being lost and migrant labour, unemployment and alcoholism were becoming the norm – a pattern that was widespread all over the developing world.

Dubbs wanted to establish local production in the villages and was planning to set up a bakery in Huslia. Patrick advised against this, for the resources and equipment would all have to be imported. Dubbs could provide the training for whatever project they settled on, but it needed to be the students who took the initiative in establishing projects that focused on local resources.

In this forested and hunting environment Patrick suggested carpentry and a tannery, stressing that, above all, ownership of the projects must be local.[41] Dubbs carried out a feasibility study to assess the available resources, skills and needs, but it is not clear whether any productive enterprise along the lines suggested by Patrick was ever established. Huslia today, with a resident population of about 400, 93 per cent of whom are indigenous Alaskans, 25 per cent of whom live below the poverty line, is the capital of mushing (dog-sleigh racing) in Alaska.[42]

From Alaska Patrick flew to Canada, where he had a few weeks' holiday. While there he secured Canadian University Service Overseas (CUSO) support for some FEP projects. Returning to Africa in the southern winter, he attended a Popular Theatre workshop in Harare in July, followed by a workshop on co-operatives in Gaborone. He presented a paper at a symposium on education at the National Museum and Art Gallery in Gaborone in August, before flying to Tanzania to attend an ANC Education Council meeting at SOMAFCO. In October he was in Paris for a meeting with the United Nations Educational, Scientific and Cultural Organization (UNESCO) Education Institute. It was at about this time that he wrote *Looking Forward from Serowe*, a special ninety-five-page supplement to the FEP journal, which became, in effect, his personal manifesto.[43]

* * *

Patrick's main focus through 1984 was to revive *Mmegi wa Dikgang*, the newspaper he had founded in Serowe in 1968 and which had survived fitfully through the early 1970s. He intended to re-establish the paper as a full-sized tabloid weekly that would provide an independent voice on local and world news, as an alternative to the government's *Daily News*, which he perceived to be mainly concerned with promoting government policies.

In practice, *Mmegi*'s direct competitor was the weekly *Botswana Guardian*, which was a spin-off from the *Mafeking Mail*, still being printed in Mafikeng.[44] *Mmegi* was to be printed by the Serowe Printers' Brigade as part of Patrick's drive to revive the Serowe brigades.[45] It soon overtook the *Botswana Guardian* in sales and popularity.

Figure 15.2: Mma Kentlahetse working on the *Co-operative News* at the Serowe Printers' Brigade. The relaunch of *Mmegi wa Dikgang* as a national weekly in 1984 saved the Printers' Brigade through the 1980s and allowed it to become an independent co-operative. (By kind permission of Peter Jensen)

To help with the paper Patrick hired a young graduate teacher, Methaetsile Leepile, as his editorial assistant. Leepile had been a student at Swaneng Hill School for five years in the 1970s and had edited the school newsletter.

In Serowe he knew Patrick by reputation, rather than personally. Since graduating he had edited the History Association Newsletter and written a few pieces for international newspapers. On Leepile's first day at work Patrick explained that *Mmegi* would be printed in Serowe and distributed nationally by bus and train. Leepile, filled with the confidence of youth, protested that Patrick had no money – how could he start a newspaper without money?

Patrick responded calmly: 'Young man – if you keep asking questions you'll get fired.' But Leepile would not let up, and Patrick, who never let a lack of money stand in the way of a good idea,[46] simply shouted: 'You're fired!'

That afternoon Patrick came to Leepile's home and demanded: 'Why aren't you at work?'

'You fired me.'

'You just annoy me. Start work on Monday.'[47]

And so, they started work on the paper, initially just the two of them. It was July 1984 and the first issue of the new-look *Mmegi* was published on Friday 31 August. Advertising was collected and the paper composed and set in Gaborone. It was then driven to Serowe on Thursday by George Moalosi, Patrick's general assistant at the FEP, the road by then being tarred as far as Palapye. It was printed overnight by Serowe Printers. Some copies were left for distribution in Serowe and Francistown and the bulk driven back to Gaborone for distribution on the Friday morning.[48]

Mmegi was 'a flagship for Patrick's ideas'.[49] In his first editorial he declared the paper's independence:

> We belong to no party. But that does not mean that we have no views, opinions or commitments. We believe that everyone's basic needs must be satisfied – and can be satisfied – now! That means education, good health, and a sound habitat, housing, clothing, water and food, freedom and welfare, public transport and the right to communicate – for everyone – now. It is the achievement of these – as rights – for all that will be the real guarantee of our democracy. Mmegi wa Dikgang will provide a forum to discuss how we are to achieve all this, now, and we will serve to remind all parties of these goals.[50]

In the early months Patrick did most of the writing himself. Leepile has described him as the finest journalist and editor he has known. He would take Leepile's copy, which had taken him five hours to compose, 'turn it upside-down, cut it in half and make it a "must read" story – all in 15 minutes'.[51] Gradually over the next five years he handed more and more work to Leepile, who took over the editorship in 1987. Leepile brought in others, such as Titus Mbuya, who joined *Mmegi* in 1989.

Mmegi in its early years was financially underwritten by the FEP, and the FEP in turn was largely funded by grants from Sida. This presented a problem for Sida, which could not afford to be seen to support a newspaper that was perceived to be critical of the Botswana government. Sven Hamrell, however, agreed with Patrick that a newspaper that disseminated information and promoted social justice suited the remit of the Dag Hammarskjöld Foundation, and a conduit was established whereby Sida provided funds to the DHF, which transferred it to *Mmegi*.[52]

At the same time Patrick began to separate the newspaper from the FEP by forming the Mmegi Publication Trust, which, by 1989, had become the paper's sole proprietor.[53] It remains to this day Botswana's leading independent newspaper. Meanwhile, the printing contract for *Mmegi* put the Serowe Printers' Brigade on a sound financial footing and allowed it, eventually, to break away from control by the SBDT board – which, to Patrick's mind, had become too much under the sway of the ruling BDP. It took a few years of legal wrangling, but eventually Serowe Printers was able to set itself up as a separate co-operative.[54]

* * *

In 1980 the 'Front Line States' – Botswana, Zambia, Tanzania, Angola and Mozambique – joined with Lesotho, Swaziland, Malawi and newly independent Zimbabwe to form the Southern African Development Coordination Conference (SADCC), a regional grouping dedicated, through inter-state cooperation, to reducing economic and communication dependence on South Africa.[55] Cooperation among SADCC states became ever more important through the 1980s as apartheid South Africa went through its death throes, striking out at its neighbours, trying to destabilise them and intimidate them into expelling all South African refugees.[56]

Figure 15.3: Patrick representing Botswana at an education/development conference. (Van Rensburg family collection; photographer unknown)

In 1985 Patrick and the Dag Hammarskjöld Foundation planned to hold a seminar on 'Another Development for SADCC Countries', to promote Patrick's education and development ideas. King Moshoeshoe II, who had followed Patrick's career since the early 1960s when he visited Serowe, made his royal palace in Maseru available for the meeting. He was very committed to EwP, had set up his own school to promote EwP ideas and was instrumental in forming a Lesotho branch of the FEP. The meeting, scheduled for late November 1985, took most of the year to organise and Patrick attended numerous planning meetings in Lesotho, Zambia, Zimbabwe and Sweden in the course of the year.

He had just 'put the paper (*Mmegi*) to bed' on Thursday 13 June and was on the train north for one of these meetings in Zimbabwe when a unit of the South African special forces conducted a raid on Gaborone in the early hours of Friday morning, 14 June 1985. Twelve people were killed; several of them were Batswana, including women and children, and the South African refugees who died were all civilians. It was clearly a terror attack, intended to pressure the Botswana government into taking a harder line on South African refugees.

Patrick appears not to have been on the target list, but the raid made him even more determined to go ahead with the seminar in Lesotho, a country which, the previous year, had also been subject to a South African raid. He made several trips to Uppsala to discuss arrangements with Sven and Olle, who totally supported his plans.

The seminar, which took place from 18 to 22 November 1985, was well attended by delegates from across the region and was judged a great success. Unlike the case with a previous conference held in Lesotho, Patrick was able to attend, direct flights having been established between Gaborone and Maseru.

The seminar concluded that collective self-reliance within and among countries was what was needed, with pressure being applied on governments, aid donors and regional organisations to move urgently towards these goals.[57] Moshoeshoe II, who had attended the entire seminar, took the resolutions very seriously and Patrick, the DHF and Lesotho's Matsieng Development Trust ran another seminar in Maseru in December 1987. Entitled 'Another Development for Lesotho', it was attended by 250 participants, mostly from within Lesotho, plus ten 'high qualified international resource persons from Africa, Asia and South America'.

Lesotho was going through a turbulent period politically and the participants concluded that the seminar at least 'fulfilled a long felt need for a public discussion of Lesotho's development priorities'.[58] Patrick sought to disseminate his ideas as widely as possible internationally and the collected papers from both seminars were published by the FEP and printed by the Serowe Printers' Brigade, with financial assistance from the DHF.[59]

* * *

Although Patrick had long since moved on from Swaneng Hill School, he still clung to the idealism he had nurtured during his first decade in Botswana. From 1986 to 1988 he studied rural development projects in China and India and was convinced that he could establish an autonomous rural community in Botswana that would demonstrate the practicality of his model of education for rural development.

He had already identified a site in the Mokgware Hills, 50 kilometres south-east of Serowe. It had the natural resources from which could be developed a coal mine, a cement factory, an iron works and pottery units. It was a very ambitious project that would involve education and production on a co-operative basis, combining the best of early Swaneng Hill School, the brigades of the 1970s and Boiteko. It would be called *Thuto Le Tiro* ('Education with Work').

He won the support of the Serowe *kgotla*, who, in 1988, approved allocation of the land. All that remained was government approval and financial support from international donors, but despite great hopes and numerous promises, ultimately, on both these issues the project stalled. Nevertheless, *Thuto Le Tiro* remained Patrick's ideal through much of the 1990s and his son Tom worked on the project at the FEP in Gaborone in the early 1990s. It was a good scheme on paper, but it never materialised in practice in Botswana.[60]

* * *

The last of the series of 1980s SADCC seminars took place in Zimbabwe in April 1989. It was a two-part conference. The initial meeting, 'Curriculum for Development', held in Harare on 20–22 April, was followed by the main five-day conference at Victoria Falls: 'Education and Training for Employment'. The latter was attended by representatives from all nine of the SADCC countries, with seven of the delegations headed by their ministers of education.

The FEP was represented by Professor Kuhanga, John Conradie and Patrick, as seminar director. Patrick's paper, 'Critical innovations in education for employment', was presented on the third day at Victoria Falls and, according to his own account, 'it gave rise to a heated discussion'.[61] But Patrick had ensured that a suitable cooling off was enjoyed that evening as the eighty delegates were treated to a cruise on the Zambezi – what tourists have dubbed 'the booze cruise'.

A hot topic in the social milieu of the sunset cruise would have been the political events in Southern Africa. The apartheid state was clearly in retreat. Its attacks on the South West African People's Organisation (SWAPO) had been checked in Angola, the UN was scheduled to conduct pre-independence elections in Namibia later in the year,[62] and South Africa itself, under severe international sanctions and simmering rebellion at home, was becoming ungovernable. It may have been difficult to believe on the Zambezi in April 1989, but it was becoming increasingly clear that the history of Southern Africa was about to enter a whole new trajectory.

16 | Education with Production and South Africa, the 1990s

In October 1989 F. W. de Klerk, newly sworn in as South African state president, ordered the release of all but one of the country's high-profile political prisoners. It was clear that De Klerk was seeking new paths out of the morass of apartheid, and the stage-managed release of Nelson Mandela could be only months away.

SOMAFCO was celebrating the tenth anniversary of its founding and, with a feeling that the end of apartheid was nigh, a number of educators from South Africa travelled north to Morogoro. For many it was their first meeting with their exiled ANC counterparts. The main topic of discussion was the ANC's education policy for a liberated South Africa, and it was Patrick's 'first opportunity to present the Education with Production (EwP) curriculum to a mainly South African audience'.[1] He distributed copies of a complete alternative curriculum that the FEP, with the assistance of experts from six SADCC countries, had worked out in detail through the 1980s. It included languages, Mathematics and Science alongside four specific EwP subjects.[2]

Apart from one or two exceptions within the ANC leadership, however, the party had never really been committed to EwP. Indeed, the underlying focus of SOMAFCO itself had never been totally clear. Was the college mainly for political education and training for 'the struggle'? Was it somewhere to keep the exiled youth occupied and partially trained in practical skills, thus paying lip service to the fashion for EwP? Or was it to gain higher education abroad to create an élite who would someday rule South Africa? This dilemma was never clearly resolved.

Perhaps the last thing the ANC and SOMAFCO wanted was someone like Patrick van Rensburg – an outside expert who knew *exactly* what he wanted, and that was to create an educational model for social and economic transformation that could and should be replicated in a liberated South Africa.[3] It was clearly going to be an uphill struggle to get EwP on the South African education agenda. There was, however, a glimmer of hope in the presence of a small delegation from Kangwane, the segregated Swazi 'homeland' or 'bantustan', in what was then the Eastern Transvaal (now Mpumalanga province).

Kangwane was one of the poorest, most neglected regions of South Africa; just the sort of fertile soil for the germination of a replicable EwP programme. The delegation was led by the local chairman of the education department of the Congress of South African Trade Unions (Cosatu), Chris Seoposengwe, who had already discussed with local progressive groups and the homeland government the setting up of an 'alternative' school in the region. He was very taken with EwP and invited Patrick to help launch a project in Kangwane.[4] Patrick explained that for the time being he would have to decline the invitation as he was still banned from the country, but he promised to visit as soon as he was free to do so.

Meanwhile, if this really was the endgame of apartheid, it had enormous implications for the whole of the SADCC region and it was important that the people, upon whom a democratic future depended, were properly informed. Patrick, already the founder of an important independent national newspaper, took up the cause.

At his urging, the Dag Hammarskjöld Foundation and the FEP jointly organised a seminar entitled 'Democracy and the Media in Southern Africa'. It was directed and hosted by Patrick from 1 to 5 December 1989 at his favourite holiday spot, the Chobe Game Lodge in northern Botswana. Unlike any other regional seminar that Patrick had directed in the previous two decades, this one was attended by a delegation from the Republic of South Africa. Patrick proudly described it as 'a unique event; it was the first time that journalists from the alternative or democratic press in South Africa had met with colleagues from the Front Line States in a gathering of this type'.[5]

The seminar concluded that unfolding events in Eastern Europe, including the fall of the Berlin Wall four weeks previously, had emphasised the importance of the role of independent media and that these lessons needed to be applied in Southern Africa during this era of great change.

Ahead of the Chobe meeting Patrick had already submitted to the DHF board of trustees a proposal for setting up a regional weekly newspaper. Like *Mmegi*, 'now considered one of the liveliest and best-informed newspapers in the region', it would be an inexpensive tabloid, addressed to a broad spectrum of public opinion, with a blend of serious and popular content and style.

'Its comprehensive, analytical coverage and strong focus on news should,' Patrick argued, 'facilitate the achievement of its objectives of promoting awareness at all levels of the need for closer regional identity and collective self-reliant action.'[6] Individual national newspapers were vulnerable to government and other interference, whereas a regional paper would be better at strengthening participatory democracy, social justice and mechanisms for protecting human rights.

Full of enthusiasm for the new project, Patrick advocated a feasibility study, to be worked on jointly by the DHF and the FEP. But the tumultuous events in South Africa in 1990 soon took over and ultimately, as with so many of Patrick's progressive projects, his idea of a regional newspaper failed to get off the ground. To some extent the role was taken up in 1993 by the weekly paper the *Mail & Guardian*, which, together with input from the British *Guardian Weekly* and some comment from the *Washington Post*, emerged out of the *Weekly Mail* that had replaced the *Rand Daily Mail* in 1985.

* * *

Once the African National Congress (ANC), the Pan Africanist Congress (PAC) and other political parties were unbanned and Nelson Mandela walked free in February 1990, exiled South Africans were able to apply to have their individual banning orders lifted, which would allow them to return to their country without fear of arrest.

The ANC, now free to act in South Africa, provided the government in Pretoria with a list of its members who needed clearance for return. Patrick, however, was not among those given priority in this way, which appears to confirm that, despite doing so much for its cause throughout his years of exile, he was never actually a card-carrying member of the ANC.

Another possible mark against him as far as the ANC hierarchy was concerned was that he had been a friend in Botswana to many exiled members of the PAC, the ANC's political rival. But that was typical of Patrick: a friend to all South African exiles, but not a party-political man. He had experienced the mild restrictions of the long-defunct Liberal Party, and that was enough for him. He had avoided membership of the Botswana National Front for this very reason and had no desire to surrender his freedom to a South African political party. Nor was he someone who would lobby on his own behalf. This meant that, as an individual, he went to the back of the queue for repatriation.

He was allowed one short visit, in August 1990, but did not get clearance to freely enter South Africa until 1991, making him one of the last of the banned South Africans in Botswana to be allowed to return to the country of his birth.[7] He continued, however, to use a Botswana passport and had to renew his visa every thirty days.[8]

He settled in an apartment in Bertrams, an inner-city suburb of Johannesburg, a little to the north-east of the central business district, where he bought a small block of maisonettes 'with a soft loan from a friend in the UK'. He let out the downstairs and kept the upstairs apartment for his own accommodation. He immediately opened an FEP office, which, initially, he operated single-handedly from his living room.[9]

For the next decade Johannesburg became the joint headquarters, with Gaborone, of FEP International, with financial backing in the early years from a Canadian non-governmental organisation. By 1992 the Johannesburg FEP had its own office and two full-time staff members – Ahmed Moonda as coordinator South Africa, in charge of the day-to-day running of the office, and Koketso Selebogo as youth coordinator.[10] Rosemary Forbes, who had returned to Botswana in 1991 to work for INTERFUND, paid off the Bertrams house to provide Patrick with security of accommodation in Johannesburg. Having been tempted back to Botswana after three years in Canada because of Patrick, she found that he was spending most of his time in South Africa.[11]

* * *

From the moment he returned to South Africa in 1991, Patrick knew that the task he faced was monumental. The country had a 'highly-developed, diversified economy' alongside 'vast pools of stagnant underdevelopment in its rural areas and urban slums'. Apartheid, 'with its mix of racial capitalism, based on super-exploitation of Black peasants and workers', meant that 'most people still live[d] their lives in poverty'. The 'highly undemocratic nature' of apartheid education had enshrined great inequality in the structure of society, something that would take 'time, commitment and innovative approaches to correct'. EwP, however, would make a start in this direction, for it not only offered 'substantial potential economic, social and learning benefits', but its productive capability would also help fund his new approach to education.[12]

Following up on his discussion with Cosatu's Chris Seoposengwe at SOMAFCO's anniversary in 1989, the first South African project in which Patrick and FEP South Africa became involved was in Kangwane. While Patrick waited for clearance to return to South Africa, officials from Cosatu, together with members of the teachers' union in Kangwane, made several trips to Gaborone to see at first hand his plans for *Thuto Le Tiro* ('Education with Work'), his rural community project in Botswana.

The fact that *Thuto Le Tiro* had not yet been implemented did not seem to matter. Patrick seems to have been able to convince his visitors that it soon would be. It was realised that the Botswana curriculum and education concept needed to be adapted slightly to suit the South African context, but most of this work and consultation was completed by the end of 1990.[13]

Once Patrick was allowed to return to South Africa he was able to hold direct discussions in Kangwane and make final adjustments to the project document. If he could not get *Thuto Le Tiro* implemented in Botswana he would do so in Kangwane. With the support of the Kangwane Ministry of Education, a group of teachers was able to visit Windhoek in newly independent Namibia, where introductory EwP courses were being held for teachers from all the SADCC countries.[14]

At this stage the day-to-day preparation of the Kangwane project was largely in Patrick's hands, with some part-time assistance from Chris Seoposengwe. Patrick managed to get funding for a feasibility study and an architectural planning study for the project, the latter done by the man responsible for designing the buildings for SOMAFCO. By the time these studies were completed Patrick and the Kangwane authorities had found a suitable site for the study centre. Like the Mazimba farm in Tanzania, it had some disused and derelict buildings that could be renovated and adapted for accommodation, classrooms and production workshops. The Kangwane Work and Study Centre (KWSC) opened its doors to its first students at the end of 1991.

Through 1991–1992 Patrick's time was split between Johannesburg and Kangwane, with occasional hurried visits to Gaborone, where he had left the FEP office in the hands of John Conradie and *Thuto Le Tiro* in the hands of his son Tom. On those occasions he would drive through the night to the Botswana border, sleep in the car and go through the border as soon as it opened in the morning, turning up at Rosemary and Joanna's flat in time for breakfast.[15]

Back in Kangwane he set up a Youth Education Trust (YET) to run the KWSC, with trustees drawn from the area. He was elected chairman of the trust. The Kangwane ministry seconded fourteen committed teachers to the project, production managers were recruited, and the students began enjoying integrated education and training, involving themselves in all the sorts of basic productive skills that Patrick had pioneered with the brigades in Botswana. These included growing their own vegetables, building their own classrooms and dormitories, and equipping them with self-built wooden and metal furnishings. As in Serowe, some brigades were set up to cater for primary school 'drop-outs'.[16]

All appeared well on the surface, but from the start there were major problems and rivalries over the management and funding of the project and the selection of students. According to Patrick, Chris Seoposengwe, based in Johannesburg, brought a number of high-profile personal contacts onto the board of trustees and had himself appointed project director.[17] He received some funding from a Swiss Christian NGO on the understanding that it would be spent on educating returning exiles. Without consulting Patrick or the YET board, and using the slogan 'bringing SOMAFCO home', he admitted fifty students to the KWSC whom he claimed were refugees.

As Patrick recalled, 'it was the view of ANC personnel dealing with repatriates that almost all the group members so admitted were not exiles, but from Soweto'. Seoposengwe quit as project director in February 1992, but his 'Committee of Parents' sent more students, and conflict between the committee and the YET board escalated, culminating in accusations of misappropriation of funds. Patrick and a bookkeeper, with the aid of the bank, managed to satisfy the Swiss NGO about the accounts, but by that time Patrick had resigned as chairman of the YET board.

Following the democratic elections of 1994, the former 'bantustans' of apartheid South Africa were dissolved. Kangwane was incorporated into the new Mpumalanga province. Patrick would have known that with the unfolding liberation of South Africa through the early 1990s the life of the Kangwane Ministry of Education was severely limited, but he had been hoping that his project would be so successful that its principles would become part of education policy in post-apartheid South Africa.

As we shall see below, however, the incoming ANC government failed to commit to Patrick's ideas and YET's Work and Study Centre lost the support it had had from the now dissolved Kangwane Ministry of Education. As Patrick later recalled sadly, 'a dream project became a nightmare and never fully recovered, [although] it limped through to 1996, with at least credible results in Cambridge examinations'.[18]

* * *

Despite these problems, Patrick felt able to report to the DHF in 1992 that 'already a student constituency supportive of Education with Production is developing'.[19] He should strike while the iron was hot and get in touch with those involved in training the teachers of the future.

He approached various universities and received a positive response from Professor Peter Kallaway of the Faculty of Education of the University of Cape Town (UCT). Kallaway already knew a great deal about the FEP and EwP and had extensive connections with people involved with Patrick and his work. They had a mutual friend in Jonathan Paton, son of Alan, a friendship which, in Patrick's case, went back to his days in the Liberal Party in the late 1950s.

Coincidentally, Kallaway's first master's student (in the late 1970s) had chosen 'the Brigades' as the topic for his dissertation and Kallaway had known John Conradie, the co-director of the FEP in Gaborone, for years – their mothers had grown up together in East London.

Kallaway thus knew Patrick well by reputation and was pleased to invite him to make a presentation about his educational work to what turned out to be 'a large and appreciative audience' at UCT's Faculty of Education. Patrick discussed with Kallaway the formulation of a course on EwP that would be one of a series of optional courses for the Bachelor of Education (BEd) degree.

The syllabus they settled on covered the international history, theory and practice of EwP, including the wide range of potential productive projects, with case studies and practical examples, mostly from his own experience. For 20 per cent of the final assessment, students would be required to do practical fieldwork, reporting on an EwP project or writing part of a text for a supplementary reader in one of the EwP school subjects.[20]

Although Kallaway then moved to the University of the Western Cape (UWC), the mixed-race university in the Cape Town suburb of Bellville, in 1993/1994, Patrick was offered the post of part-time visiting professor at UCT, initially for two years, from 1993. The following year he extended the same course to the University of Natal (today's University of KwaZulu-Natal) in his old hometown of Pietermaritzburg.

It became a gruelling schedule that consumed much of his time, especially in the second year. He would fly down to Cape Town in the evening, stay overnight with Kallaway, prepare his lecture in the morning, deliver it at UCT in the afternoon and fly straight back to Johannesburg. Sometimes he would even drive there and back, often sleeping in the old FEP car.

With Pietermaritzburg added to the schedule, he was clocking up 4 000 kilometres a week. Ever since the founding of Swaneng Hill School Patrick had led by example – that of commitment and sheer physical hard work. Now, with this punishing schedule, he appears to have felt that he could single-handedly inspire, convince and persuade people of his great solution for development: EwP. It was a schedule, reflective of his obsessive personality, that was impossible to maintain for long.

In the two years between 1993 and 1994 about 150 students in the two universities took the course and, on the whole, it was enthusiastically received. But the weekly travel took its toll and the whole project was very costly. The universities each paid the FEP a fee for Patrick's lectures, but this did not even cover his travel costs, which became a heavy burden on the foundation's finances. In the end, after two years of worthwhile work getting his message across to a small section of the younger generation of budding educators, he had to abandon the BEd course: 'Apart from cost, the time to prepare lessons, and to mark assignments and examinations meant that I was simply unable to deal adequately with the increasing demands of other FEP work,' he wrote.[21]

* * *

If EwP was ever going to work in South Africa it was time for others to take up the baton. The outlook for this, however, was not promising. When the Sida-funded National Education Policy Initiative (NEPI) held a conference on 'Human Resources for a New South Africa' in Durban in May 1992 Patrick was not there. Peter Kallaway, who attended the conference, thinks he was not even invited.[22] In 1993 NEPI published *The Framework Report*. It mentioned the Kangwane Project, with some reflections on EwP in South Africa, but when the ANC government drew up its final education policy it ignored the report and neither Patrick nor the FEP even got a mention.[23]

Patrick was to take this apparent rejection of his life's work deeply personally and unfairly translated it into an emerging élitism of the sort he had fought against for so many years in Botswana.

Back in the late 1950s he had known many of the ANC leaders personally and he and his work for the struggle were well known to them. Forty years on, though, Patrick was largely unknown to the vastly expanded leadership of the ANC. As he saw it, however, those in the field of education knew exactly who he was and the alternative education he was promoting and chose to ignore it.[24] He believed they wanted for their children the privileged academic education that had previously been available only to white children. Most parents and educators 'could not conceive of the involvement of their students in any kind of real work while they [were] at school'.[25]

What Patrick may not have appreciated in this crucial period of transition to a post-apartheid South Africa was the importance of democratisation in all spheres of government, including education. All ideas were being considered and EwP had to compete with others. Nor was he unique in proposing the integration of academic education and technical training, an idea strongly promoted by Cosatu.

The incoming administration was presented with decades' worth of racist inequity in education, and the driving force of policy in all spheres of government was to right this crying injustice rather than tinker too deeply with the system itself. It was decided after much discussion that integration of academic and technical education would best be handled through a focus on new national qualifications for more traditional curricula, as set out in the National Qualifications Framework, rather than the adoption of a new, unfamiliar and not widely tested curriculum such as EwP.[26]

Patrick's failure to be drawn into the ANC's education policy discussions may have been linked to the fact that his contacts with ANC exiles were primarily with those at SOMAFCO. Beyond that he did not have access to ANC decision-making. The ANC's head of education when the organisation came to power in 1994 was John Samuel, a professional educationist who had not left South Africa and who did not have a background in EwP. And Patrick was not a man given to lobbying politicians.

* * *

If Patrick could not get across to educational authorities at national level, he would try at local level. Through 1990–1994, as the ANC and the De Klerk government negotiated a settlement for the future of South Africa, it became clear that responsibility for education was going to be devolved to provincial level and Patrick felt that this was where he should focus his efforts.

During a short break in his lecture schedule he spent a week in Sweden in June 1993, discussing the issue with Sven Hamrell and Olle Nordberg. He reported on the 'recent satisfactory performance of the Kangwane Work and Study Centre' and the strong support there from students and staff, as well as the production and technical personnel.

He proposed a series of regional seminars, which the DHF agreed to support.[27] By this time the FEP in Botswana had published a number of textbooks and teachers' guides, which were available for the EwP curriculum.[28] These would be presented at the seminars to demonstrate that EwP was a viable curriculum with appropriate materials ready and waiting to be used. Patrick was back in Uppsala in November for the detailed planning of the seminars, which, it was hoped, would take place the following year.

At about this time Olle Nordberg took over as executive director of the DHF, while Sven Hamrell remained as special adviser. In these capacities the two men visited South Africa in February 1994. They hoped, with Patrick, to discuss the proposed cycle of seminars with national and provincial governing bodies, but the timing of their visit could not have been worse. All politicians and most government officials were tied up in electioneering for the most significant general election in South Africa's history and Olle and Sven were not able to meet with any of the national education authorities.

Once the 1994 elections were over, however, and the new ANC government under President Nelson Mandela was firmly ensconced in power, the new provincial authorities took over responsibility for education and it was to them that the proposed seminars were addressed. Patrick and the DHF proposed three regional seminars, each of which would draw representatives from three of the nine new provinces.[29]

Much of Patrick's time in the early months of 1995 was taken up with planning meetings and administrative matters, with Olle Nordberg joining him in South Africa in June. The first seminar, for North West province and the Free State, was held in Mafikeng in September 1995. The Northern Cape province had been unable to attend.

There were seventy-five participants, including Patrick's stalwart supporter Joseph Ki-Zerbo from Burkina Faso, and the ministers of education from Botswana, Lesotho and Namibia, as well as the members of the executive councils responsible for education from both provinces. The speech from Botswana's minister of education, Dr Gaositwe Chiepe, was particularly persuasive. Serowe was her hometown and, as an education officer, she had known Patrick from his first arrival, in 1962.

She was thus able to draw on her personal knowledge of his work, especially that of the brigades, through which he had developed the theory and practice of EwP.[30] Similarly, the ministers from Lesotho and Namibia expressed strong support for EwP. In the first of his two papers for the seminar Patrick stressed that EwP must not focus on cheap manual labour; it must be well organised and managed, diversified according to local circumstances and based on socially useful and productive activities.

He illustrated his talk with examples of EwP-related activities in South Africa in the previous few years: the Kangwane project, his BEd course and an urban renewal project that he had recently been involved in, in

Bertrams.[31] Subsequently, a number of the delegates came to Botswana to see the work of the brigades, although these were by then a shadow of their former selves.

The second seminar, for Gauteng (the southern region of the former Transvaal) and Mpumalanga, was held in Hazyview, Mpumalanga, in December 1995. There were administrative difficulties with arranging further seminars. In the end they took place in the Western Province (May 1996),[32] KwaZulu-Natal (1997) and the Northern Cape (1998).[33] By then the national Department of Education had given the provinces permission to implement EwP directly themselves, should they choose to do so; but the steam had gone out of the drive for change.

As noted above, the priority of the ANC's education policy was to redress education inequality and rid education and training of the legacy of racism.[34] Individual schools and community centres initiated some productive activities, but these were purely local initiatives. Provincial and national education authorities preferred to stick to the tried and trusted academic and technical models, now protected by new standardised national qualifications.

* * *

Throughout the seminar programme of the mid-1990s, however, Patrick was simultaneously throwing himself into a project for urban renewal in Bertrams, the suburb in which he lived and in which the FEP had its office. Bertrams was a mixed residential area, housing both the families of Portuguese who had left Mozambique in the 1970s and poor black South Africans from the rural areas, who had taken advantage of the government's increasing inability to enforce its residential restrictions and had moved to the city in search of a livelihood.[35] Needless to say, the latter were to be found in the really run-down parts of the neighbourhood.

As Patrick was to observe: 'Bertrams' vacant lots, derelict buildings, empty offices and factories, its squatters, street kids, its many unemployed, and drug dealers who operated openly and with impunity, were a problem.'[36] But for him, 'some or all of this constituted a challenge for the concept and practice of Brigades'.[37]

He could see there was scope for urban renewal in the suburb and, at his initiative, the FEP became the driving force behind a project that would offer both brigade-type training for building high-quality, low-cost housing on some sort of co-operative basis and training for literacy, numeracy and other technical skills as the opportunity arose.

Setting up a *Thuto Le Tiro* type of project in a long-established city setting, however, was very different from doing so in the vacant areas of land on which he had been able to work in Botswana. It involved architects and engineers and the need to win the support of public works and planning departments. This all took time, but, in 1993, he finally won approval and an urban renewal grant from the Johannesburg City Council (JCC).

The expectation of government investing in this part of Johannesburg was associated with the 1995 Rugby World Cup, the final of which would be played at Ellis Park Stadium, near Bertrams. This may have influenced the JCC's decision to allocate a grant. In the event, the World Cup–associated urban renewal turned out to be a false promise, though in the meantime Patrick was able put the grant to immediate use. The skeleton staff of the FEP was expanded to five and the Bertrams Development Brigade (BDB) was established. Patrick characterised the BDB as

… an attempt to keep up with a growing influx of unemployed and underemployed people of all ages, but mainly youths, and a race against the continuing deterioration of a small but growing number of houses, which their unscrupulous slumlord owners packed with tenants from among these homeless migrants.[38]

In 1994–1995 the BDB completed six semi-detached low-cost houses and 'trained 78 young men in literacy, numeracy and construction skills'.[39] The houses were built jointly by Bertrams trainees and a professional building contractor, who undertook much of the on-the-job training. Each of the six houses had two bedrooms, a kitchen, a living area and a bathroom.

When they were completed and ready for occupation, in September 1995, they won a national competition for low-cost housing in the 'urban renewal' category. Most of that first batch of trainees, recruited from among residents in the Bertrams area and from the youth clubs of Soweto, had very little primary schooling and many had literacy and numeracy problems. Patrick had persuaded the Johannesburg Technical College to provide special lessons in technical theory and other non-productive practical tuition at all appropriate levels, including literacy classes, for which the FEP paid the college. On completion of their training 86 per cent found employment with contractors and sub-contractors on large building projects.[40]

By the mid-1990s, however, the general environment and buildings of Bertrams had deteriorated so badly that the banks, regarding the whole area as a decaying slum, refused to give loans to homebuyers, even those wanting to buy into the small group of prize-winning BDB houses. The FEP itself had taken out a heavy mortgage to pay off the contractors and, as a result of the attitude of the banks, only two of the houses were sold in the next five years.

By 2000 the FEP still owed the bank R140 000, 'secured by four good-quality but unsaleable houses'.[41] The BDB could not afford to continue construction under these circumstances, yet the whole purpose of this worthy urban renewal project was to continue to provide education, both theoretical and on-the-job practical training, linked to the construction of new, affordable housing.

In order to get Bertrams Phase II off the ground, Patrick came to a verbal agreement with Cope Housing Association, a co-operative housing model based on a Norwegian design for low-income earners. It had been founded in Johannesburg in 1989 with high hopes that it would help solve South Africa's acute housing crisis. In the 1990s it supported six housing co-operatives in Johannesburg, one of which was the FEP's in Bertrams.

With Cope's access to various sources of funding and social housing subsidies, the FEP was able to continue with its mission, recruiting more trainees and managing their education, training and production. Under this arrangement, over the four years to 1999, the FEP, through the BDB, built fifty-four housing units for Cope. They were in four two-storey blocks, a project considerably more complex than the initial one-storey

Bertrams buildings, and the FEP had to bring in a small outside contractor to meet the standards of the building trade.

Before it was completed, however, the project ran into serious difficulties involving the different demands and expectations of both the FEP's main international funder, which was focused on the education of unemployed youth, and various South African sources of funds, mostly relating to low-cost housing.

Both tied the FEP to deadlines that proved impossible to meet because the inexperienced trainees tended to work slowly. It was the sort of complaint that Patrick had confronted with the Serowe brigades, but he maintained, both then and now, that the extra cost entailed was more than offset by the training and high level of subsequent employment that was achieved.

His problems were compounded by the resignation of the FEP coordinator, Ahmed Moonda, in 1996 and the heavy extra burden this threw upon his shoulders. The correspondence about the FEP's Johannesburg office in this period is dominated by issues of rent, mortgages and pursuit of defaulters.[42] At times Patrick must have felt like little more than a landlord – the last role he would ever have imagined for himself. Furthermore, there was no recognition from the South African authorities, either local or national, of what he was doing for the education of unemployed youth and for his contribution to urban renewal in a run-down district of Johannesburg.

* * *

In 1995 Rosemary Forbes got a job in Johannesburg and moved there with Joanna, imagining they would be living with Patrick. But as they moved into the house she had paid for, Patrick, increasingly disillusioned with South Africa, was turning his attention to Botswana once more.[43]

He still divided his time between the two countries, but, in the next few years, Gaborone increasingly became his main base, while visits to Johannesburg became irregular and usually dependent on some specific work that needed to be done. One visit to South Africa at this time, however, was to receive recognition from the state president.

Figure 16.1: Patrick at a social gathering in Gaborone. (By kind permission of Andrew Gunn)

On 20 July 1996 Patrick was invited by President Mandela to 'a luncheon in honour of the veterans of our struggle for freedom'.[44] The invitation was for 11:00 to 15:00 at the Presidential Guest House, Church Street, Pretoria, dress: smart/casual. Rosemary and Joanna accompanied him.[45]

The occasion was very much personal recognition from Nelson Mandela of Patrick's work for the boycott campaign in the 1950s, for the help he gave refugees settling in and passing through Botswana, and perhaps, too, for his efforts to try to help SOMAFCO develop its curriculum.

The extent of recognition of his work on an alternative and more comprehensive model of education, developed during thirty years in exile, and his promotion of EwP in South Africa in the 1990s, was the nomination by the North West province branch of the FEP for the 'Presidential and Premier Education Award 1996'.

There can be little doubt that from the time of his return to South Africa Patrick had harboured unspoken hopes that he might be offered a high position in the Department of Education, perhaps even the post of minister. As far as he could see, the failure of EwP to take off was always the result of a lack of political commitment.

He believed that with his experience and vision he could have transformed South Africa's education system and helped the country progress into a more egalitarian future. But it was not to be. He had to be satisfied with a handshake and personal thanks from President Mandela.

There have been unconfirmed rumours that because of his fluency in French Patrick was offered the post of ambassador to France, but that he turned it down. Whether that was true or not, he would not have been interested in a job of luxury and status, with no power to affect the education system of his country. For Patrick it was the Department of Education or nothing. But by this point he had already turned his mind back to Botswana.

17 | Return to Botswana

During the final decade of apartheid in South Africa, Botswana was a beneficiary of a significant amount of direct investment by multinational manufacturing corporations, including South African-based companies, bringing to the country productive activities as diverse as vehicle assembly and the production of spaghetti.

Since it was in a customs union with South Africa, investment in Botswana was a safe hedge against the possibility of full-blown economic sanctions against the apartheid regime. The truth of this cynical corporate viewpoint was revealed by the speed with which this investment was shifted to South Africa the moment it became clear that apartheid was collapsing.

With the accompanying rise in levels of unemployment by the mid-1990s, the Botswana government's reliance on foreign investment to drive the diversification of its economy could be seen to be failing. This was reflected in the results of the general election of October 1994 that saw a surge in support for the opposition Botswana National Front (BNF), which tripled its number of Parliament members – to 13 of 40 – taking all four seats in Gaborone.

Against this political background, Patrick's refocus on Botswana could be said to have started in February 1995 with a long article in *Mmegi*, the independent weekly newspaper he had re-founded in 1984. The article, highly critical of the general trend of government policy, was written in response to President Quett Masire's address at the opening of Parliament.

Politically, the government was, for once, looking vulnerable, and now seemed a good time to put forward alternative economic and development strategies – as much to push the opposition into forming a coherent programme for government as it was to prompt the government into a change of direction.

In his speech Masire recognised the slowdown in the country's economic growth but, according to Patrick, he failed to recognise its root causes: the government was too heavily involved in partnerships with transnational corporations whose investment priority was minimal investment for maximum profit. In particular, there was a lack of balance in rural development between enrichment of a few (mostly large-scale cattle ranchers) and rural stagnation for the majority, leading to rural–urban migration and environmental degradation.

Government schemes for rural development had not alleviated poverty. For instance, there was still no minimum wage for cattle herders, while village development committees were dominated by the well off, who hijacked government schemes and benefits.[1]

What was needed, argued Patrick, was a fundamental change in education policy. There had been two commissions on education since independence, but they merely highlighted what he called the 'reactionary conservatism' of government and its bureaucracy, which only addressed the needs of the people as elections approached.

The 1993 Education Commission had recommended that government 'improve general education to prepare students more effectively for life, citizenship and the world of work'. He pointed out that the FEP's *Thuto Le Tiro* proposal would have fitted the recommendations of the commission, for it combined an academic and vocational curriculum to beyond Junior Certificate (JC) level; but government had ignored it.

Since the late 1970s the government had been against what it called the 'vocationalisation' of secondary schools, as at Swaneng Hill, and had killed it off. Instead, it had chosen to increase the number of junior secondary schools; but this had not solved the problem. With only 27 per cent gaining access to senior secondary school, there were more JC school leavers than jobs. In 1994 government had added a vocational year for JC leavers, but this only postponed the problem by one year. If the brigades, Patrick wrote, had not been neglected, they could have absorbed a lot of these school leavers and really prepared them for the independent world of work.[2]

The BNF, on the other hand, had long claimed EwP as its educational policy, and its strong showing in the 1994 election seems to have prompted President Masire to take a fresh look at his party's preference for the academic model of formal school education. In a move clearly intended to facilitate this, Masire appointed the professional educationist Dr Gaositwe Chiepe as his new minister of education.[3]

It was a move Patrick would have regarded as both wise and long overdue. Dr Chiepe had welcomed and encouraged his incorporation of technical skills and practical experience into academic education at Swaneng Hill and Shashe River schools. As a 'Tiger' – a Tiger Kloof alumna – she was familiar with the teaching of technical skills at secondary level, but, unlike many of her contemporaries, she appreciated that Patrick 'did not just teach students how to make bricks, he taught them how to lay them in actual building' and all at no expense to government.[4]

Development Studies had been offered at senior secondary level since the 1970s, but it had fallen into abeyance in most schools following Minister K. P. Morake's condemnation of it as 'teaching socialist ideas'. A couple of schools kept it on and from the late 1980s teachers began calling for it to be re-introduced at Cambridge level.

Patrick was asked to review the syllabus and the subject was re-approved. Development Studies was examined at School Certificate (Form V) level again in 1994.[5] As Patrick would have expected, Dr Chiepe was a lot more open-minded than her predecessors and, with her appointment, there was noticeably less hostility within the Ministry of Education towards the whole of the alternative school curriculum that Patrick was proposing. Besides, the Revised National Policy for Education (RNPE), published in 1994, recommended the inclusion of vocational training in schools, to give students more hands-on experience.[6]

The recommendations of the RNPE, the shock of the upsurge in support for the BNF and the appointment of Dr Chiepe all coincided with and perhaps influenced Patrick's renewed focus on the affairs of Botswana. It appeared that his time had come, and he was ready for it. EwP was no longer just a theoretical concept. The FEP had produced a detailed curriculum, with accompanying textbooks, for three additional subjects: Cultural Studies, Fundamentals of Production, and Environmental and Social Studies.

Trials and workshops were undertaken in 1995–1996, with Patrick fully engaged with teachers and officers from the Ministry of Education. In 1995 teachers joined colleagues from elsewhere in the SADC region for an EwP workshop in Namibia, co-directed by Patrick, and there was a visit to a school in Johannesburg to see the practical aspect of Cultural Studies.

Patrick was an active participant in all these meetings. He held lengthy discussions with teachers in particular, realising that, provided there was continued national political support, the future of EwP lay in their hands. He was part of a team of officers from the Ministry of Education who conducted in-service training and support for the teachers and trainers of the EwP subjects.

The team was headed by Modisaotsile Hulela, senior education officer, secondary schools, and included Philip Bulawa, a Swaneng Hill alumnus from the 1970s, Education Officer Sebofo Motswane, and the future president of Botswana, Mokgweetse Masisi, then in the curriculum department of the Ministry of Education.[7]

They visited the schools in pairs. Patrick was paired with Bulawa. The first task was to win over the head teachers. One school head, Swaneng alumna Mrs Maunganidze, was particularly enthusiastic. The teachers, too, were excited, especially to be rubbing shoulders with the legendary Patrick van Rensburg. The young teachers in particular appreciated the relevance of the new subjects that prepared their students for life. It involved so much more than classroom work, such as training them in the techniques and practices of field research.[8]

The two-year examined course began in Form IV in 1997 and it seemed that at last Patrick's innovative Education with Production was receiving the attention it was due in Botswana, the country of its birth. He feared, however, that its acceptance into the mainstream of Botswana's education system depended too much on the support of a handful of individuals and was aware that there were forces in the ruling establishment that still saw it as a threat to their capitalist comfort zone.

They correctly perceived that the underlying direction of EwP subjects was informing the future electorate about the social and economic inequality of Botswana society and the failure of current government policy to correct it. Furthermore, the subjects were so designed that they were taught through the pedagogy of research and enquiry rather than passive absorption and the students were thus being trained to question and challenge the status quo.

* * *

In order to secure the future of EwP in Botswana Patrick turned to the BNF. He had long been on close terms with the president of the party, Dr Kenneth Koma, and the party's vice-president, Michael Dingake, a founding member of the Mmegi Publishing Trust.

With EwP long established as the BNF's national educational policy[9] and with Kenneth Koma's promise that Patrick would become minister of education if the BNF should ever come to power, Patrick was finally drawn to official membership of the party. In 1997 he became a member of the central committee, with responsibility for education, and this was his position at the time of the Special Congress of the BNF, held in Palapye over the Easter weekend of 1998.

Patrick had never sought personal power for its own sake; he had only ever wanted the power to implement his educational vision. He had always built alliances of support for his projects based upon personal friendships. Once he had a friend who was politically attuned to his way of thinking, whom he liked and who supported his current project, he trusted that friend implicitly.

Most of the time he was a very good judge of people and he had proved adept at gaining the friendship and trust of many of the key leading figures in Serowe in the 1960s and 1970s. When it came to national politics, however, he was out of his depth. He was politically naïve enough to believe that he could rely upon his long-standing personal friendship with Kenneth Koma and appears to have been unaware of, or had chosen to ignore, the warning signs in the months leading up to the 1998 congress.

The BNF had a long history of disunity, usually caused by personal rivalries over membership of the central committee or candidacy for safe seats for local or general elections. Disappointed candidates would accuse their opponents of disloyalty or right-wing factionalism. Rivalry often led to breakaway factions forming alternative parties, sometimes putting up just one or two candidates at the next election, but always enough to split the opposition vote and give the BDP yet another easy ride to victory.[10]

After the relatively successful general election of 1994, in which the BNF won a record 13 seats out of 40, the party was convinced it was on the brink of winning power in 1999. President Masire, who had retired at the end of March 1998, had been, despite his short stature, a giant in the ruling BDP since its foundation and the BNF was convinced it would have an easier ride against his successor, the relative newcomer and former vice-president, Festus Mogae.

The prospect of imminent power, however, intensified pre-existing rivalries within the party. In the months leading up to the Palapye congress factional rivalry had effectively split the party in two. The majority of the central committee supported party vice-president Mike Dingake, while a rival, the so-called Concerned Group, won the ear of party president Kenneth Koma, who, the previous year, had been a supporter of Dingake.

With eighty-year-old Koma on the brink of retirement, competition for the vice-presidency and shadow Cabinet posts was at the forefront of nearly everybody's mind. Patrick appears to have tried to steer clear of the factionalism, trusting that his former friendship with Koma would ensure him the education post. But Koma, seeing Patrick as a friend of Dingake, decided that he could not be trusted.

The delegates who assembled in Palapye on Saturday 11 April did not even get beyond settling the agenda. The central committee, which included Patrick, and its supporters reassembled for the second day and started the meeting without Koma, Dingake or the Concerned Group present. When the Concerned Group turned up, fighting broke out, missiles were hurled, people were injured.

The police were called to restore order and the congress was abandoned. That night Koma announced the suspension of the whole of the central committee, and Dingake responded by suspending Koma from the presidency of the party.[11] A week later the case came before the High Court, which decided in Koma's favour.[12] Dingake responded to the court's decision by announcing the formation of a breakaway party, the Botswana Congress Party (BCP). He took with him eleven of the thirteen BNF MPs and formed the official opposition in Parliament.[13]

Patrick was in despair. He had tried to avoid involvement in factionalism, but through his position on the central committee he was totally associated with the Dingake faction. Dingake invited him to join his new party, but Patrick declined. He had had his fill of national politics and disassociated himself from both the BNF and Dingake's party. That did him no good politically. As far as the BDP government was concerned, he had shown his true colours in joining the BNF and he lost what little credibility he had left with the education establishment. The BDP was able to capitalise on the opposition's disarray and romped home at the 1999 election, regaining six seats in Parliament, taking 33 of 40.

Dr Chiepe had retired from politics before the election, which lost Patrick his key supporter at the Ministry of Education. It would only be a matter of time before his pilot programme of EwP subjects was removed from the Cambridge Certificate curriculum. In 2000 it was announced that they would be scrapped, with their final year of examination taking place in 2001.

A slightly watered-down version of Development Studies survived, but the official line was that the existing Social Studies and Business Studies covered what was necessary from EwP's Cultural Studies and Fundamentals of Production.[14] Almost certainly the real underlying motive for the removal of these subjects was to put an end to the 'perverting of the youth' through exposure to Patrick's socialist ideas.

Figure 17.1: A ceremony in 2009 to honour the two founders of Boiteko, Patrick van Rensburg (*left*) and Joel Pelotona (*right*), with Otsogile Pitso (*centre*). Joel and Otsogile had both been fundamental and dedicated supporters and practitioners of Patrick's ideals from the very beginning. (By kind permission of the Van Rensburg family collection)

It was at about this time that Patrick wrote his final published book, *Making Education Work: The What, Why and How of Education with Production*. It was published by the FEP in 2001, in conjunction with the ever-loyal Dag Hammarskjöld Foundation. The book laid out the history and theory of EwP, together with Patrick's experience in practice in Botswana and South Africa and the Southern African region. He reserved a special place in the book for a verbal assault on the Botswana government's rejection of his EwP curriculum, seeing it as a product of broader social forces in the country:

> Botswana's deeply conservative and hierarchical society is the historical outcome of its own traditional rule ... It is a society that has readily accommodated the divisions of modern capitalism that are reflected in one of the worst among international ratings of contrasts of rich and poor ...
>
> Botswana's elite is more entrenched than ever today, some of them enriching themselves more than ever before from the country's diamond-generated wealth. The education system is largely geared to reproducing the existing society, with the children of the elite learning how to join their parents. In the past, a good number of the more well-to-do might have spared a thought for the deprived and given support to approaches to education that might help uplift them. Very few of the better-off would do either now.[15]

This was his parting shot at the élites of Botswana. With the opposition split and in disarray, he could see that the government was 'under no pressure to pay heed to education with production'. The country was clearly too 'heavily dependent upon diamonds as its predominant source of national income and manufactures little of what it consumes', most of its citizens preferring 'to consume what they earn, rather than invest'. In any case, there was little in the way of production for them to invest in. Most of Botswana's artisans came from Zimbabwe, and Botswana had very few entrepreneurs of its own. Patrick declared: 'This is the country that just threw out Fundamentals of Production, with its related practical course work, from its high school curriculum.'[16]

* * *

Having given up on his brief stint in Botswanan politics after the deeply shaming BNF fiasco of Easter 1998, Patrick returned to South Africa to spend more time living with Rosemary and Joanna in Johannesburg. Thus far Joanna had seen him as a distant father figure – always coming and going – and she lacked any real relationship with him. In the latter half of 1998, however, with Rosemary away visiting her mother, Patrick was left in charge of his twelve-year-old daughter.

He drove her up to Maun for a holiday in the Okavango Delta and their time together cemented a close relationship. Twenty years later Joanna retained vivid images of that trip, on a boat in the river with crocodiles, and her father talking about the fauna and flora of the wilderness, for which he had a passionate regard.[17]

Early in 2001 Rosemary and Joanna returned to Canada and it was at this point that Patrick completed *Making Education Work*.

As for South Africa, by 2001 he had realised that his vision for the country of his birth, that vision that had driven him through decades of education and development work, was nothing more than a dream. He had tried to follow up on the EwP seminars for which he had received so much support from Olle and Sven of the DHF, but only one official from the national Department of Education had ever turned up to a seminar and a follow-up EwP workshop promised for 1998 had failed to materialise. He sadly concluded that where South Africa was concerned

> [t]he government has opted to maintain the socio-economic policies it inherited and seems to believe that it can run them better than its predecessor. It is committed to … globalisation, as if it were a leading industrialised country.
>
> … there is very little socialist or revolutionary zeal in South Africa. Consumerism prevails.
>
> … South Africa seems now to hold alternatives in contempt, seeing them as beneath its dignity as an advanced industrialised country.[18]

Patrick was mugged in Bertrams at least once at about this time, but that was fairly standard fare for the area and the time. Nevertheless, with Rosemary and Joanna now back in Canada, Johannesburg no longer held the attraction it had once had. In the years that followed he based himself increasingly in Gaborone, where he lived in a one-bedroom flat on the first floor of the FEP and *Mmegi* office block that had been constructed by Tshwaragano Enterprises near the Maruapula shopping mall.

Some years before, *Education with Production* had ceased publication as a separate journal due to costs, and Patrick, now in his seventies, devoted much of his energy to trying to establish a development project on another property in Gaborone and writing a regular weekly column for *Mmegi*, sometimes critical of Botswana society and policies, at other times reflecting on the affairs of the world. He also began to write the autobiography that was to be his *magnum opus*.

* * *

The autobiography would relate his whole life and work, warts and all, from his earliest memories to the new millennium. Having been reunited and reconciled with his South African family, he was now able to confront his childhood and upbringing. Although he was not to start work on the book until the late 1990s, the process of family reconciliation had started as early as 1980.

On his first trip into newly liberated Zimbabwe that year he had looked up his mother, Cecile, whom he knew to be living in Harare.[19] He was also reunited with his half-sister, Jean Bain, whom he had not seen since she was a small child in Natal. It was an important and cathartic meeting for both mother and son. Patrick was glad to be reunited and reconciled with his mother, feeling, perhaps, a sense of guilt that in his youth he had rejected her attempts to reclaim him as her son. The reconciliation now was probably partly built on an admission of his true paternity.

Apart from this all-important point, Cecile revealed that she had been following his career, from a distance, and that she was very proud of him, even though it was clear to Patrick that she still harboured the racial prejudice typical of the white settler culture of South Africa and Rhodesia. Rosemary, who on another occasion met Cecile and Jean with Patrick in Harare, could see that Patrick's mother was 'an old-fashioned racist', but Patrick was very forgiving of this attitude, understanding from his own experience how difficult it was for her to overthrow the deeply ingrained prejudices of her white South African background. It was clear to Patrick's son Tom that the relationship with Cecile remained very positive.

Through his years of exile Patrick had kept photographs of his South African family and had shown them to his sons as they were growing up. They were thus always aware that their father had an extended family that they were not able to meet. Tom has recalled that his father went to considerable trouble to make contact with his family once he was allowed into the former Rhodesia and South Africa.

Patrick kept in fairly regular touch with his mother following their initial reunion in 1980 and on his visits to Liz and their sons in Leicester in the 1980s was able to show them photographs of Cecile's grandchildren. In 1988, while Tom, in his mid-twenties, was on a visit to Southern Africa, Patrick took him to meet his grandmother. Tom, recalling that they had tea together in her flat in Harare, remembered her simply as 'a very nice little old lady'.[20]

Later, as soon as the opportunity arose, Patrick made contact with other members of his extended family, in Durban and Pietermaritzburg, probably initially during the brief visit to South Africa that he was allowed in August 1990. In Pietermaritzburg he found the man he had known as 'Uncle Pat', now in his eighties, to be the same kind, open man he had always known. The only difference now was that it was openly acknowledged between the two of them that Patrick Maxwell was Patrick van Rensburg's father.

Maxwell had three sons, all of whom acknowledged the importance of Patrick's work and were very pleased to welcome him into the Maxwell family.[21] In 1994, the year he had taught the BEd course on EwP at the University of Natal in Pietermaritzburg, Patrick had had an almost weekly opportunity to meet with his father, and later, when Rosemary went on holiday with Patrick to Natal, she, too, met him and 'liked him enormously'.

When Patrick Maxwell died in 1998, all four sons spoke at his funeral. Rosemary recalls with wry amusement that Patrick's speech went on for an embarrassingly long time.[22] But for Patrick it was important that he spoke of his own life of exile by way of explaining why he had not been around for thirty years. After their father's death the three Maxwell brothers decided on their own initiative to divide the family inheritance equally among the four of them. Thus Patrick came into R90 000, which he promptly lodged in the FEP account.[23]

Through the 1990s and early 2000s Patrick visited his old haunts and homes in both Pietermaritzburg and Durban and, through meetings with members of his mother's extended family, was able to recapture memories of his childhood and early adult life. In due course those stimulated and fed into his story of his life.

He began to plan his autobiography in the late 1990s, but was not able to spend long periods working on it until the early years of the new century. Much of the writing was done between 2001 and 2005, during extended trips to Gatineau in western Quebec, where he stayed with Rosemary and Joanna. Tom Holzinger, who visited him there, found him in Rosemary's basement, writing away: 'I am a has-been before my time,' he quipped.[24]

The early chapters of the autobiography, up to about 1970, are remarkably detailed and follow a clear narrative. They explain his family background and early upbringing in what is clearly as much detail as he can remember, with anecdotes added, sometimes fairly randomly. Thereafter he writes candidly of his adult maturing and the adoption of an Afrikaner identity alongside a gradual awakening of unease about the government's racial policies.

Once the break with apartheid is recorded, a new energy is evident in the manuscript, as he writes of his life as an increasingly committed anti-apartheid activist. His search for a role in exile is revealing, and it is clear that he began to find it during his travels with Liz through Africa in 1962. By the time he reached Dar es Salaam he was ripe for conversion to the 'new religion' of 'Third World Development'. He thus arrived in Bechuanaland committed to the importance of rural development based on self-reliance built on grass-roots activism.

The tale of the founding of Swaneng Hill School and the brigades follows a detailed narrative through the 1960s. It is a story he told many times to potential donors to persuade them to loosen their purse strings. His rendering of the story is supported by the memories of his volunteer colleagues, Batswana and expatriate. Thereafter, from about 1970, when he left Swaneng Hill, the narrative and focus of the autobiography begin to fade. Subsequent chapters covering the 1980s and the establishment of the FEP are fairly perfunctory; the return to South Africa in the 1990s even more so. It remained, in effect, an unfinished work, and his attempts to have it published proved unsuccessful.

It was becoming clear from the mid-2000s that his memory and remarkable powers of concentration were not what they had been when he could sit down and dash off a book in a matter of months. In his late seventies, in 2008, he was diagnosed as suffering from Alzheimer's disease. He struggled on as best he could, and when it was suggested that he give up on his work, he replied, 'I might as well be dead'.[25]

Figure 17.2: Family gathering, Montreal, 2010. *Right to left*: Tom van Rensburg with his wife Katie Manifold and their daughter Maya on the lap of Joanna Forbes, and Patrick. (By kind permission of Rosemary Forbes)

Despite the struggles with concentration and memory loss, he did not lose his sense of humour. When Joanna got hold of a copy of *Guilty Land* and gave it to him for Christmas, he was thrilled, declaring himself 'the last Maoist standing!'[26] He remained a great one for telling jokes, mostly against himself, and never ceased to repeat them, laughing uproariously every time. He loved to mimic and, especially, to mock politicians: ' "Gentlemen," he would say, imitating the voice of a politician, "these are my principles. If you don't like them, I have others." '[27] When asked by a journalist in 2010 whether he had lived a planned or unplanned life, he replied, 'Yeah. It's not like you planned all those things that went wrong!'

In 2010 he was invited to the Right Livelihood Award's fortieth anniversary ceremony and Jakob von Uexkull recalls him thoroughly enjoying himself on the dance floor at the party afterwards.[28] That year marked his last visit to Canada. Joanna wanted him present for her university graduation. He came, but on the way back he got lost in Johannesburg's Oliver Tambo Airport. He failed to turn up in Gaborone and was missing for twenty-four hours. The ever-reliable FEP employee, friend and companion George Moalosi drove to the airport, found him and brought him home to the flat in Gaborone. It was to be the last international trip Patrick would make on his own.

His last public appearance was at the golden jubilee of Swaneng Hill School, laid on by the school's alumni,[29] although by the time it was organised it was 2014 and the fifty-first anniversary. It was a large gathering, with alumni and staff from all the decades of the school, some having travelled from overseas to be there.

Mothusi and his family looked after Patrick on that day. Alumna Pelonomi Venson, then minister of education, paid generous tribute to Patrick for his inspirational work in the field of education, as well as for the foundation of *Mmegi*, which she had edited in its early version in Serowe. She pledged to bring back elements of Patrick's vision to the education system of Botswana, where an upgrade in technical training was so desperately needed.[30]

Patrick made a speech; the last public occasion on which he did so. It was rambling at first, but, with great courage, he pulled it together and everybody was pleased and proud to see the great man acquit himself so well. Liz arrived in Botswana the following week, in time to attend the gathering for the presentation by the alumni of the Motswana artist Philip Segola's portrait of Patrick. The rest of Patrick's family, Tom and his family (in Ireland) and Rosemary and Joanna (in Canada), were unable to attend.

Figure 17.3: Presentation of Philip Segola's portrait of Patrick, 2014. *Left to right*: Tsetsele Fantan (née Sekgoma, secretary of the Alumni Association of Swaneng Hill School), Patrick, Puseletso Elizabeth Kidd (née Manake, Swaneng alumna), Liz van Rensburg, Methaetsile Leepile (Swaneng alumnus and former editor of *Mmegi wa Dikgang*) and Barulanganye Mudongo (former head girl and later teacher at Swaneng Hill School). (By kind permission of the Van Rensburg family collection)

Earlier that year, in February 2014, friends and family had decided Patrick could no longer continue to look after himself in Gaborone and Mothusi took him to live with him in the family house in Serowe, close to Swaneng Hill School and Boiteko. The latter had by this time been converted into a co-operative shopping mall complex, of which Mothusi was the manager.

In the years that followed Patrick was a shadow of his former self and, with his mind rambling, he spoke much of Durban. Unable to comprehend how much it had changed since his youth, he fantasised about returning there. In Serowe, however, he was free to wander in familiar surroundings where people knew him and could steer him home when he looked lost.

Figure 17.4: Three generations of Van Rensburgs – Patrick, Mothusi and Mothusi's son, Tom – visiting the Khama Rhino Sanctuary, Serowe, 2016. (Photographer: Kevin Shillington)

He loved to be taken to game parks, nearby in Botswana or across the border in South Africa, where he felt at ease communing with the animals and the environment. Joanna came to teach at a secondary school near Gaborone and Rosemary visited at least once a year. In these declining years Patrick remained a quiet and gentle man, still with some clarity of mind, and it was here, in the home he had built in Serowe, that he passed away peacefully in his sleep on 23 May 2017.

Epilogue

Patrick van Rensburg's obituaries reminded many and informed the young of the great life he had lived, to the benefit of so many, and after his cremation a large gathering of family, friends and colleagues, government ministers, politicians and a former president assembled at Swaneng Hill School on 24 June 2017 for a memorial service in celebration of a life so well lived for the betterment of humankind.

It was one of those rare occasions when Botswana's opposition parties were united, and their leader, Duma Boko, a Madiba alumnus, was one among many who spoke that day. He pledged that 'when' the opposition came to power 'two years later', 'education with production' would be implemented throughout the country. 'If we had listened to Patrick van Rensburg 30 years ago,' he declared with the confidence of a politician in opposition, 'Botswana would be a First World country today.' In the event, the 2019 general election did not go his way and the BDP continued as the only governing party in Botswana's history.

It is inevitable that Patrick van Rensburg should be remembered more for his work as an alternative educationist than for his role as an anti-apartheid activist, although he had thrown himself into activism with an intensity that was characteristic of his obsessive personality. As was intended, his *Guilty Land* informed an audience way beyond South Africa (where it was banned) and influenced many in Europe and America. A number of the expatriate volunteers who came to work on Patrick's projects in Botswana were initially prompted in that direction after reading it.

The late 1950s and early 1960s, however, were years of widespread and dramatic activism in South Africa and the wider African continent, and it was inevitable that Patrick's role should be overshadowed by those

301

of the pantheon of heroes of the anti-imperialist, anti-racist struggle of those years.

From the moment he contemplated reinventing himself as a radical educationist, Patrick read other people's work voraciously and adapted and adopted their ideas as he saw fit. The implementation of his version of Education for Development, however, came mostly through his practical experience of founding a self-help school and finding practical solutions – co-operatives, brigades – to problems as they arose, combined with the inspiration that he drew from his volunteer colleagues, Batswana and expatriate. And, although he had had a preview of Nyerere's thinking through conversations with Joan Wicken and others in Dar es Salaam in 1962, it was not until 1967 and 1968 that Nyerere's *Arusha Declaration* and *Education for Self-Reliance* were actually printed. By then Patrick's educational philosophy was well advanced.

Patrick was a living example of the spirit of voluntarism and the value of working for the common good. He introduced some of his volunteers to a lifelong belief in socialism. Robert Oakeshott, who contributed so much to Patrick's work in Serowe, was himself influenced by the Van Rensburg charisma and, after leaving Botswana, went on to found a builders' co-operative, Sunderlandia, in the north-east of England, and later co-founded what was to become the Employee Ownership Association.

Patrick's immediate legacy in Southern Africa is to be seen in the three schools he founded, even though they have long since become standard academic secondary schools. Their alumni, particularly those from the 1960s and 1970s, have carried a certain self-confidence and sense of duty and responsibility; a product of the Van Rensburg inspiration and leadership through voluntarism, practical training, his ever-questioning pedagogy and his course in Development Studies.

It is significant that the record of Cambridge School Certificate results held in the Botswana National Archives shows that from the late 1960s through the 1970s Swaneng Hill School was always on top in terms of high-level passes when it came to Development Studies. This was where it had been born and where it was really taken to heart.

Patrick van Rensburg will probably best be remembered in Botswana for the brigades and the co-operative movement, which, in the late 1960s and early 1970s, spread throughout the country. By then the brigades were not all run for the advancement of the rural economy as Patrick would have preferred, but he was eternally pragmatic and was pleased to observe some elements of his ideal being implemented many years later.

Many of the country's citizens were able to use the practical skills acquired in the brigades to help build the infrastructure for which Botswana is renowned, and many successful Batswana benefited from the second opportunity the brigades offered to those who had failed to squeeze through the bottleneck of competition for secondary school.

Elsewhere in Serowe, through Boiteko, many adults with little formal schooling gained the confidence and skills to take their place in the modern sector. Ultimately, Patrick aimed to promote autonomous and active citizens with a sense of civic duty, unafraid to challenge an unfair status quo and, to a considerable extent, he achieved this in Botswana.

In the optimistic view of Tom Holzinger:

> Patrick's greatest legacy remains the village development trusts who work to improve local communities. Beginning with the first Youth Development Association in Serowe, such trusts have spread everywhere in Botswana. They especially allow elders, teachers, and retired civil servants to bring their ingenuity and wisdom to bear on local problems and find local solutions.[1]

Education with Production in its broadest sense is still relevant today. Elements of it have been tried throughout history, from early post-revolution China – 'walking on two legs' – to Cuba and various countries in Africa, from Ghana, where Patrick first got his inspiration, to Tanzania and countries within the SADC region, most of the latter under Patrick's influence.

For Patrick, EwP was not an occasional add-on but a whole way of life. With the professional assistance of numerous colleagues, he laid out a viable curriculum, to the satisfaction of the Cambridge International Examinations Syndicate. His aim: a non-élitist education for all that introduces even the most gifted of academic students to manual skills for life and combines training the brain with training the hands, thus inculcating a respect for the dignity of labour. Those not academically gifted learn the skills to earn a living in some productive enterprise, together with sufficient understanding of society to enable them to hold their own as equal citizens of the world. These were honourable aims when he evolved them. They remain so today.

It could be argued that where Education with Production failed to take hold it was most often for want of political commitment. Certainly, Patrick considered that it failed in South Africa because the ANC believed it to be beneath the dignity of the First World country its leaders considered South Africa to be.

This judgement, however, misunderstood the primacy of the transitional government's focus on correcting the decades of racism that had infected all spheres of South African life. Within this context it is worth noting that Patrick's EwP may have been perceived in South Africa as too closely aligned to Bantu Education's focus on the sort of low-level technical skills the apartheid regime had considered appropriate for limited rural development in the 'bantustans' or the lower echelons of the industrial urban economy.

There remain, however, individual projects promoted by some NGOs in South Africa that show what could be achieved on a wider scale when faced with the challenges of education and employment in the twenty-first century. In Lesotho, EwP suffered from too great a reliance on the personal support of King Moshoeshoe II and faded after his untimely death. In Zimbabwe, where, to a limited extent, EwP was firmly established, all ZIMFEP's farm-based schools fell victim to the land crisis of the early 2000s and were illegally confiscated by the government in 2004.[2]

In Botswana, on the other hand, Pelonomi Venson followed through on her pledge of 2014 with the 'Education and Training Sector Strategic Plan', published in April 2015, and produced in collaboration with the European Union. It proposed setting up 'Pathways' in the education system, with students at the Junior Certificate level able to choose between a vocational and an academic pathway for their further education. By 2017 this was already being piloted in some schools.

At the same time, brigades would be given more prominence. According to Philip Bulawa, this was just what Patrick had been proposing, but politics had got in the way. Echoing the thoughts of Duma Boko, Bulawa believes that 'had we listened to Patrick then, the EU would have come here to learn from us. Now we are spending millions on this, and his ideas were free.'[3]

There were few who had not known Patrick van Rensburg personally, had not 'passed through his hands', so to speak, at Swaneng, who could understand why this man who had founded three schools, the brigades and numerous co-operatives, and had received large tranches of aid from foreign donors, was not a wealthy man.

There was nothing he actually owned apart from the house he had built in Serowe that was the home of his son Mothusi and his family. At a workshop at Swaneng in the mid-1990s, where Patrick was presenting his EwP curriculum, he was asked by one of the participants why he, who had achieved so much for the country, was not rich. His reply was, 'I am a socialist.'[4]

As far as Patrick was concerned, that said it all: no further explanation of his life was needed.

Notes

Introduction

1   Jakob von Uexkull, telephone interview, 9 December 2018.
2   See www.rightlivelihoodaward.org/ (accessed 7 November 2018).
3   See www.rightlivelihoodaward.org/laureates/patrick-van-rensburg/ (accessed 7 November 2018).
4   Patrick van Rensburg, *Guilty Land* (London: Jonathan Cape and Penguin Special, 1962).
5   Thomas Holzinger, 'A Personal Memoir of Patrick van Rensburg' (unpublished typescript/s, 31 May 2017).
6   Holzinger, 'Personal Memoir'.
7   Neil Parsons, *Report on the Botswana Brigades, 1965–1983* (Gaborone: National Institute of Research, University of Botswana, 1983), ii.

Chapter 1   Origins and Identity in South Africa

1   Their African workers were similarly imprisoned, in separate concentration camps in which conditions were even worse. See, e.g., Denis Judd and Keith Surridge, *The Boer War* (London: Murray, 2002), 194–196.
2   The following account of Patrick's grandparents was gleaned by him from various family sources through his childhood and recorded in the early chapters of his unpublished memoir.
3   Patrick van Rensburg, unpublished memoir, edited by Liz van Rensburg, Chapter 1, 2. Hereafter referred to in the notes simply as Van Rensburg, Memoir.
4   Van Rensburg, *Guilty Land*, 9.
5   Van Rensburg, Memoir, Chapter 1, 1.
6   Van Rensburg, Memoir, Chapter 1, 2.
7   Van Rensburg, *Guilty Land*, 9.
8   Van Rensburg, Memoir, Chapter 1, 2.
9   Van Rensburg, Memoir, Chapters 1 and 2.
10   Van Rensburg, Memoir, Chapter 1, 1.
11   Van Rensburg, Memoir, Chapter 1, 15.

Chapter 2 An Anglophone South African, 1936–1948

1   Van Rensburg, Memoir, Chapter 1, 6.
2   The book by James Hilton, set in an English private school, was first published in 1934. A film version, with Robert Donat playing Mr Chipping ('Chips'), appeared in 1939. The film was very likely seen by Patrick and many of the boys at Ixopo, hence their use of the nickname. In his Memoir Patrick does not provide any other name for the teacher.
3   *Outspan*, 'A South African weekly for everybody', was a popular illustrated magazine filled with a mixture of factual essays, articles and fictional stories. Founded in 1927, it was edited in this period (1939–1953) by Gordon Makepeace. In 1957 it changed its name to *Personality* and ceased publication in 1965.
4   Van Rensburg, Memoir, Chapter 1, 18.
5   Van Rensburg, Memoir, Chapter 1, 19.
6   Van Rensburg, Memoir, Chapter 1, 14.
7   Van Rensburg, Memoir, Chapter 1, 14.
8   Van Rensburg, Memoir, Chapter 2, 27.
9   Van Rensburg, Memoir, Chapter 2, 26.
10   Van Rensburg, Memoir, Chapter 2, 26.
11   Rosemary Forbes, Skype interview, 1 June 2019; Tom van Rensburg, Skype interview, 4 June 2019; see also Chapter 16.
12   Van Rensburg, Memoir, Chapter 2, 29.
13   In British pre-decimal currency there were 20 shillings to the pound (£).
14   Van Rensburg, Memoir, Chapter 2, 35.
15   Van Rensburg, Memoir, Chapter 2, 35.
16   Van Rensburg, Memoir, Chapter 2, 36.
17   Van Rensburg, Memoir, Chapter 2, 37.
18   Van Rensburg, *Guilty Land*, 14–15.
19   Van Rensburg, Memoir, Chapter 2, 37.

Chapter 3 The Making of an Afrikaner, 1949–1953

1   Van Rensburg, Memoir, Chapter 2, 37–38.
2   Paula Ensor (daughter of Michael Ensor), interview, 8 February 2017.
3   In his memoir he spells the name 'van Todder', but 'van Tonder' is likely to be the correct Afrikaans spelling.
4   Van Rensburg, Memoir, Chapter 3, 43–44.
5   Van Rensburg, *Guilty Land*, 16.
6   Van Rensburg, *Guilty Land*, 15.
7   His study notes on the subject were drawn from the work of the Cambridge scholar I. A. Richards, whose *The Principles of Literary Criticism* and *Practical Criticism* were published by Kegan Paul in London in 1924 and 1929 respectively.
8   Van Rensburg, Memoir, Chapter 3.
9   This was decades before women were even allowed to *play* the sport, let alone umpire it.

10 I use 'Transvaal' here for the republic north of the Vaal River, which the found-
    ers called the *Zuid-Afrikaansche Republiek* (South African Republic), so as not to
    confuse with the modern 'Republic of South Africa', founded in 1961 when South
    Africa left the Commonwealth.
11 Anglophone South Africans tended to call it Dingaan's Day, after the defeated
    Zulu king. Since 1994 it has been changed to the Day of Reconciliation.
12 The forenames 'Henry Francis' suggest a possible ancestral link with Anglophone
    Natal, for one of the two British traders who founded Port Natal (Durban) in
    1824 was called Henry Francis Fynn.
13 Van Rensburg, Memoir, Chapter 3, 54.
14 Van Rensburg, Memoir, Chapter 3, 61.
15 Van Rensburg, Memoir, Chapter 3, 51.
16 Joanna Forbes, interview, Gaborone, 15 February 2017.
17 Now Namibia.
18 Anne Yates and Lewis Chester, *The Troublemaker: Michael Scott and His Lonely
    Struggle against Injustice* (London: Aurum Press, 2006), 78.
19 Yates and Chester, *The Troublemaker*, 71. Scott made this graphic allegation in
    a court case. The *sjambok* (Afrikaans) was a long whip made of rhino hide and
    widely used on South African farms.
20 The UN met in Long Island until the opening of its headquarters in Manhattan in
    1952.
21 Yates and Chester, *The Troublemaker*, 96–97.

Chapter 4 Diplomat and Rebel, 1953–1957

1 South Africa, as a self-governing (though 'white') Dominion within the British
   Commonwealth, was regarded as an independent nation and so had a seat at the
   UN. The only other African countries with seats at that time were Egypt, Ethiopia
   and Liberia. The remaining nations of Africa were yet to gain their independence
   from colonial rule and so were not represented.
2 Dosoo Framjee Karaka, *Nehru: The Lotus Eater from Kashmir* (London: Verschoyle,
   1953).
3 Michael Dutfield, *A Marriage of Inconvenience: The Persecution of Ruth and Seretse
   Khama* (London: Unwin Hyam, 1990); Thomas Tlou, Neil Parsons and Willie
   Henderson, *Seretse Khama: 1921–1980* (Gaborone: Botswana Society; Braamfontein: Macmillan Boleswa, 1996), 75–96; BBC film, *A United Kingdom*, 2016.
4 Tlou, Parsons and Henderson, *Seretse Khama*, 87 and 408–409, fns 38 and 39.
5 Van Rensburg, Memoir, Chapter 4, 81–84.
6 Van Rensburg, Memoir, Chapter 4, 81.
7 *Der Tag*, German for 'The Day', was used by German naval officers as an after-din-
   ner toast before and during World War I, referring to the day when the Imperial
   German Navy would establish supremacy over the British Royal Navy. It subsequently came to mean any day of reckoning, and had such resonance among
   Afrikaners that they used the German rendition rather than the Afrikaans, *Die Dag*.

8   Van Rensburg, Memoir, Chapter 4, 81–82.
9   Helen Joseph, *Side by Side* (London: Zed Books, 1986), 36.
10 Van Rensburg, Memoir, Chapter 4, 93.
11 Van Rensburg, Memoir, Chapter 4, 95.
12 Van Rensburg, Memoir, Chapter 5, 98.
13 Thomas Kanza, *Conflict in the Congo: The Rise and Fall of Lumumba* (translated from the French) (Harmondsworth: Penguin Books, 1972), 19–20.
14 Van Rensburg, Memoir, Chapter 5, 100.
15 Van Rensburg, Memoir, Chapter 5, 100.
16 Van Rensburg, Memoir, Chapter 5, 100 onward.
17 Van Rensburg, Memoir, Chapter 5, 106.
18 Published by Bonnier, Stockholm, 1954.
19 Published in English in South Africa in 1954 by A. W. Blaxall of Heidelberg, Transvaal.
20 Van Rensburg, Memoir, Chapter 5, 102.
21 Chester Bowles, *Africa's Challenge to America* (Berkeley and Los Angeles, CA: University of California Press, 1956).
22 Van Rensburg, Memoir, Chapter 5, 107.
23 Van Rensburg, Memoir, Chapter 5, 108.

Chapter 5 Anti-Apartheid Activist, 1957–1959

1   Van Rensburg, Memoir, Chapter 5, 109.
2   *The Star*, 5 June 1957.
3   Named after the former South African prime minister, who had died in 1950. In 1994 the airport was renamed Johannesburg International and in 2006 renamed again. It is now Oliver Tambo International.
4   *Rand Daily Mail*, 8 June 1957.
5   See https://en.wikipedia.org/wiki/John_Brown_(abolitionist)#cite_note-Territorial_Kansas_Online-53 (accessed 16 October 2017).
6   Van Rensburg, Memoir, Chapter 6, 114–115.
7   Randolph Vigne, *Liberals against Apartheid: A History of the Liberal Party of South Africa, 1953–1968* (Basingstoke: Palgrave Macmillan, 1997), 66–68.
8   'Qualified franchise' refers to the concept that so-called non-white people should only have the right to vote in local or general elections if they met certain qualifications, through ownership of property, level of income or education. White people automatically had the right to vote, without qualification.
9   Van Rensburg, Memoir, Chapter 6, 116.
10 Van Rensburg, Memoir, Chapter 6, 116; Vigne, *Liberals against Apartheid*, 68.
11 Van Rensburg, Memoir, Chapter 6, 116.
12 Van Rensburg, Memoir, Chapter 6, 116.
13 Van Rensburg, Memoir, Chapter 6, 116.
14 Van Rensburg, Memoir, Chapter 6, 119.
15 Van Rensburg, Memoir, Chapter 6.
16 Van Rensburg, Memoir, Chapter 6, 123.

17 Paula Ensor, interview, Cape Town, 8 February 2017.

18 Gangathura Mohambry Naicker.

19 Van Rensburg, Memoir, Chapter 6, 121.

20 Liz van Rensburg, private communication, 1 July 2018.

21 Hendrik Verwoerd was minister of native affairs and the mastermind of the apartheid system.

22 The residents of Sophiatown, Indian, 'coloured', Chinese and African, proved able to mix freely in peace and harmony, the very epitome of a non-racial South Africa and anathema to Verwoerd's racist ideology. For more on Sophiatown, see Van Rensburg, *Guilty Land*, 112–115, and Trevor Huddleston, *Naught for Your Comfort* (New York: Doubleday, 1956), 117–136.

23 Van Rensburg, Memoir, Chapter 6, 120–121. *Kwela* was also slang for a police van, or 'Black Maria'.

24 For Huddleston's story and portrayal of South Africa, and in particular Sophiatown, see his *Naught for Your Comfort*.

25 Derek Hudson, interview, Wincanton, 2 October 2017. Derek was to meet Patrick in exile in Botswana in the 1960s. He himself went on to become the first director of the Bank of Botswana.

26 *Contact* 1(5), 5 April 1958.

27 Van Rensburg, Memoir, Chapter 6, 126.

28 *Rand Daily Mail*, 5 May 1958, 8.

29 *Rand Daily Mail*, 20 May 1958, 2.

30 *Rand Daily Mail*, 2 June 1958, 8.

31 *Rand Daily Mail*, 2 June 1958, 8.

32 Van Rensburg, Memoir, Chapter 6, 128.

33 *Rand Daily Mail*, 23 August 1958, 1.

34 *Rand Daily Mail*, 23 August 1958, 1; Van Rensburg, Memoir, Chapter 6, 128.

35 *Rand Daily Mail*, 23 August 1958, 1; 30 October 1958, 11.

36 *Rand Daily Mail*, 3 September 1958, 9. Prime Minister Strijdom had died in office two weeks previously.

37 *Rand Daily Mail*, 26 November 1958, 12.

38 *Contact* 2(8), 18 April 1959.

39 Alfred Hutchinson, *The Road to Ghana* (London: Victor Gollancz, 1960; Johannesburg: Penguin Classics, 2006, with Afterword by Es'kia Mphahlele), 7–8.

40 Hutchinson, *Road to Ghana*; Van Rensburg, Memoir, Chapter 7, 152.

41 *Rand Daily Mail*, 14 October 1958, 1.

42 Van Rensburg, Memoir, Chapter 6, 131.

43 Van Rensburg, Memoir, Chapter 6, 131.

44 *Contact*, 29 September 1958, 11.

Chapter 6 Boycott, 1959–1960

1 Nkrumah had led the British colony of 'The Gold Coast' to independence as 'Ghana' on 6 March 1957. He became the country's executive president when Ghana became a republic in 1960.

2 Hutchinson, *Road to Ghana*.

3 *Contact*, 21 February 1959, 2.

4 Vigne, *Liberals against Apartheid*, 104–105; *Rand Daily Mail*, 31 March 1959, 9.

5 Van Rensburg, Memoir, Chapter 6, 124.

6 Van Rensburg, Memoir, 134.

7 Botswana National Archives (BNA), Senate House (London) Special Collections, M837, microfilm of Liberal Party Transvaal correspondence, enclosed in Jack Unterhalter (Transvaal Chairman) to Peter Brown (National Chairman), 24 April 1959.

8 Christabel Gurney, '"A Great Cause": The Origins of the Anti-Apartheid Movement, June 1959–March 1960', *Journal of Southern African Studies* 6(1), March 2000, 127.

9 BNA, Senate House, M837, Unterhalter to Brown, 17 June 1959. *Wit Baaskap* is Afrikaans slang (literally, 'White Boss-ship') for 'white supremacy'.

10 Van Rensburg, *Guilty Land*, 38–39.

11 BNA, Senate House, M837, Unterhalter to Brown, 15 July 1959.

12 *Sunday Times* (Johannesburg), 12 July 1959, 1.

13 Van Rensburg, Memoir, Chapter 6, 140.

14 Vigne, *Liberals against Apartheid*, 36–37.

15 From Senator Leslie Rubin's speech to the Senate, 9 September 1958, quoted in *Contact*, 20 September 1958. In 1960 Rubin was to go into voluntary exile, first as an academic in Ghana (where he would meet and help Patrick under very different circumstances) and later at Howard University, Washington, DC, from where he helped organise a Defence and Aid Fund to assist the victims of apartheid; see his obituary in *The Guardian*, 16 April 2002.

16 Although the Defence and Aid Fund did not add 'International' to its title until the early 1960s, I use IDAF throughout to avoid any confusion.

17 Van Rensburg, Memoir, Chapter 7, 140–141.

18 Anti-Apartheid Movement Archive, AAM 005, Patrick van Rensburg (PvR) to Miss Symonds (Secretary to Canon Collins), 30 September 1959.

19 AAM 005, PvR to Michael Scott (Africa Bureau), 26 October 1959. Although written a couple of months after the event, this letter references PvR's discussion with Scott about the boycott.

20 AAM 005, Peter Brown to PvR, 21 September 1959.

21 Gurney, '"A Great Cause"', 135.

22 AAM 005, PvR to Miss Symonds, 30 September 1959.

23 AAM 005, for numerous letters, from 23 September 1959.

24 *Manchester Guardian*, 20 October 1959. The *Manchester Guardian* moved to London in 1964 and became simply *The Guardian*.

25 *Manchester Guardian*, 27, 28 October 1959; *The Times*, 28 October 1959; *Daily Telegraph*, 28, 29 October 1959.

26 AAM 005, Holland to PvR, 26 October 1959.

27 Van Rensburg, Memoir, Chapter 13, 247.

28 AAM 002, Minutes of meeting, 4 November 1959.

29 Van Rensburg, Memoir, Chapter 7, 146.

30 Van Rensburg, Memoir, Chapter 7, 146.
31 Van Rensburg, Memoir, Chapter 7, 147.
32 *Cape Argus*, 9 February 1960, interview with Eric Louw.
33 *Contact*, 20 February 1960.
34 AAM 005, PvR to Paton, 4 November 1959.
35 AAM 005, PvR to Guinness, 18 November 1959.
36 The description comes from an article about him in *Contact*, 29 November 1958.
37 Polly Loxton, via Liz van Rensburg, email, 23 April 2018.
38 Van Rensburg, Memoir, Chapter 7, 147–148.
39 AAM 006, for numerous copies of the memorandum, with signatures appended.
40 AAM 005, Holland to PvR, 20 and 23 October 1959.
41 *The Times*, 25 November and 8 December 1959.
42 AAM 006.
43 AAM 005, PvR to Albert Luthuli, 4 November 1959.
44 AAM 005, Enclosed in Peter Brown to PvR, 12 December 1959. See AAM 002 for
    a copy of the signed memorandum.
45 Christabel Gurney, personal communication, August 2019.
46 AAM 005.
47 AAM 005, Brown to PvR, 12 December 1959.
48 AAM 005, Alan Paton to PvR, 31 December 1950.
49 AAM 005, PvR to Paton, 4 January 1960.
50 Gurney, '"A Great Cause"', 138–139.
51 Van Rensburg, Memoir, Chapter 7, 150. Although these thoughts were recorded
    many years later, they appear to be a genuine reflection of his attitude at the time.

Chapter 7 Into Exile, 1960–1961

1 Colin Legum, *Pan-Africanism: A Short Political Guide* (Westport, CT: Praeger, first
   published 1962, revised edition 1965); Richard Gott, John Major and Geoffrey
   Warner (eds), *Documents on International Affairs 1960* (London: Oxford University
   Press, 1964), 349–351.
2 Van Rensburg, Memoir, Chapter 7, 151. The Belgian government had called
   Congolese nationalist leaders to a meeting in Brussels, which had started on 20
   January 1960, just a few days before the opening of the Tunis conference.
3 UK National Archives (UKNA), Cabinet publication C. (60) 66, 155 (*my emphasis*).
   This Cabinet Office pamphlet, originally published as 'SECRET', contains full details
   of Prime Minister Macmillan's Africa tour, including his major speeches in each
   country that he visited as well as the minutes of his private meetings with South
   African Prime Minister Dr Verwoerd and Foreign Affairs Minister Eric Louw
   (whose name was spelt in Britain as the English 'Lowe').
4 Quoted in *Contact*, 20 February 1960.
5 Translation, quoted in Van Rensburg, Memoir, Chapter 7, 153.
6 Quoted in *Contact*, 20 February 1960.
7 *Contact*, 20 February 1960.
8 Hutchinson, *Road to Ghana*, 193.

9 Van Rensburg, Memoir, Chapter 16, 281. For Ghana's Brigades, see Peter Hodge, 'The Ghana Workers Brigade: A Project for Unemployed Youth', *The British Journal of Sociology* 15(2), June 1964, 113–128.

10 Van Rensburg, Memoir, Chapter 7, 154.

11 Tom Lodge, 'The Sharpeville Crisis', in *Black Politics in South Africa since 1945* (Johannesburg: Ravan Press, 1983), 201–230. Two anti-pass demonstrators were killed and 49 wounded in the Cape Town 'township' of Langa.

12 Van Rensburg, Memoir, Chapter 7, 154.

13 Van Rensburg, *Guilty Land*, 42–43.

14 Van Rensburg, Memoir, Chapter 7, 155.

15 Van Rensburg, *Guilty Land*, 44–45.

16 Van Rensburg, *Guilty Land*, 43–44; Van Rensburg, Memoir, Chapter 7, 156.

17 Vigne, *Liberals against Apartheid*, 134.

18 Van Rensburg, *Guilty Land*, 46–47.

19 Van Rensburg, Memoir, Chapter 8, 162.

20 Van Rensburg, Memoir, Chapter 8, 163.

21 Early white visitors to much of sub-Saharan Africa, and subsequent colonial officials, insisted on referring to indigenous towns as 'villages', regardless of their size. 'Towns' or 'cities', in their view, were urban centres constructed in their European cultural image.

22 Neil Parsons, 'The Pipeline: Botswana's Reception of Refugees, 1956–68', *Social Dynamics* 34(1), March 2008, 19.

23 Garth Benneyworth, 'Bechuanaland's Aerial Pipeline: Intelligence and Counter Intelligence Operations against the South African Liberation Movements, 1960–1965', *South African Historical Journal* 70(1), 2018, 113–119; Jeff Ramsay, 'Roots of Botswana's Nationalist Politics (Part 21): MK, MI6 and the Pipeline', *Weekend Post*, 17 May 2019.

24 Ronald Watts, 'Memoirs of a Refugee "Pipeline": The Serowe Route, 1960–1961', *Botswana Notes & Records* 29, 1997, 107.

25 Watts, 'Refugee "Pipeline"', 106; UKNA, DO 157/9, No. 7 of 1960 (October).

26 Watts, 'Refugee "Pipeline"', 110–111.

27 Van Rensburg, Memoir, Chapter 8, 164. A rondavel was a typical African-style circular dwelling, usually thatched and with walls built of poles, wattle and daub or mud bricks. In his subsequent work in Bechuanaland/Botswana, Patrick was to adapt and 'modernise' the concept, retaining the thatch but using more durable baked clay bricks.

28 Patrick van Rensburg, 'The Making of a Rebel', 152.

29 My thanks to Patrick Kidner (email, 27 October 2019) for confirming the name of the LMS missionary couple. Kidner, an administrative cadet in the colonial administration at the time, lived next door to Ronald and Theresa Watts.

30 UKNA, DO 157/9, No. 7 of 1960 (October), para 7(a).

31 In his memoir, Patrick refers to fifty refugees, but Watts, in a letter dated 14 September 1960, writes that the number was nineteen, including the two children: Watts, 'Refugee "Pipeline"', 111.

32 Van Rensburg, 'Making of a Rebel', 153.

33 Watts, 'Refugee "Pipeline"', 111.
34 Steenkamp, a Kenyan-born Afrikaner, had come to Bechuanaland as a cadet district officer in 1955 and took out Botswanan citizenship at independence in 1966. He became permanent secretary in the Office of the President and was for many years effectively head of the civil service: *Sunday Standard* (Botswana), 5 June 2019, reprint of an interview of 28 October 2007.
35 Van Rensburg, 'Making of a Rebel', 155.
36 Van Rensburg, 'Making of a Rebel', 156–157.
37 Van Rensburg, 'Making of a Rebel', 157.
38 Van Rensburg, 'Making of a Rebel', 157.
39 Van Rensburg, 'Making of a Rebel', 158.
40 The Boycott Movement had morphed into the Anti-Apartheid Movement in the aftermath of Sharpeville and now campaigned for a widespread and continuous boycott of South Africa.
41 Van Rensburg, 'Making of a Rebel', 158.
42 Van Rensburg, 'Making of a Rebel', 158.
43 Van Rensburg, 'Making of a Rebel', 158.
44 Liz van Rensburg, email communication, April 2019.
45 Van Rensburg, 'Making of a Rebel', 160–161.
46 Van Rensburg, Memoir, Chapter 10, 177.
47 Van Rensburg, Memoir, Chapter 10, 175.
48 Van Rensburg, Memoir, Chapter 10, 175.
49 Van Rensburg, Memoir, Chapter 10, 175.
50 Van Rensburg, Memoir, Chapter 10, 176.
51 Van Rensburg, Memoir, Chapter 10, 176.
52 The Penguin Special series 'was defined by its crusading engagement with topical issues of the day and by its centre-left political stance and it is often cited as shifting public and political opinion', www.bristol.ac.uk/penguinarchiveproject/research/specials/ (accessed 6 November 2017).
53 Van Rensburg, Memoir, Chapter 11, 202.
54 Van Rensburg, Memoir, Chapter 11, 201.
55 Van Rensburg, Memoir, Chapter 11, 201.
56 Van Rensburg, Memoir, Chapter 11, 202.

Chapter 8 Return to Africa, 1961–1962

1 Liz van Rensburg, private communication, 9 March 2018.
2 Van Rensburg, Memoir, Chapter 11, 206.
3 B. C. Thema, 'Moeng College: A Product of "Self-Help"', *Botswana Notes & Records* 2(1), 1969, 71–74.
4 C. J. Driver, *Patrick Duncan: South African and Pan-African* (London: James Currey, 2000 [first edition, Heinemann, 1980]), 198–199.
5 Van Rensburg, 'Making of a Rebel', 186.
6 Van Rensburg, Memoir, 204.
7 Van Rensburg, Memoir, 203.
8 Van Rensburg, Memoir, 205.

9   Quoted in a brief memorial notice by Professor Stephen Lambert-Humble MBE, in *Working for Oral Health in the Commonwealth* 2(2), April 2015, 5, www.comdental.org/resource/bulletin-04-2015.pdf (accessed 4 December 2017).

10 Van Rensburg, Memoir, Chapter 12, 210.

11 Inserted in the version of Van Rensburg, Memoir, edited by Liz van Rensburg, Chapter 12, 211.

12 Inserted in the version of Van Rensburg, Memoir, edited by Liz van Rensburg, Chapter 12, 211.

13 Inserted in the version of Van Rensburg, Memoir, edited by Liz van Rensburg, Chapter 12, 211, 212.

14 Inserted in the version of Van Rensburg, Memoir, edited by Liz van Rensburg, Chapter 12, 211; extract from Liz's diary.

15 Inserted in the version of Van Rensburg, Memoir, edited by Liz van Rensburg, Chapter 12, 211, 214.

16 Quoted in Van Rensburg, Memoir, 215. Wau is a city in the western part of what is today South Sudan.

17 Quoted in Van Rensburg, Memoir, 217.

18 Quoted in Van Rensburg, Memoir, 218.

19 Quoted in Van Rensburg, Memoir, 220.

20 The Mau Mau uprising was a war between the Kenya Land and Freedom Army, also known as Mau Mau, and the British colonists.

21 'Dar es Salaam' is Arabic for 'the house of peace' or 'haven of peace'. Tanganyika, one of the former German colonies mandated to Britain after World War I, gained its independence in December 1961 under the inspirational leadership of former teacher Julius Nyerere. It became a republic a year later and merged with Zanzibar to form the Republic of Tanzania in 1964.

22 *The Guardian*, obituary of Joan Wicken, 21 December 2004.

23 Liz van Rensburg, private communication, 16 June 2019.

24 Van Rensburg, Memoir, Chapter 12, 226.

25 *The Guardian*, obituary of Michael Stern, 1 August 2002.

26 Liz van Rensburg, private communication, 2017.

27 The Central African Federation was still ruled from the federal capital Salisbury (Harare) in Southern Rhodesia (Zimbabwe), although it was clear to all except some self-deluding white settlers that it was on its last legs. Owing to the extent of African opposition in the northern territories, it finally broke up in December 1963, allowing Nyasaland and Northern Rhodesia to become independent the following year as the republics of Malawi and Zambia respectively.

28 Van Rensburg, Memoir, Chapter 12, 227.

29 Guy and Molly Clutton-Brock, *Cold Comfort Confronted* (London and Oxford: Mowbray, 1972).

30 Clutton-Brock, *Cold Comfort*, 99.

31 Clutton-Brock, *Cold Comfort*, 100–104.

32 Vernon Gibberd, interview, 17 July 2017.

33 Watts, 'Refugee "Pipeline"', 106.

34 UKNA, DO 157/9, Secret: Bechuanaland Protectorate Central Intelligence Committee Report, No. 11 of 1961 (November).

35 UKNA, DO 157/9, Secret: Intelligence Report, No. 5 of 1960.

36 Van Rensburg, Memoir, Chapter 12, 229.

37 Van Rensburg, Memoir, 230.

Chapter 9 The Founding of Swaneng Hill School, 1962–1963

1 Van Rensburg, Memoir, Chapter 13, 235.

2 Van Rensburg, Memoir, Chapter 13, 235.

3 Neil Parsons, interview, 21 November 2016. Parsons, who had been a Voluntary Service Overseas teacher at Moeng from 1962 to 1963, had learned the story from the Stanleys.

4 Neil Parsons, interview, 21 November 2016.

5 *Kgosi* (Chief) Mokhutshwane Sekgoma, interview, Serowe, 26 June 2018.

6 Tlou, Parsons and Henderson, *Seretse Khama*, 132, 159, 167.

7 Van Rensburg, Memoir, Chapter 13, 236.

8 *Mmegi*, 2 October 2003, translation of 'Profile: Patrick van Rensburg'.

9 Van Rensburg, Memoir, Chapter 13, 235–237. The South African rand (R) had replaced the British pound (£) in February 1961, at the rate of R2 to £1. This exchange rate remained the same until British devaluation in 1967. Bechuanaland was within the South African Monetary Area; thus the rand became the protectorate's legal currency. This remained the case until ten years after independence, when, in August 1976, Botswana launched its own currency, the pula (P), initially on a par with the rand.

10 This was shortly before primary school enrolment was extended to seven years.

11 Van Rensburg, Memoir, Chapter 13, 239.

12 Van Rensburg, Memoir, Chapter 13, 240.

13 Paulo Freire, *Pedagogy of the Oppressed* (New York: Herder & Herder, 1970; first published in Portuguese, 1968), 77.

14 Freire, *Pedagogy*.

15 Neil Parsons, interview, 21 November 2016, recalling Stanley's description.

16 Quoted in Van Rensburg, Memoir, Chapter 13, 241. Neil Parsons, who was at the *kgotla* meeting, has dated it to October 1962.

17 Van Rensburg, Memoir, Chapter 13, 241.

18 The date of Saturday 13 October is confirmed by the date of the October full moon for 1962, www.timeanddate.com.

19 Masire would serve as Botswana's president from 1980 to 1998.

20 *Gamangwato* was the Setswana name for the territory of the Bamangwato, which, in colonial terms, was the 'Bamangwato Reserve'. In preparation for independence in 1966 it became 'Central District'.

21 Patrick van Rensburg, *Swaneng Hill School* (Fundraising pamphlet No. 1, *Mafeking Mail* n.d. [late 1963]), 5.

22 Van Rensburg, Memoir, Chapter 13, 241–242.

23 Otsogile Pitso, interview, 15 February 2017.

24 Van Rensburg, *Swaneng Hill School*, 5–6; Van Rensburg, Memoir, Chapter 13, 242–243; //theswanengstory.files.wordpress.com/2015/09/martins-account-first-secti.pdf, 3 (accessed 17 September 2017).

25 Van Rensburg, *Swaneng Hill School*, 5–6; Van Rensburg, Memoir, Chapter 13, 242–243; //theswanengstory.files.wordpress.com/2015/09/martins-account-first-secti.pdf, 3 (accessed 17 September 2017).

26 Steinberg was founding treasurer of the Bechuanaland Democratic Party and from 1965 the first member of Parliament for the Boteti district (north-west of Serowe). It was his cattle post that became Orapa diamond mine.

27 Driver, *Patrick Duncan*, 208–209, 213–220; Van Rensburg, Memoir, Chapter 13, 243–244.

28 Neil Parsons, interview, 21 November 2016.

29 Liz van Rensburg, private communication.

30 Neil Parsons, interview, 21 November 2016; Van Rensburg, Memoir, Chapter 13, 246–247.

31 Tlou, Parsons and Henderson, *Seretse Khama*, 298.

Chapter 10 Challenging 'The Ladder to Privilege', 1963–1965

1 Quote from an article by Tom Holzinger in *Mmegi*, 15 November 2013, reprinted in https://theswanengstory.wordpress.com/swaneng-school/student-selection/ (accessed 19 September 2017).

2 For a near-contemporary account of those early school years, see Patrick van Rensburg, 'Memo on the future of Swaneng Hill School' (1965), a cyclostyled report circulated to the education department and others. I am grateful to Mike Hawkes, British volunteer teacher at Swaneng at that time, for lending me a copy of this memorandum.

3 Van Rensburg, *Swaneng Hill School*, 4.

4 Tom Holzinger, interview, Dorset, 1 June 2017.

5 Julia Majaha-Jartby, interview, London, 16 September 2017.

6 Van Rensburg, Memoir, Chapter 14, 253.

7 Both went on to become Cabinet ministers in independent Botswana.

8 Linchwe's installation as chief took place on 6 April 1963. See Sandy Grant, 'A Chronological Career Summary: Chief Linchwe II Kgafela', *Botswana Notes & Records* 17, 1985, 47–48.

9 Naomi Mitchison, *Return to the Fairy Hill* (London: Heinemann, 1966), 42.

10 Van Rensburg, Memoir, Chapter 14, 255.

11 Van Rensburg, Memoir, Chapter 14, 257–259.

12 Markievicz (1868–1927) participated in the Irish Easter Rising of 1916 and in 1918 became the first woman to be elected to the British Parliament, although, representing the Irish republican party Sinn Féin, she refused to take up her seat, which would have involved swearing loyalty to the British Crown.

13 Mike Hawkes, Skype interview, 13 March 2018.

14 *Rand Daily Mail*, regular reports through August/September 1963.

15 The Central African Federation broke up in December 1963 and Zambia, with Kenneth Kaunda as president, gained its independence in October 1964.

16 Kaunda was at the time a member of the Northern Rhodesian legislature, elected on a restricted franchise in October 1962. He was also president of the United National Independence Party, the largest African nationalist party in the country.

17 Liz van Rensburg, private communication, 9 March 2018.

18 *Kgosi* Mokhutshwane Sekgoma, interview, Serowe, 26 June 2018.

19 Van Rensburg, Memoir, Chapter 14, 257.

20 Mike Hawkes, Skype interview, 13 March 2018.

21 Van Rensburg, Memoir, Chapter 14, 250–260.

22 Mike Hawkes, Skype interview, 13 March 2018.

23 See www.theguardian.com/society/2017/sep/15/trevor-bottomley-obituary (accessed 3 February 2018).

24 See Chapter 9.

25 Van Rensburg, 'Making of a Rebel', 238.

26 Van Rensburg, Memoir, Chapter 15, 268.

27 Patrick van Rensburg, *Education and Development in an Emerging Country* (Uppsala: The Scandinavian Institute of African Studies, 1967), 11.

28 See https://theswanengstory.wordpress.com, Martin's second account, MK02/14.

29 Gaositwe K. T. Chiepe, interview, 21 February 2017.

30 Van Rensburg, 'Memo on the future of Swaneng Hill School', 4.

31 Lord (Frank) Judd, interview, Westminster, 19 April 2018.

32 Lord Judd, interview, 19 April 2018.

33 Neil Parsons, interview, 21 November 2016, recalling a conversation in London (1964/1965) with B. C. Thema (former principal of Moeng College), who had (as required by regulations) resigned from the teaching service in order to enter BDP politics in preparation for Bechuanaland's first general election in March 1965.

34 Liz van Rensburg, private communication, 17 February 2019.

35 See https://saih.no/english/who-we-are (accessed February 2019).

36 Van Rensburg, Memoir, Chapter 15, 278.

37 Van Rensburg, Memoir, Chapter 15, 278.

Chapter 11 The Alternative Educationist, 1965–1967

1 Van Rensburg, *Education and Development*, 11.

2 Alasdair McEwen, letter home, 28 April 1965, 2–3, in //theswanengstory.wordpress.com/swaneng-people-2/swaneng-staff-2/ (accessed 17 September 2017).

3 Alasdair McEwen, letter home, 28 April 1965, 4.

4 Liz van Rensburg, report, 'Swaneng Hill School Newsletter', October 1965.

5 Hodge, 'The Ghana Workers Brigade'.

6 Van Rensburg, Memoir, Chapter 15, 272.

7 Van Rensburg, Memoir, Chapter 15, 273.

8 Alasdair McEwen, letter home, 28 April 1965, 2–3.

9   Van Rensburg, *Education and Development*, 24. This pamphlet was based on a series of lectures delivered in Scandinavia in January 1967, but the ideas expressed had evolved in Serowe in 1965/1966.

10 The phrase comes from Alasdair McEwen's letter home, 28 April 1965, 3.

11 Van Rensburg, Memoir, Chapter 15, 285.

12 Van Rensburg, 'Memo on the future of Swaneng Hill School', 10.

13 Van Rensburg, 'Memo on the future of Swaneng Hill School', 11.

14 E. F. Schumacher, 'How to Help Them Help Themselves', *The Observer*, Review Section, 29 August 1965.

15 See www.centerforneweconomics.org/buddhist-economics (accessed 17 September 2017).

16 See www.centerforneweconomics.org/content/how-help-them-help-themselves (accessed 17 September 2017).

17 Schumacher, 'How to Help Them'. Schumacher was to become best known for his book *Small is Beautiful: A Study of Economics as if People Mattered* (London: Blond and Briggs, 1973).

18 Bessie Head, *Serowe: Village of the Rain Wind* (London: Heinemann 1981), 173.

19 Van Rensburg, Memoir, Chapter 16, 298–299; see also https://theswanengstory. wordpress.com for Diane Fewster, 'The Fewsters' Experience', April 2013.

20 Mike Hawkes, phone interview, 28 May 2018.

21 Thomas Moseki, interview, Serowe, 25 June 2017.

22 Thema was, in fact, minister of labour and social services, but his portfolio included the Department of Education.

23 Interview, Queen Notha, Lawrence Notha's widow, Serowe, 25 June 2018.

24 Sheila Bagnall, *Letters from Botswana, 1966–1975*, edited by Sandy Grant (Odi, Botswana: Leitlho Publications, 2001), 1 October 1966, 20–24.

25 Van Rensburg, 'Making of a Rebel', 241.

26 Gillian S. Eilersen, *Bessie Head: Thunder Behind Her Ears* (Cape Town: David Philip, 1995), 3–62.

27 Van Rensburg, Memoir, Chapter 17, 302.

28 Bagnall, *Letters*, 3 November 1966, 29–30.

29 *The Guardian*, Robert Oakeshott obituary, 3 August 2011.

30 [Robert Oakeshott], '… and for Botswana?', From a Correspondent, *The Economist*, 18 June 1966, 1300.

31 Tom Vernon, 'Bechuanaland', *The Economist*, 25 June 1966, Letters.

32 Bagnall, *Letters*, Staff List, June 1967, 87.

33 *The Guardian*, 3 August 2011.

34 Van Rensburg, Memoir, Chapter 17, 305.

35 Head, *Serowe*, 140–141, for the evidence of Jacklyn Cock, a South African volunteer who taught Development Studies at Swaneng Hill School from 1969.

36 Van Rensburg, Memoir, Chapter 17, 305.

37 Van Rensburg, Memoir, Chapter 17, 306.

38 Botswana National Archives (BNA), BNB 1089/B1, 'Swaneng Development Plan'.

39 Van Rensburg, Memoir, Chapter 17, 306.
40 Van Rensburg, Memoir, Chapter 17, 306.
41 Oakeshott Letters, Robert Oakeshott (R. O.) to his mother, Serowe, 'Good Friday' [12 April] 1968.

Chapter 12 Expansion and Replication, 1967–1969

1   BNA, BNB 1089/B1, 'Swaneng Development Plan'.
2   Quoted in Van Rensburg, Memoir, Chapter 18, 317.
3   For the ongoing controversy surrounding the death of Dag Hammarskjöld, see Susan Williams, *Who Killed Hammarskjöld? The UN, the Cold War and White Supremacy in Africa* (London: Hurst Publishers, 2016).
4   Later president of Finland (1994–2000) and Nobel Peace laureate (2008).
5   Van Rensburg, Memoir, Chapter 18, 313–314.
6   Van Rensburg, *Education and Development*, 18.
7   Van Rensburg, *Education and Development*, 27. Martin Kibblewhite was also acknowledged, in a footnote, for his work on the building course taught to all students in the secondary school from 1964.
8   Interview, Alison Kirton, 4 August 2017.
9   Oakeshott Letters, R. O. to mother, 8 August 1968, in which he thanks her for sending him a copy of the radical historian Christopher Hill's *Reformation to Industrial Revolution: A Social and Economic History of Britain, 1530–1780* (first published in 1967); see also Oakeshott's letters throughout 1968–1969.
10 Liz van Rensburg, private communication, 2 April 2019.
11 J. K. Nyerere, *Education for Self-Reliance* (Dar es Salaam: Ministry of Information and Tourism, 1967).
12 Van Rensburg, Memoir, Chapter 18, 326.
13 See Chapter 14.
14 Ditshwanelo Makwati, interview, Gaborone, 4 March 2016.
15 Tom Holzinger, Skype interview, Montreal, 19 March 2018.
16 Bagnall, *Letters*, 31 July 1967, 99.
17 Bagnall, *Letters*, 1 August 1967, 100; Tom Holzinger, interview, 1 June 2018.
18 Ditshwanelo Makwati, interview, 4 March 2016.
19 Oakeshott Letters, R. O. to mother, 17 March and 10 June 1968.
20 Oakeshott Letters, R. O. to mother, 17 March 1968.
21 Liz van Rensburg, private communication, 30 May 2018.
22 Van Rensburg, Memoir, Chapter 18, 328–329.
23 Oakeshott Letters, R. O. to mother, 5 and 29 February 1968.
24 Bagnall, *Letters*, 2 August 1967, 101.
25 Bagnall, *Letters*, 2 August 1967, 101.
26 Bagnall, *Letters*, 20 September 1967, 104–106.
27 Bagnall, *Letters*, 20 September 1967, 106.
28 Bagnall, *Letters*, 22 November 1967, 123.
29 Bagnall, *Letters*, 22 November 1967, 123.

30 Bagnall, *Letters*, 123, 8 December 1967, 126.
31 Van Rensburg, Memoir, Chapter 19, 336.
32 Bishi Mmusi, interview, 27 June 2018.
33 Bagnall, *Letters*, 4 January 1968, 128.
34 Oakeshott Letters, R. O. to mother, 17 March and 12 April 1968.
35 Oakeshott Letters, R. O. to mother, 17 March 1968.
36 Bagnall, *Letters*, 5 April 1968, 142.
37 The former president Quett Ketumile Masire, interview, Gaborone, 17 February 2017, a few months before his death. The Swaneng staff member supervising the building of the lime kiln was Peter Fewster.
38 Quett Masire, interview, 17 February 2017.
39 Quett Masire, interview, 17 February 2017.
40 Bagnall, *Letters*, 20 June 1968, 159.
41 Van Rensburg, Memoir, Chapter 19, 349–350.
42 Bagnall, *Letters*, 29 June 1968, 159–160.
43 Van Rensburg, Memoir, Chapter 19, 349–350.
44 *Botswana Daily News*, 28 June 1968.
45 Bagnall, *Letters*, 3 July 1968, 161.
46 BNA, BNB 2587 for the early editions of *Mmegi wa Dikgang*, July, August 1968.
47 Bagnall, *Letters*, 3 September 1968, 177.
48 Neil Parsons, private communication, 26 May 2019.
49 Vernon Gibberd, interview, 17 July 2017.
50 Bagnall, *Letters*, 3 November 1968, 191.
51 Today the distance has been reduced to 500 kilometres by a fully tarred road directly north-west from Serowe via Orapa, but in those days the only serious option, other than by Oakeshott's suggested oxwagon across the desert, was to take the long route round via Palapye and Francistown.
52 Bagnall, *Letters*, 3 February 1969, 208.
53 Oakeshott Letters, R. O. to mother, 3 November 1968.
54 Oakeshott Letters, R. O. to mother, 23 November 1968.
55 Oakeshott Letters, R. O. to mother, 23 November 1968.
56 J. W. Hanson, *Secondary Level Teachers in Supply and Demand in Botswana* (East Lansing, MI: Michigan State University, Institute for International Studies in Education, 1969); the quotations are taken from Bagnall, *Letters*, 9 March 1969, 215–216.
57 The 'swatter' at Moeding was Rev. Ken Smith, said to be a notorious beater of boys.
58 Bagnall, *Letters*, 13 March 1969, 216–217.
59 Neil Parsons, private communication, 26 May 2019.
60 Bagnall, *Letters*, 13 March 1969, 217.

Chapter 13 Time of Crisis, 1969–1971

1 Carl Marstrand, 'Formation of Serowe Farmers' Brigade', https://theswanengstory.wordpress.com/brigades-boiteko/ (accessed 15 September 2017).

2 Nthaga Keoraletse, interview, Serowe, 26 June 2018. At the time of interview Keoraletse was passing on his skill in this declining traditional craft to a younger generation, supervising the thatching of a building in the compound of Serowe's Khama Memorial Museum.

3 Tom Holzinger, interview, 1 June 2018.

4 Tom Holzinger, interview, 1 June 2018.

5 See https:// theswanengstory.files.wordpress.com: Vernon Gibberd's reflections on the Farmers' Brigade, Chapter 4 (accessed 15 September 2017).

6 Patrick van Rensburg, 'Swaneng Hill School Newsletter' 2 (69), December 1969, 8–9.

7 Patrick van Rensburg, *The Serowe Brigades: Alternative Education in Botswana* (Basingstoke: Van Leer Foundation/Macmillan Education, 1978), 16.

8 Oakeshott Letters, R. O. to mother, 24 September 1970.

9 Quett Masire, interview, 17 February 2017, for Botswana government thinking at this time. Masire was at that time (1966–1980) vice-president and minister of finance and development planning.

10 Bagnall, *Letters*, 26 December 1969, 249.

11 Bagnall, *Letters*, 26 December 1969, 249.

12 Bagnall, *Letters*, 26 December 1969 and 2 January 1970, 249–250; Van Rensburg, Memoir, Chapter 20, 359–360.

13 Van Rensburg, Memoir, Chapter 20, 360.

14 Jacklyn Cock, *Maids and Madams* (Johannesburg: Ravan Press, 1980).

15 Bagnall, *Letters*, 14 January 1970, 252.

16 Bagnall, *Letters*, 13 May 1970, 261.

17 Bagnall, *Letters*, 21 May 1970, 262.

18 Bagnall, *Letters*, 22 May 1970, 263.

19 The account of what followed is drawn from Bagnall, *Letters*, 28–29 May 1970, 264–166; Van Rensburg, Memoir, Chapter 21, 267–269; Tom Holzinger, interview, 1 June 2018.

20 Oakeshott Letters, R. O. to mother, June 1970.

21 After a chequered career in education in Ghana, Nigeria and Zambia, Setidisho joined the Ministry of Education in Botswana and went on to become vice-chancellor of the University of Botswana.

22 From his initials and the name of the villain in the first (1962) James Bond film of that name.

23 Van Rensburg, 'Making of a Rebel', 231.

24 Van Rensburg, 'Making of a Rebel', 231.

25 Van Rensburg, Memoir, Chapter 21, 368.

26 Interview, Tom Holzinger, 1 June 2018.

27 The previous June, Sheila had moved from the bedsit flat next to the common room into a house specially built for her: Bagnall, *Letters*, 20 June 1969, 219.

28 As Jackie and Dottie reported to Sheila: Bagnall, *Letters*, 28 May 1970, 266.

29 Van Rensburg, Memoir, Chapter 21, 368–369.

30 Bagnall, *Letters*, 30 May 1970, 267.

31 Van Rensburg, Memoir, Chapter 21, 369.

32 Oakeshott Letters, R. O. to mother, 29 May 1970.

33 Bagnall, *Letters*, dated 8 June 1970, though clearly completed several days later, 269; Van Rensburg, Memoir, Chapter 21, 269.

34 Patrick van Rensburg, *Report from Swaneng Hill: Education and Employment in an African Country* (Uppsala: DHF, 1974), 57.

35 Bagnall, *Letters*, 18 June and 8 July 1970, 269–270.

36 For a revised, published version of this paper, see Patrick van Rensburg, 'A New Approach to Rural Development', *Botswana Notes & Records* 3, 1971, 201–215.

37 Bagnall, *Letters*, 3 September 1970, 275.

38 Reported in Bagnall, *Letters*, 13 September 1970, 277.

39 Bagnall, *Letters*, 13 September 1970, 278.

40 Mike Hawkes, Skype interview, 13 March 2018.

41 Mike Hawkes, Skype interview, 13 March 2018.

42 *Kutlwano* IX(12), December 1970, 20–23; *Mmegi wa Dikgang* 2(1), February 1971, 7.

43 Bagnall, *Letters*, 5 and 11 November 1970, 286–288.

44 Bagnall, *Letters*, 25 November 1970, 289.

45 Bagnall, *Letters*, 5 November 1970, 286–287.

Chapter 14 Education with Production, the 1970s

1 Liz van Rensburg, private communication, 14 September 2018.

2 Liz van Rensburg, private communication, 14 September 2018.

3 Eilersen, *Bessie Head*, 121.

4 Eilersen, *Bessie Head*, 137.

5 Eilersen, *Bessie Head*, 137–138.

6 Eilersen, *Bessie Head*, 157.

7 Neil Parsons, private communication, 27 May 2019.

8 Eilersen, *Bessie Head*, 135–138.

9 For a revised, published version of this paper, see Van Rensburg, 'A New Approach', 201–215.

10 Van Rensburg 'A New Approach', 203.

11 Quoted from Van Rensburg's report in the 'Swaneng Hill School Newsletter' 2(69), December 1969, 7.

12 Jenny (Peel) Wielandt, personal communication, May 2019. Jenny worked in Serowe as Patrick's secretary from November 1973 to January 1977, during which time she met and married Danish volunteer Benny Wielandt, who arrived in 1974 to set up the Plumbers' Brigade.

13 Patrick van Rensburg, *Looking Forward from Serowe* (Gaborone: Foundation for Education with Production, 1984), 37–38.

14 Wouter van der Wall Bake, Skype interview, 20 December 2018.

15 SYDT, *Serowe Brigades, 1965/66–1975/76* (Serowe: SYDT, 1976).

16 Frank Taylor, interview, Gabane, 19 June 2018.

17 Frank Taylor, interview, 19 June 2018. Frank subsequently set up Pelagano Village Industries in Gabane, based on his alternative model of rural training for

enterprise. It is still there, although it has not become the engine for widespread community development that Patrick was trying to achieve in Serowe. Today Gabane is largely a dormitory town for nearby Gaborone.

18 Joel Pelotona, interview, Serowe, 11 March 2016.

19 Titia van der Wall Bake, Skype interview, 20 December 2018.

20 Van Rensburg, *Report from Swaneng Hill*, 99–104.

21 Van Rensburg, *Report from Swaneng Hill*, 99–104.

22 See https://theswanengstory.wordpress.com/brigades-boiteko/ (accessed 20 September 2017).

23 Eilersen, *Bessie Head*, 184.

24 BNA, Khama Memorial Museum (Serowe), Bessie Head Papers, file 53, letter dated 26 February 1976. I am grateful to Tom Holzinger for acquiring a copy of this letter for me.

25 Kopano Lekoma and Liz van Rensburg, 'Report on Boiteko', in SYDT, *Serowe Brigades*, 45–47.

26 Van Rensburg, *Looking Forward*, 65.

27 D. D. Makwati, 'Boiteko Agricultural Management Association', *FEP Newsletter* 18/19, 'Women in Production', 4–5.

28 Liz van Rensburg, private communication.

29 Karl Marx, *Capital*, Vol. I (Harmondsworth: Penguin, 1976), 613–619, quoted in Stephen Castles and Wiebke Wüstenberg, *The Education of the Future: An Introduction to the Theory and Practice of Socialist Education* (London: Pluto Press, 1979), 37–39.

30 See Chapter 15.

31 Published by Monthly Review Press, New York, 1967.

32 *Sunday Standard* (Botswana), 1 June 2015, 'Remembering Cde Goabamang Kenneth Koma', on the 50th anniversary of the founding of the Botswana National Front.

33 *Mmegi*, 29 June 2012.

34 Frank Youngman, who attended some of the study groups, personal communication, June 2019.

35 Quett Masire, interview, 17 February 2017.

36 Patrick van Rensburg, 'The Serowe Experience', Paper presented to the FEP/NIR Seminar on Education, Development and Social Transformation, Gaborone, 1982, 9.

37 Parsons, *Report on the Botswana Brigades*, 43.

38 Quoted in Parsons, *Report on the Botswana Brigades*, 43.

39 Parsons, *Report on the Botswana Brigades*, 43.

40 *Botswana Daily News*, 12 July 1977.

41 *Botswana Daily News*, 12 July 1977.

42 The combined University of Botswana, Lesotho and Swaziland, based in Roma in Lesotho, had been established in the 1960s. In 1975 Lesotho nationalised the university, leaving Botswana and Swaziland to form the combined University of Botswana and Swaziland, each with its own university college campus. These became separate universities in 1981.

43 *Botswana Daily News*, 21 November 1977. His lecture at the University College of Botswana had been on Thursday 17 November.

44 *Botswana Daily News*, 25 November 1977.

45 *Botswana Daily News*, 28 November 1977.

46 *Botswana Daily News*, 30 November 1977.

47 *Botswana Daily News*, 30 November 1977.

48 Liz van Rensburg, private communication, December 2018.

49 Archives of the DHF, A2: 8 (1972), Draft proposal for a seminar in 1973, 3.

50 Patrick van Rensburg, *Report from Swaneng Hill: Education and Employment in an African Country* (Uppsala: DHF, 1974).

51 DHF, A2: 9 (1974), Minutes of DHF Board Meeting, Uppsala, 14 December 1974, Document 2: Report on Seminar in Dar-es-Salaam, 20 May–31 May 1974.

52 *Daily News* (Tanzania), 21 May 1974.

53 Upper Volta was renamed Burkina Faso in 1984.

54 Van Rensburg, *Report from Swaneng Hill*, 150.

55 Patrick van Rensburg, 'The Need for a Revolution in Education', *Africa* 45, May 1975, 34–36.

56 Olle Nordberg, private communication, 6 November 2018.

57 The proceedings of the conference were published in *Development Dialogue* 2, 1978, 2.

58 These questions, which were fundamental to his thinking at the time, found their way into the title of a later publication: Patrick van Rensburg, *Making Education Work: The What, Why and How of Education with Production* (Gaborone and Johannesburg: FEP; Uppsala: DHF, 2001).

59 Thomas Masego van Rensburg, now a senior lecturer in Environmental Economics at the National University of Ireland, Galway, is today known simply as Tom.

60 Tom van Rensburg, interview, Serowe, 24 June 2017.

61 Mothusi van Rensburg, interview, Serowe, 17 February 2017. Mothusi today manages the Boiteko co-operative retail park in Serowe.

62 Tom van Rensburg, interview, 24 June 2017.

63 Liz van Rensburg, private communication.

Chapter 15 Foundation for Education with Production and Spreading the Word, the 1980s

1 Frank Youngman, personal communication, June 2019. Youngman attended some of the study groups.

2 I am grateful to Neil Parsons for pointing out this perception: personal communication, May 2019.

3 Queen Notha (Lawrence's widow), interview, 25 June 2018.

4 Tariq Mellet, interview, Blouberg, South Africa, 8 February 2017. Mellet was an ANC member who attended the course, though he was not part of the SOMAFCO group, already being resident in Botswana as a refugee.

5 DHF Archive, A2: 11 (1983), 1.

6 Séan Morrow, Brown Maaba and Loyiso Pulumani, *Education in Exile: SOMAFCO, the ANC School in Tanzania, 1978 to 1992* (Pretoria: HSRC Press, 2004), 86–92.

7 DHF Archive, A2: 11 (1983), 1.

8   See www.sahistory.org.za/topic/june-16-soweto-youth-uprising (accessed June 2018).

9   Morrow, Maaba and Pulumani, *Education in Exile*, 86–92.

10 Morrow, Maaba and Pulumani, *Education in Exile*, 86–92.

11 In 1987 Zanu would incorporate the Zimbabwe African People's Union, to become Zanu-PF (Patriotic Front).

12 Being a leap year, there was a 29 February.

13 Janice McLaughlin, *Education with Production in Zimbabwe: The Story of ZIMFEP* (Gaborone: FEP; Harare: ZIMFEP, 2002), 4–5; Fay Chung, *Reliving the Second Chimurenga: Memories of Zimbabwe's Liberation Struggle* (Uppsala: The Nordic Africa Institute; Harare: Weaver Press, 2006/2007), 200–224.

14 At that time the Zimbabwean capital still went under the colonial name 'Salisbury'. It was only renamed 'Harare' on the second anniversary of independence, but to avoid later confusion I prefer to use the name Harare from the moment of independence.

15 FEP Archive, unsorted papers.

16 DHF Archive, A2: 11 (1983), 2, Report by Patrick van Rensburg on the Lusaka seminar.

17 Neil Parsons, private communication, May 2019.

18 Chung, *The Second Chimurenga*, 252–253.

19 Chung, *The Second Chimurenga*, 271.

20 Chung, *The Second Chimurenga*, 271–272.

21 FEP Archives, unsorted papers, copy of the minutes of FEP Board Meeting, June 1981.

22 McLaughlin, *The Story of ZIMFEP*, 18.

23 Chung, *The Second Chimurenga*, 272; Fay Chung, private communication, 11 April 2018.

24 McLaughlin, *The Story of ZIMFEP*, 33.

25 Frank Youngman, private communication, June 2019.

26 Rosemary Forbes, interviews, Gaborone, 13 March 2016 and 15 February 2017.

27 Rosemary Forbes, interviews, 13 March 2016 and 15 February 2017.

28 Castles and Wüstenburg, *Education of the Future*.

29 Chung, *The Second Chimurenga*, 254.

30 Frank Youngman, private communication, June 2019.

31 See Van Rensburg, *Making Education Work*, 64–78, for more detail on the EwP curriculum.

32 The RLA Archive, Sven Hamrell to Jakob von Uexkull, 17 February 1981. I am grateful to Kajsa Övergaard of the Right Livelihood Foundation for sending me a copy of this letter.

33 Van Rensburg, *The Serowe Brigades*.

34 RLA, *Roll of Honour, 1980–2000* (Stockholm: RLA, 2000), 1, www.rightlivelihoodaward.org/laureates/ (accessed 15 September 2018).

35 www.rightlivelihoodaward.org/speech/acceptance-speech-patrick-van-rensburg/ (accessed 15 September 2018).

36 www.rightlivelihoodaward.org/honour/about-the-right-livelihood-award/ (accessed 15 September 2018).

37 Jakob von Uexkull, telephone interview, 9 December 2018.
38 RLA Archive, letter, Patrick van Rensburg, Gaborone, to Jakob von Uexkull, Isle of Man, 6 May 1982. I am grateful to Kajsa Övergaard for sending me a copy of this letter.
39 FEP Archive, unsorted papers on the Grenada seminar.
40 Tom Holzinger, private communication. Holzinger met Patrick in Canada shortly after the overthrow and killing of Maurice Bishop.
41 FEP Archive, correspondence and report about the Alaska project.
42 www.yksd.com/Domain/34 (accessed 18 January 2019); www.citytowninfo. com/places/alaska/huslia (accessed 18 January 2019).
43 Published by FEP, Gaborone, 1985.
44 Neil Parsons, private communication, May 2019.
45 It was also in 1984 that Ditshwanelo Makwati helped revive Boiteko in Serowe.
46 Rosemary Forbes, interview, 13 February 2017.
47 Methaetsile Leepile, interview, Gaborone, 3 March 2016.
48 George Moalosi, interview, Gaborone, 4 March 2016.
49 Methaetsile Leepile, interview, 3 March 2016.
50 *Mmegi wa Dikgang* I(1), 31 August 1984, 4.
51 Methaetsile Leepile, interview, 3 March 2016.
52 DHF Archive, A2: 14 (1991), Report on seminar 'Democracy and the Media in Southern Africa', December 1989.
53 Titus Mbuya, interview, Gaborone, 9 March 2016.
54 Patrick van Rensburg, 'Dismemberment of the Brigades: A Very Disreputable Transaction', *SARE with FEP* 8, 2002, 62–63.
55 SADCC became SADC (the Southern African Development Community) in 1992, with the addition of Namibia. South Africa joined the group in 1994 following its first democratic election.
56 For contemporary analysis of the consequences of South Africa's policy towards its neighbours at this time, see P. Johnson and D. Martin, *Destructive Engagement: Southern Africa at War*, with a Foreword by Julius Nyerere (Harare: Zimbabwe Publishing House, 1986).
57 DHF Archive, A2: 12 (1986), 9, for a report on the seminar.
58 DHF Archive, A2: 13 (1988), 1.
59 M. Sefali and P. van Rensburg (eds), 'Applicability of Another Development to SADCC: Agenda for Action', paper presented at a seminar on Another Development for Lesotho, Maseru, Lesotho, 18–22 November 1985 (Gaborone: FEP, 1987); P. van Rensburg (ed.), 'Education with Production', paper presented at a seminar on Another Development for Lesotho, Maseru, Lesotho, 14–18 December 1987 (Gaborone: FEP, 1989).
60 Tom van Rensburg, Skype interview, 20 March 2019.
61 DHF Archive, A2: 13 (1989), 1, for Patrick's report on the seminar.
62 The elections, won overwhelmingly by SWAPO, took place in November 1989 and Namibia celebrated its independence on 21 March 1990, the 30th anniversary of the Sharpeville massacre.

Chapter 16 Education with Production and South Africa, the 1990s

1 Van Rensburg, *Making Education Work*, 60–61.
2 Patrick van Rensburg, 'Education with Production: An Overview', *Education with Production* 11(2), April 1996. The curriculum was published the following year as *Education with Production Curriculum* (Gaborone: FEP, 1990).
3 I am grateful to Professor Peter Kallaway, Faculty of Education, University of Cape Town, for this insight; interview, Kenilworth, 7 February 2017.
4 Van Rensburg, *Making Education Work*, 82–83; Ron Singer, '"I'll Teach You to Build a School"', *Front Porch Review* 4, April 2012.
5 DHF Archives, A2: 14 (1991), Introduction to Van Rensburg's report on the seminar.
6 DHF Archives, A2: 14 (1991), Van Rensburg's report, 5.
7 Van Rensburg, *Making Education Work*, 83.
8 Singer, '"I'll Teach You"'.
9 Van Rensburg, *Making Education Work*, 98.
10 *Working to Learn: Newsletter of the Foundation for Education with Production* 2, 1995, 1.
11 Rosemary Forbes, interviews, 13 March 2016 and 15 February 2017.
12 Van Rensburg, *Making Education Work*, 104–106.
13 Van Rensburg, *Making Education Work*, 104–106.
14 Van Rensburg, *Making Education Work*, 104–106. After the first non-racial elections were held in Namibia in 1989, the country gained its independence on 21 March 1990 and was admitted to the Southern African regional grouping. In 1992, in anticipation of impending South African liberation, SADCC was reformed as the Southern African Development Community (SADC), with its secretariat in Gaborone.
15 Joanna Forbes, interview, Gaborone, 15 February 2017.
16 Van Rensburg, *Making Education Work*, 83–84.
17 Evidence of the problems besetting the Kangwane project is drawn largely from Van Rensburg, *Making Education Work*. The project gets some mention among the unsorted papers in the FEP Archive in Gaborone, but there is little of significance there. It has not been possible to learn Seoposengwe's side of this story.
18 Van Rensburg, *Making Education Work*, 84.
19 DHF Archives, A2: 14 (1993), 6.
20 The full syllabus for the BEd course is to be found in Van Rensburg, *Making Education Work*, 97–98.
21 Van Rensburg, *Making Education Work*, 97–98.
22 Peter Kallaway, interview, 7 February 2017.
23 Peter Kallaway, interview, 7 February 2017.
24 Tom Holzinger, with whom Patrick discussed these issues, interview, 1 June 2018.
25 Van Rensburg, *Making Education Work*, 106.
26 See www.africa.upenn.edu/Govern_Political/ANC_Education.html (accessed 27 October 2018).
27 DHF Archives, A2: 14 (1993), 6.

28 Gay Seidman, *Working for the Future* (1987), a textbook for Development Studies at School Certificate level, with a *Teachers' Guide* (1990); Judy Seidman, *In Our Own Image* (1990), a Cultural Studies textbook, with a *Teaching Guide* (1995); Paul Brickhill, *Fundamentals of Production* (2 vols, 1992–1993); J. Moody, *Working with English* (3 vols, 1992–1994).

29 DHF Archives, A2: 15 (1994), 12.

30 Dr Chiepe's speech was published in *Education with Production* 11(2), April 1996, 81–90. Chiepe had spent most of her public career since independence in a range of senior Cabinet posts and had only just been appointed minister of education. As we shall see in the following chapter, her appointment was to renew opportunities for Patrick's ideas in Botswana.

31 DHF Archives, A2: 15 (1995), 10.

32 DHF Archives, A2: 15 (1994), 15.

33 Van Rensburg, *Making Education Work*, 104.

34 See www.africa.upenn.edu/Govern_Political/ANC_Education.html (accessed 27 October 2018).

35 The Group Areas Act, which defined where people lived according to 'racial' classification, was scrapped in 1991.

36 Van Rensburg, *Making Education Work*, 98.

37 Van Rensburg, *Making Education Work*, 98.

38 Van Rensburg, *Making Education Work*, 99.

39 FEP, *Working to Learn* (Johannesburg: Newsletter 2), 1995, 2.

40 FEP, *Working to Learn* (Johannesburg: Newsletter 2), 1995, 2.

41 Van Rensburg, *Making Education Work*, 99.

42 From the unsorted papers in the FEP Archive in Gaborone.

43 Rosemary Forbes, interview, 15 February 2017.

44 His invitation, found among his papers in the FEP Archive.

45 Rosemary Forbes, personal communication.

Chapter 17 Return to Botswana

1 *Mmegi*, 3–9 February 1995, 14.

2 *Mmegi*, 3–9 February 1995, 15.

3 Dr Chiepe's professional career: Education Officer 1948–1962, Senior Education Officer 1962–1965, Deputy Director of Education 1965–1967, Director of Education 1968–1970, on sabbatical as Botswana High Commissioner to the UK 1966–1974; ministerial posts held: Commerce and Industry 1974–1977, Mineral Resources and Water Affairs 1977–1984, External Affairs 1984–1995, Education 1995–1999.

4 Gaositwe K. T. Chiepe, interview, 21 February 2017.

5 M. Hulela and S. Motswane, interview, Gaborone, 18 June 2018.

6 M. Hulela, interview, 18 June 2018.

7 Philip Bulawa, interview, Gaborone, 18 June 2018.

8 Philip Bulawa, interview, 18 June 2018.

9 BNF, *The Social Democratic Programme of the Botswana National Front* (Gaborone: BNF, 1995), 20, para. 35.

10 C. J. Makgala, *Elite Conflict in Botswana: A History* (Pretoria: Africa Institute of South Africa, 2006), 130–139.

11 *Mmegi*, 17–23 April 1998.

12 *Botswana Daily News*, 20 April 1998.

13 M. Dingake, *The Politics of Confusion: The BNF Saga 1984–1998* (Gaborone: Bay Publishing, 2004); M. Dingake, interview, 5 March 2016.

14 Van Rensburg, *Making Education Work*, 126–130; M. Hulela and S. Motswane, interview, 18 June 2018.

15 Van Rensburg, *Making Education Work*, 129.

16 Van Rensburg, *Making Education Work*, 129.

17 Joanna Forbes, interview, 15 February 2017.

18 Van Rensburg, *Making Education Work*, 129–131.

19 Rosemary Forbes, Skype interview, 1 June 2019.

20 Tom van Rensburg, Skype interview, 4 June 2019.

21 Tom van Rensburg, Skype interview, 4 June 2019.

22 Rosemary Forbes, Skype interview, 1 June 2019.

23 Rosemary Forbes, Skype interview, 1 June 2019; Tom van Rensburg, Skype interview, 4 June 2019.

24 Tom Holzinger, interview, 1 June 2018.

25 Joanna Forbes, interview, 15 February 2017.

26 Joanna Forbes, interview, 15 February 2017.

27 Holzinger, 'Personal Memoir'.

28 Jakob von Uexkull, telephone interview, 9 December 2018.

29 Tsetsele Fantan, interview, 9 March 2016.

30 Pelonomi Venson, then minister of foreign affairs, interview, 20 February 2017.

Epilogue

1 Holzinger, 'Personal Memoir'.

2 Fay Chung, email communication, 11 April 2018.

3 Philip Bulawa, interview, 18 June 2018.

4 M. Hulela, interview, 18 June 2018.

Bibliography

1. Primary Sources
Archives

Anti-Apartheid Archive, AAM/002, AAM/005, AAM/006 (Bodleian Library, Oxford).

Archive of the Foundation for Education with Production (FEP), unsorted papers (Gaborone).

Archives of the Dag Hammarskjöld Foundation (DHF), A2: 8 (1972); A2: 9 (1974); A2: 11 (1983); A2: 12 (1986); A2: 13 (1988); A2: 13 (1989); A2: 14 (1991); A2: 14 (1993); A2: 15 (1994); A2: 15 (1995).

Botswana National Archives (BNA):

BNB 1089/B1, 'Swaneng Development Plan'.

BNB 2587, early Serowe editions of *Mmegi wa Dikgang*.

Khama Memorial Museum (Serowe), Bessie Head Papers.

Senate House (London) Special Collections, M837, microfilm of Liberal Party Transvaal correspondence.

UK National Archives (UKNA):

C. (60) 66, Cabinet publication.

DO 157/9, Secret: Bechuanaland Protectorate Central Intelligence Committee Report, No. 5 of 1960; No. 7 of 1960 (October); and No. 11 of 1961 (November).

Unpublished private papers

Oakeshott Letters, Robert Oakeshott to his mother, 1968–1970.

Van Rensburg, Patrick, 'Memoir' (unpublished autobiography, edited by Liz van Rensburg).

Van Rensburg, Patrick, 'The Making of a Rebel' (unpublished autobiography).

Newspapers

Botswana Daily News.

Cape Argus.

Contact (news review, Cape Town, 1958–1962).
Daily News (Tanzania).
Kutlwano.
Manchester Guardian/The Guardian.
Mmegi wa Dikgang (shortened to *Mmegi* in 1989).
Rand Daily Mail.
Sunday Standard (Gaborone).
The Economist.
The Natal Mercury.
The Star (Johannesburg).
The Sunday Times (Johannesburg).
The Telegraph.
The Times.
Working to Learn (FEP Newsletter).

Websites consulted

https://theswanengstory.wordpress.com/
www.africa.upenn.edu/Govern_Political/ANC_Education.html
www.rightlivelihoodaward.org/laureates/

Selected publications by Patrick van Rensburg

Van Rensburg, P. *Guilty Land*. London: Jonathan Cape and Penguin Special, 1962.
Van Rensburg, P. and Boyd, A. *An Atlas of African Affairs*. London: Methuen University Paperbacks, 1962.
Van Rensburg, P. *Swaneng Hill School*. Fundraising pamphlet No. 1. *Mafeking Mail* n.d. [late 1963].
Van Rensburg, P. *Education and Development in an Emerging Country*. Uppsala: The Scandinavian Institute of African Studies, 1967.
Van Rensburg, P. 'A New Approach to Rural Development'. *Botswana Notes & Records* 3 (1971), 201–215.
Van Rensburg, P. *Report from Swaneng Hill: Education and Employment in an African Country*. Uppsala: Dag Hammarskjöld Foundation, 1974.
Van Rensburg, P. 'The Need for a Revolution in Education'. *Africa* 45 (May 1975), 34–36.
Van Rensburg, P. *The Serowe Brigades: Alternative Education in Botswana*. Basingstoke: Van Leer Foundation/Macmillan Education, 1978.
Van Rensburg, P. 'Education and Production as a Lever for Another Development'. *Development Dialogue* 2 (1982), 81–88.
Van Rensburg, P. 'The Serowe Experience', *Education, Development and Social Transformation*. Gaborone: FEP/NIR, 1982.

Van Rensburg, P. *Looking Forward from Serowe*. Gaborone: FEP, 1984.

Van Rensburg, P., ed. 'Education with Production'. Paper presented at a seminar on Another Development for Lesotho, held in Maseru, Lesotho, 14–18 December 1987. Gaborone: FEP, 1989.

Van Rensburg, P. 'Education with Production: An Overview'. *Education with Production* 11(2) (April 1996), 89–108.

Van Rensburg, P. *Making Education Work: The What, Why and How of Education with Production*. Gaborone and Johannesburg: FEP; Uppsala: DHF, 2001.

Van Rensburg, P. 'Dismemberment of the Brigades: A Very Disreputable Transaction'. *SARE with FEP* 8 (2002), 62–63.

2. Secondary Sources

Alley, R. *Leaves from a Sandan Notebook*. Christchurch: Caxton Press, 1950. Republished as *Sandan: An Adventure in Creative Education*. Gaborone: FEP, 1989.

Armstrong, T. *King Cotton*. London: Collins, 1947.

Badisang, B., Mashingaidze, E. T. and Tau, K. D. *Patrick van Rensburg: Annotated Bibliography*. Gaborone: FEP/Motaki Publishing, forthcoming 2020.

Bagnall, S. *Letters from Botswana, 1966–1975*, edited by Sandy Grant. Odi, Botswana: Leitlho Publications, 2001.

Benneyworth, G. 'Bechuanaland's Aerial Pipeline: Intelligence and Counter Intelligence Operations against the South African Liberation Movements, 1960–1965'. *South African Historical Journal* 70(1) (2018), 113–119.

Benson, M. *Tshekedi Khama*. London: Faber & Faber, 1960.

Botswana National Front (BNF). *The Social Democratic Programme of the Botswana National Front*. Gaborone: BNF, 1995.

Bowles, C. *Africa's Challenge to America*. Berkely and Los Angeles, CA: University of California Press, 1956.

Brickhill, P. *Fundamentals of Production: A Practical Approach* (2 vols). Gaborone: Foundation for Education with Production, 1992–1993.

Castles, S. and Wüstenberg, W. *The Education of the Future: An Introduction to the Theory and Practice of Socialist Education*. London: Pluto Press, 1979.

Chiepe, G. K. T. 'The Botswana Brigades, 1965–1995'. *Education with Production* 11(2) (April 1996), 81–90.

Chung, F. *Reliving the Second Chimurenga: Memories of Zimbabwe's Liberation Struggle*. Uppsala: The Nordic Africa Institute; Harare: Weaver Press, 2006/2007.

Clutton-Brock, G. and Clutton-Brock, M. *Cold Comfort Confronted*. London and Oxford: Mowbray, 1972.

Coombs, P. H. and Manzoor, A. *Attacking Rural Poverty: How Non-formal Education Can Help*. Baltimore: World Bank and Johns Hopkins University Press, 1974.

Dingake, M. *The Politics of Confusion: The BNF Saga 1984–1998.* Gaborone: Bay Publishing, 2004.

Driver, C. J. *Patrick Duncan: South African and Pan-African.* London: James Currey, 2000 (first edition, Heinemann, 1980).

Dutfield, M. *A Marriage of Inconvenience: The Persecution of Ruth and Seretse Khama.* London: Unwin Hyam, 1990.

Eilersen, G. S. *Bessie Head: Thunder Behind Her Ears.* Cape Town: David Philip, 1995.

Fanon, F. *The Wretched of the Earth.* Translated by C. Farrington. Harmondsworth: Penguin, 1963.

Fewster, K. 'EWP Schools and the Early Brigades in Botswana'. *Education with Production* 11(2), April 1996, 45–73.

Foster, P. 'Education for Self-Reliance: A Critical Evaluation'. In *Education in Africa: Research and Action.* Edited by R. Jolly. Nairobi: East African Publishing House, 1969, 81–102.

Foundation for Education with Production (FEP). *Education with Production Curriculum.* Gaborone: FEP International, 1990.

Foundation for Education with Production (FEP). 'The EWP Curriculum: Fundamentals of Production'. *Education with Production* 11(2) (April 1996), 109–153.

Frank, A. G. *Capitalism and Underdevelopment in Latin America: Historical Studies of Chile and Brazil.* New York: Monthly Review Press, 1967.

Freire, P. *Pedagogy of the Oppressed.* Translated by M. Ramos. New York: Herder & Herder, 1970.

Freire, P. *Education: The Practice of Freedom.* London: Writers and Readers Publishing Cooperative, 1976.

Gott, R., Major, J. and Warner, G., eds. *Documents on International Affairs 1960.* London: Oxford University Press, 1964.

Grant, S. 'A Chronological Career Summary: Chief Linchwe II Kgafela'. *Botswana Notes & Records* 17 (1985), 47–48.

Gurney, C. '"A Great Cause": The Origins of the Anti-Apartheid Movement, June 1959–March 1960'. *Journal of Southern African Studies* 6(1) (March 2000), 123–144.

Hanson, J. W. *Secondary Level Teachers in Supply and Demand in Botswana.* East Lansing, MI: Michigan State University, Institute for International Studies in Education, 1969.

Head, B. *When Rain Clouds Gather.* London: Gollancz, 1969.

Head, B. *Maru.* London: Gollancz, 1971.

Head, B. *A Question of Power.* London: Davis-Poynter, 1973.

Head, B. *Serowe: Village of the Rain Wind.* London: Heinemann, 1981.

Healy-Clancy, M. 'Mass Education in the Gendered Politics of Development in Apartheid South Africa and Late-Colonial British Africa'. In *Empire and Education in Africa: The Shaping of a Comparative Perspective,* edited by P. Kallaway and R. Swartz. New York: Peter Lang, 2016, 177–201.

Hodge, P. 'The Ghana Workers Brigade: A Project for Unemployed Youth'. *The British Journal of Sociology* 15(2) (June 1964), 113–128.

Huddleston, T. *Naught for Your Comfort*. New York: Doubleday, 1956.

Hunter, M. *Race for Education: Gender, White Tone and Schooling in South Africa*. London: Cambridge University Press and International African Institute, 2019.

Hutchinson, A. *The Road to Ghana*. London: Victor Gollancz, 1960.

Hutchinson, A. *The Road to Ghana*, with Afterword by Es'kia Mphahlele. Johannesburg: Penguin Classics, 2006.

James, C. L. R. *The Black Jacobins*. London: Secker & Warburg, 1938.

Johnson, P. and Martin, D., eds. *Destructive Engagement: Southern Africa at War*, Foreword by Julius Nyerere. Harare: Zimbabwe Publishing House, 1986.

Joseph, H. *Side by Side*. London: Zed Books, 1986.

Judd, D. and Surridge, K. *The Boer War*. London: Murray, 2002.

Kallaway, P. 'The Need for Attention to the Issue of Rural Education'. *International Journal of Educational Development* 21(1) (January 2001), 21–32.

Kanza, T. *Conflict in the Congo: The Rise and Fall of Lumumba*. Translated from the French. Harmondsworth: Penguin Books, 1972.

Legum, C. *Pan-Africanism: A Short Political Guide*. Westport, CT: Praeger, 1965 (first published 1962).

Lekoma, K. and Van Rensburg, E. 'Report on Boiteko'. In SYDT, *Serowe Brigades: 1965/66–1975/76*. Serowe: SYDT, 1976, 45–47.

Lodge, T. *Black Politics in South Africa since 1945*. Johannesburg: Ravan Press, 1983.

Makgala, C. J. *Elite Conflict in Botswana: A History*. Pretoria: Africa Institute of South Africa, 2006.

Makwati, D. D. 'Boiteko Agricultural Management Association'. *FEP Newsletter* 18/19, 'Women in Production', 3–7.

Marx, K. *Capital* Vol. I. Harmondsworth: Penguin, 1976.

Masire, Q. K. J. *Very Brave or Very Foolish: Memoirs of an African Diplomat*, edited by S. Lewis Jr. Gaborone: Macmillan Botswana, 2006.

McLaughlin, J. *Education with Production in Zimbabwe: The Story of ZIMFEP*. Gaborone: Foundation for Education with Production; Harare: ZIMFEP, 2002.

Mitchison, N. *Return to the Fairy Hill*. London: Heinemann, 1966.

Moody, J. *Working with English* (3 vols). Gaborone: Foundation for Education with Production, 1992–1994.

Morrow, S. Maaba, B. and Pulumani, L. *Education in Exile: SOMAFCO, the ANC School in Tanzania, 1978 to 1992*. Pretoria: HSRC Press, 2004.

Morton, F. and Ramsay, J., eds. *The Birth of Botswana: A History of the Bechuanaland Protectorate from 1910 to 1966*. Gaborone: Longman Botswana, 1987.

Nyerere, J. K. *Education for Self-Reliance*. Dar es Salaam: Ministry of Information and Tourism, 1967.

Parsons, N. 'The Pipeline: Botswana's Reception of Refugees, 1956–68'. *Social Dynamics* 34(1) (March 2008), 17–32.

Parsons, Q. N. *Report on the Botswana Brigades, 1965–1983*. Gaborone: National Institute of Research, University of Botswana, 1983.

Ramsay, J. 'Roots of Botswana's Nationalist Politics (Part 21): MK, MI6 and the Pipeline'. *Weekend Post*, 17 May 2019. www.weekendpost.co.bw/wp-column-details.php?col_id=183 (accessed 30 May 2019).

Richards, I. A. *The Principles of Literary Criticism*. London: Kegan Paul, 1924.

Richards, I. A. *Practical Criticism*. London: Kegan Paul, 1929.

Right Livelihood Award (RLA). *Roll of Honour, 1980–2000*. Stockholm: Right Livelihood Award, 2000.

Schumacher, E. F. 'How to Help Them Help Themselves'. *The Observer*, Review Section, 29 (August 1965). https://centerforneweconomics.org/publications/how-to-help-them-help-themselves/ (accessed 3 January 2018).

Schumacher, E. F. *Small is Beautiful: A Study of Economics as if People Mattered*. London: Blond and Briggs, 1973.

Sefali, M. and Van Rensburg, P., eds. 'Applicability of Another Development to SADCC: Agenda for Action'. Paper presented at a seminar on Another Development for Lesotho, Maseru, Lesotho, 18–22 November 1985. Gaborone: Foundation for Education with Production, 1987.

Seidman, G. *Working for the Future*. Gaborone: Foundation for Education with Production, 1987.

Seidman, G. *Working for the Future: Teachers' Guide*. Gaborone: Foundation for Education with Production, 1990.

Seidman, J. *In Our Own Image*. Gaborone: Foundation for Education with Production, 1990.

Seidman, J. *In Our Own Image: Teaching Guide*. Gaborone: Foundation for Education with Production, 1995.

Serowe Youth Development Trust (SYDT). *Serowe Brigades, 1965/66–1975/76*. Serowe: SYDT, 1976.

Singer, R. '"I'll Teach You to Build a School"'. *Front Porch Review* 4 (April 2012). http://frontporchrvw.com/issue/april-2012/article/ill-teach-you-to-build-the-school (accessed 20 August 2018).

Thema, B. C. 'Moeng College: A Product of "Self-Help"'. *Botswana Notes & Records* 2(1) (1969), 71–74.

Thompson, A. R. *Education and Development in Africa*. New York: St Martin's Press, 1981.

Tlou, T., Parsons, N. and Henderson, W. *Seretse Khama: 1921–1980*. Gaborone: Botswana Society; Braamfontein: Macmillan Boleswa, 1996.

Vanqa, T. P. *The Development of Education in Botswana (1937–1987): The Role of Teachers' Organisations*. Gaborone: Lightbooks, 1998.

Vigne, R. *Liberals against Apartheid: A History of the Liberal Party of South Africa, 1953–1968*. Basingstoke: Palgrave Macmillan, 1997.

Watts, R. 'Memoirs of a Refugee "Pipeline": The Serowe Route, 1960–1961'. *Botswana Notes & Records* 29 (1997), 106–111.

Watts, R. *Eyes on Africa: A Fifty Year Commentary.* York: William Sessions, 2005.

Williams, S. *Who Killed Hammarskjöld? The UN, the Cold War and White Supremacy in Africa.* London: Hurst Publishers, 2016.

Yates, A. and Chester, L. *The Troublemaker: Michael Scott and His Lonely Struggle against Injustice.* London: Aurum Press, 2006.

Youngman, F. 'Sandan School: A Chinese Experiment in Combining Education with Production'. *Education with Production* 1(2) (1982), 67–81.

Index

Page numbers in italics refer to illustrations.